My Son Is an Alien

My Son Is an Alien

A Cultural Portrait of Today's Youth

Marcel Danesi

ROWMAN & LITTLEFIELD PUBLISHERS, INC.
Lanham • Boulder • New York • Toronto • Oxford

ROWMAN & LITTLEFIELD PUBLISHERS, INC.

Published in the United States of America
by Rowman & Littlefield Publishers, Inc.
A wholly owned subsidiary of The Rowman & Littlefield Publishing Group, Inc.
4501 Forbes Boulevard, Suite 200, Lanham, Maryland 20706
www.rowmanlittlefield.com

PO Box 317, Oxford OX2 9RU, UK

British Library Cataloguing in Publication Information Available

Library of Congress Cataloging-in-Publication Data
Danesi, Marcel, 1946–
    My son is an alien : a cultural portrait of today's youth / Marcel
Danesi.
        p. cm.
Includes bibliographical references and index.
    ISBN 0-7425-2854-5 (cloth : alk. paper) — ISBN 0-7425-2855-3 (pbk. :
alk. paper)
    1. Teenagers—United States. 2. Adolescence—United States. 3.
Popular culture—United States. I. Title.
    HQ796.D248 2003
    305.235'0973--dc21
                                    2003010539

Printed in the United States of America

♾ ™ The paper used in this publication meets the minimum requirements of
American National Standard for Information Sciences—Permanence of Paper
for Printed Library Materials, ANSI/NISO Z39.48-1992.

Contents

Contents

Why Another Book on Teenagers?

In 1994, I wrote a book analyzing the lifestyle features that characterize adolescence.[1] Shortly after its publication, something unexpected happened. Instead of getting the attention of my colleagues in academia, as I had hoped, to my surprise the book caught the attention of parents, educators, and representatives of the media. As never before in my academic career, I was invited to speak to community groups and teacher organizations, and to take part in radio and television programs dealing with adolescence. And to my even greater surprise, the book was put on reading lists sponsored by parent groups throughout North America.

At first, I hesitated to take on speaking engagements. Eventually, I felt the obligation to do so, given that I had ventured upon the study of adolescence as a parent myself and as a concerned academic in daily contact with young people. My aim was to report factually on how I conducted the research for the book, staying away from advice-giving of any kind. After one particular lecture, which I remember vividly to this day, I was especially adamant in telling a distraught parent that I had no advice to offer him with respect to his rebellious teenage son, citing a phrase I recalled by the satirist Erica Jong (1942–): "Advice is what we ask for when we already know the answer but wish we didn't." Undeterred, the gentleman retorted that what I had brought to light that evening in my presentation allowed him to understand many things that were obscure to him before. As he put it, "More than advice, you gave me valuable insights on the relation between culture and adolescence." He went on to suggest that I put these insights together in a book for a general audience of parents because, he added, "Most books dealing with adolescence are much too opinionated."

That parent's eloquence had an effect on me. Shortly thereafter, I decided to take his suggestion and embarked upon a three-year information-gathering project with the help of a team of research assistants that I assembled at the University of Toronto. The team collected facts on teen lifestyle and language trends, and it interviewed 200 adolescents in various cities across North America. The outcome of that project is the present book, which I sincerely hope will provide readers with some of those insights that I apparently gave a worried parent several years ago. In that regard, I would like to quote Holden Caulfield, the adolescent protagonist of *The Catcher in the Rye* by J. D. Salinger (1919–): "What really knocks me out is a book that, when you're all done reading it, you wish the author that wrote it was a terrific friend of yours and you could call him up on the phone whenever you felt like it."[2] I hope to be read in precisely that spirit—as the reader's friend. The reader is, in fact, invited to contact me at my e-mail address any time he or she wishes: marcel.danesi@utoronto.ca.

The title of this book, *My Son Is an Alien*, crystallized from a conversation with another parent. At the conclusion of a presentation in late 1995, I was accosted by a mother who told me that what I said that evening made her think of her son as an "alien from another planet." I reflected on her perceptive metaphor for a moment and then replied that for a period of time "teens do indeed seem to live on a different planet." Painting a portrait of life, or more precisely lifestyle, on that planet is the primary objective of this book.

Needless to say, troublesome and insubordinate youths have always existed. In his *Historia*, the Greek historian Herodotus (c. 485–425 B.C.) describes a Sumerian diary in which a fretful father complains about his son as someone who constantly loiters in the public square, always answers back in an insolent manner, and routinely expresses indifference toward his future. That father's portrait of a bored and defiant young boy four millennia ago closes the gap of time rather dramatically, seeming all too close to our own age. But unlike their counterparts in ancient Sumer, our young people today live in a culture that is vastly different—a culture that sees their rebellious behavior as a "natural" reflex of the coming-of-age period and may, in fact, even induce it. This book constitutes an examination of this culture-specific view.

I should comment briefly on how the relevant information for the book was gathered. Thanks to two grants—one from the Social Sciences and Humanities Research Council of Canada and one from Victoria College of the University of Toronto—a team of research assistants was hired to conduct interviews with 200 informants, utilizing open-ended questions related to the main areas of concern to be treated in this book. A common pre-prepared questionnaire was not used, because the team thought that it would stilt the interviews with the teens, who are typically wary of such social scientific methods. The researchers—all university students trained in ethnography—were told what kinds of information were needed. It was left up to each one to get the information in any way he or she could in response to the "interpersonal dynamics" of his or her specific situation. Follow-up interviews were also carried out with the parents of some of the teenagers. The parental perspective on why teens look, talk, and act the way they do is of obvious importance to the subject matter of this book.

The research was carried out between April 1999 and December 2002 in nine North American cities (Toronto, Boston, San Francisco, Vancouver, San Diego, Milwaukee, New York, Montreal, and Miami). The only criterion used in selecting the 200 teens—106 female and 94 male—was age. It was impossible to get the exact same number of informants for each age category, because written consent from teenagers, parents, and school officials was required beforehand by the ethics committee representing the granting agencies, thus limiting the team's flexibility in choosing subjects. As it turned out, the three age categories were nevertheless fairly uniform in number: (1) early teens (ages 12–15) = 77 (42 girls, 35 boys), (2) mid-teens (ages 16–18) = 72 (38 girls, 34 boys), and (3) late teens (18–early 20s) = 51 (26 girls, 25 boys). Although arbitrary, this subdivision was found to be appropriate by the teen informants themselves. Most of the interviewees were urban teens (179); only twenty-one came from rural backgrounds. This discrepancy was due, in large part, to the constraints of the grant, which provided resources that allowed us to reach a limited number of teens. However, the interview sessions revealed that little difference in overall outlook on the diverse kinds of issues treated in this book emerged between the urban and rural teens. The socioeconomic backgrounds of the teens varied considerably. In an open-ended ethnographic approach, it is extremely difficult to pigeonhole subjects into categories in a uniform manner. Overall, the interview sessions produced sufficient data from which, I believe, concrete generalizations can be drawn.

I should warn the reader from the outset that many of my comments will have a scholarly ring to them. Presenting the subject matter of this book cannot really be done in any other way without diluting it so much as to make it worthless. But I have not written it primarily for my colleagues in academia. I have written it for a general public. So, I have made a conscious effort to use straightforward language. Citations and references to the relevant literature will be used only when strictly necessary. I hope that parents, educators, and adolescents themselves will find this book useful or beneficial. I am especially interested in what the latter have to say about it. The study of adolescence is not, and certainly should not be, the exclusive privilege of adults.

First and foremost, I would like to thank the research team—Katarina Kuruc, Kate O'Neill, Kate McGee, Biagio Aulino, Tracy Tam, Dominika

Solan, Stéphanie Belanger, Pinella Buongiorno, Katie Lauder, Lindsay Kochen, and Marianna Calamia—for all their help and excellent work. Second, I must thank the many students I have had the privilege of teaching at the University of Toronto. They have always been, and continue to be, a source of inspiration and of insight. Third, I am truly grateful to Brenda Hadenfeldt and Heather Armstrong of Rowman & Littlefield, not only for enthusiastically supporting the publication of this book but also for providing me with many insightful comments on its contents during the editing phases. These have greatly improved my overall treatment of a very difficult and complex subject matter. Needless to say, any infelicities that the book may contain are my sole responsibility. Fourth, I wish to thank the many parents and teachers I have met since the publication of my previous book. They have been a constant source of encouragement and assurance.

Finally, a heartfelt thanks goes out to my family: Lucy, my wife; Alexander and Sarah, my grandchildren; Danila, my daughter; Chris, my son-in-law; and Danilo, my own father, for all the patience they have had with me over my incessant ranting about modern culture and its effect on young people. I must also beg their forgiveness for having been so grumpy and neglectful of family duties during the writing of this book.

NOTES

1. Marcel Danesi, *Cool: The Signs and Meanings of Adolescence* (Toronto: University of Toronto Press, 1994).
2. J. D. Salinger, *The Catcher in the Rye* (Boston: Little, Brown, 1951), 45.

Format of This Book

Each of the ten chapters of this book is designed to sketch out a particular facet of the adolescent portrait and then to derive specific insights from it—what it means to be a young person today; why body image in adolescence is so problematic; why teens speak a language all their own; why music plays such a crucial role in adolescence; why teens are influenced so much by peer pressure; why they smoke, take drugs, and drink alcohol; what role the school environment plays on teen life; what effects the media have on adolescents; and why there are so many perils associated with the coming-of-age process today. Each chapter constitutes an amalgam of information, commentaries, anecdotes, and opinions, most of which are derived from, or based on, the findings of the research team.

Each chapter is divided into three main sections: (1) an opening vignette, (2) an examination of the background issues related to the chapter theme, and (3) a discussion of the relevant insights.

OPENING VIGNETTE

The chapter starts with a brief dialogue taken from an interview session recorded by one of the research assistants. It is meant to set the tone for the chapter, providing the first insight from the "horse's mouth," so to speak—that is, from the teenager himself or herself.

BACKGROUND

This is the main part of the chapter. It constitutes an overview of the principal issues related to its theme. Each issue is examined historically and discussed with reference to the relevant research findings and technical literature. I have appended a glossary of technical terms at the end of the book to facilitate the reading of this section.

INSIGHTS

Parents and educators know what is going on intuitively in their own situations, but they may not always be in a position to articulate their intuitions or to back them up with relevant information. The insights provided here will, I hope, allow them to do exactly that. Each insight is fashioned from a statement made by a teenager as taped by a member of the research team.

At times, the reader might construe some of the insights offered as advice-giving and as highly opinionated. All I can say is that I have made a conscious effort to avoid engaging in the type of glib advice-giving that is found in the "How to Talk to Your Teen" books that currently glut the market. In a letter dated October 2, 1765, the English statesman Lord Chesterfield (1694–1773) stated that in some matters he refused to give advice because he did not want to "have anybody's torments in this world or the next laid to [his] charge."[1] Lord Chesterfield's point is one that I have taken to heart in writing this book. Nevertheless, I admit that as a parent and grandparent, I too have opinions about what teenagers say and do. These will occasionally rise surreptitiously to the textual surface. In such instances, I beg the reader's indulgence.

The information and data on which this book is based are bound to go out of date rather quickly. The details of the portrait will thus have to be updated by the reader as he or she goes through the book. Nevertheless, I suspect that the basic outline of the portrait will not change very much in the foreseeable future. I have appended a list of Internet sites and relevant addresses that parents, educators, and teens may find useful if a situation arises that will require them to seek further insights or professional help. I hope that the portrait I will paint in the pages that follow will strike a resounding chord in all readers. I truly hope not to disappoint anyone.

NOTE

1. P. D. Chesterfield, *Correspondence* (London: Allen & Unwyn, 1926), 26.

1

Adolescence in
Historical Context

Interviewer	How old are you?
Teen Informant	I'm almost 12.
Interviewer	Do you still consider yourself to be a child?
Teen Informant	No way, man.
Interviewer	Then, what do you consider yourself to be?
Teen Informant	I'm big, man, like my friends.

BACKGROUND

In 1930, the Italian political theorist Antonio Gramsci (1891–1937) made the following remark: "In the life of children there are two very clear-cut phases, before and after puberty."[1] Gramsci's assertion may have been accurate when he articulated it. But it no longer rings true. Today, we hardly expect adulthood to emerge after puberty—as Gramsci's statement implies. Rather, we now think of the coming-of-age period as constituting a "transitional" phase toward adulthood—a phase characterized by emotional problems that, in Gramsci's times, would undoubtedly have been viewed as bizarre.

What has happened since those times? Why is the coming-of-age period now viewed so differently from how it was not so long ago? Unraveling the events that brought about such a fundamental shift in cultural groupthink is a crucial point of departure for any study of adolescence. This will allow me to jot down a general outline of the portrait of adolescence, whose details I will provide in the remainder of this book.

ADOLESCENCE AS A SOCIAL EXPERIMENT

The starting point for any systematic examination of the relation between culture and adolescence is tracing the origins and meanings of three key terms that are crucial to the examination. The first one is *puberty*. It was coined in the medieval period to describe the stage in the human lifecycle when an individual becomes physiologically capable of sexual reproduction. The second is *adolescent*. It was also coined in medieval times, but its meaning was hardly the one we ascribe to it today. It referred, originally, to any boy who left his family in the countryside for the city in order to earn a living in a trade. The term meant literally "he who grows up (on his own)." The third is *teenager*. Although it was coined in the late 1930s, the term gained currency in the 1950s as a synonym for *adolescent*. On the one hand, it signaled the fact that the period of adolescence was becoming longer and longer, covering most of the "teen" years (thirteen, fourteen, and so on); on the other hand, it signaled the fact that adolescence had developed into a distinct lifecycle category characterized by its own sui generis lifestyle.

Two other recently coined terms require some commentary here. They are *tweenie* and *middlescent*. The former was coined in the early 1990s to describe a prepubescent child who manifests lifestyle behaviors that are more typical of adolescents than they are of children; the latter was coined in the mid-1990s by journalist Gail Sheehy to describe individuals in their twenties and thirties whose lifestyle behaviors resemble more those of adolescents than they do of adults.[2] Tweenies and middlescents are now clearly distinct market populations. The tweenies have their own TV shows (the Disney Channel and YTV), stores (Betwixt in Greenwich Village), and snacks (Hot Bites, a line of frozen miniature pizzas from Heinz); middlescents make up the primary market population targeted by companies that sell electronic devices (audio equipment, electronic games, and the like).

PUBERTY

- Puberty is the period in the human lifecycle during which the organs of sexual reproduction become fully developed.
- In females, it is marked by the arrival of menstruation, an enlargement of the breasts, the growth of pubic hair, and a broadening of the hips.
- In males, it is marked by the production of semen; a growth of facial, bodily, and pubic hair; and a deepening of the voice.

Table 1.1. The Lifecycle Today

Birth		Puberty		Death
childhood		*adulthood*		
infancy	tweeniehood	adolescence/ teenagehood	middlescence	adulthood
0	7	12	19	30	80+
		Approximate Age Ranges		

The coexistence of these terms in contemporary social discourse makes it saliently obvious that Gramsci's simple two-phase division of the life-cycle is no longer reflective of reality. That same lifecycle is now perceived to have at least five major distinct phases—infancy, tweeniehood, adolescence or teenagehood, middlescence, and adulthood. In table 1.1, the top part shows Gramsci's simple two-part division, and the bottom one the five-part division that has crystallized since his times.

The term *childhood* also requires some attention here. In previous eras, and even in other cultures today, children were not perceived to be the helpless and innocent creatures they are nowadays. The crawling stage, for instance, was hardly seen to be the "milestone" it is considered to be today. Crawling on the floor was regarded as animal-like behavior and, consequently, as something to be corrected. Infants were clothed in attire that kept them in a rigid posture, so that they could learn to stand up as early in life as possible. It was in the middle part of the romantic nineteenth century that our culture came to view childhood in a radically different way. The concept that children are innocent creatures living in a type of imaginary "fantasyland" is, in fact, a romantic idea, perpetuated by books such as *Peter Pan* (1904) by J. M. Barrie (1860–1937). This view spread quickly throughout the English-speaking world. In the twentieth century, the fantasyland image of childhood was adopted and perpetuated by the ever-expanding pop culture world. Walt Disney (1901–1966) in particular enshrined it once and for all into groupthink with his highly appealing children's movies, TV programs, books, and musical recordings.

In early tribal cultures, childhood was hardly viewed as a romantic period of development. It was seen to be a period of preparation for adulthood. The passage from one phase to the other was marked by elaborate rites that allowed the entire culture to celebrate it in a communal way. In city-based cultures, however, passage rites lost their importance as communal events already in the ancient world, being assigned primarily to the religious sphere, where they continue, to this day, to have importance—I mention the Catholic sacrament of Confirmation and the Jewish Bar Mitzvah as two cases in point. However, at no time did the ancient cultures have the romantic or fantasyland view of childhood that we have today. Infants were expected to work as soon as it became physically possible for them to do so. Children as young as five years of age tilled the fields, milked cows, gathered hay, and tended to animals. Little distinction was made between childhood and adult work roles. There were no special laws related specifically to the rearing of children.

This view of childhood remained the status quo until the Industrial Revolution when, in cities throughout Europe, more and more children were put into schools rather than sent out to work the land or carry out household chores. To be sure, many city children were also expected to go out and work, as they once did back on the farm. But, unlike the farm, the new industrial workplace was an inhospitable one. In the early factories and mechanical shops, children simply could not keep up with the pace, nor could they carry out the type of physically demanding labor required of them. As a result, they were treated with harshness and barbarity— a brutal situation that has been imprinted indelibly into our collective memory by novels such as Charles Dickens's *Oliver Twist* (1838). In a short time, specific laws were passed to protect children. It became illegal, for example, to send children out to work until after puberty. At about the same time, romantic writers started depicting childhood as a period of innocence and purity. Inspired by Jean-Jacques Rousseau's novel *Émile* (1762), novelists such as Robert Louis Stevenson (*Treasure Island*, 1883) and Rudyard Kipling (*The Jungle Book*, 1894) started carving the fantasyland image of childhood into the communal consciousness. Not surprisingly, this image does not exist in many other parts of the world today. Indeed, it is estimated that the number of what we in the West would define as "working children" is in the hundreds of millions worldwide.

The nineteenth century also produced a new "scientific" view of childhood. Influenced by social Darwinism, the practitioners of psychology (then in its infancy) claimed that children underwent adaptive stages of mental and emotional growth, as predictable as were the stages of their bodily growth. Although controversial at first, it became such a widespread idea that, to this day, it is felt to be beyond reproach. It remains, in effect, a deeply entrenched pattern of groupthink that we no longer realize came about essentially as a conjecture. Together, the fantasyland and scientific views of childhood have had a profound impact on the social, ideological, legal, and institutional fabric of Western society. There are now more laws protecting children than there are laws protecting adults. There are more books written for or about children than there are on virtually any other topic of human concern.

The romantic redefinition of childhood was the catalyst for the creation of a new age category—*adolescence*—which came about simply for a socioeconomic reason: namely, as a consequence of keeping young people in school longer so that they could be better prepared for the new industrialized workplace. The term *adolescent* came into common usage in Great Britain in the mid-1800s to refer to any person who stayed in school past puberty. As mentioned, the term was coined originally in the Middle Ages to refer to any male child who decided to move away from the family farm to work independently in some city guild or trade.[3] For five centuries subsequently, this meaning of the term remained virtually unchanged. Late in the eighteenth century, an important event took place in England, called the "Sunday school movement," which was inaugurated to help poor, working children gain a basic level of literacy. By the time of the Industrial Revolution, the movement expanded as education for one and all became a practical necessity. Those who stayed in school beyond puberty were called adolescents. The original meaning of the word was lost once and for all.

As a growing number of adolescents stayed in school for longer periods of time, they came to be perceived more and more as "older children" for the simple reason that they remained economically dependent upon adults. By the early 1900s, people started to view adolescence increasingly as a phase of preparation for adulthood. This led, inevitably, to a host of unprecedented problems—unwanted pregnancies, an increase in the incidence of sexually transmitted diseases, and alcoholism. Clearly, nature could not be fooled by what was essentially a social experiment! It was obvious to one and all that sexually mature individuals could not be told *tout court* to ignore their sexual urges and concentrate on school as they did when they were children.

To make sure that sexual urges did not get the better part of these "older children," complicated taboos emerged that were quickly incorporated into law. The new "restraining measures" brought about many unwelcome repercussions. And we continue to live with them to this day.

People at the time knew that something was amiss. But there was no turning back the clock. To rationalize the experiment, a "theory" of adolescence was desperately needed. Such a theory was provided conveniently in 1904 by the psychologist G. Stanley Hall (1844–1924), who simply claimed that adolescence was a "natural" stage in human development marked by emotional turmoil because of the fact that the adolescent was adapting to conditions that were emotionally and socially different from those that characterized the world of childhood.[4]

Hall claimed that the various phases in the lifecycle constituted a kind of "recapitulation" of the stages that characterized the evolution of the human race. Accordingly, the infant recapitulated humanity's animal stage, the adolescent the savage stage, and the adult the mature (sapient) stage. Predictably, Hall went on, the passage from one stage to the other is a difficult one for the reason that transitions require adaptation and adjustment. Undoubtedly, Hall's theory would have been quickly discarded as the fanciful speculation of an overactive academic imagination if not for the fact that society desperately needed it as a rationalization (if not justification) for having called into existence the "problems of adolescence." The theory legitimized two things at once—adolescence and developmental psychology itself. At first, there was much doubt expressed about Hall's proposal, but his view spread quickly because it was just what the social doctor ordered.

Shortly after Hall's whimsical proposal, Sigmund Freud (1856–1939), the founder of psychoanalysis, put forward another self-styled fanciful theory. Following on Hall's coattails, Freud claimed that adolescents were troublesome creatures because their repressive childhood experiences made the adjustment to adulthood "traumatic." Freud's proposal, which initially met with the hostility that it deserved, incredibly made its way into the mainstream of developmental theory. Although later psychologists attenuated it somewhat by pointing out that cultural factors other than childhood repressions play a role in adolescence, it nevertheless also became an unconscious pattern of Western cultural groupthink.[5] The contemporary version of Freudian "trauma theory" goes somewhat like this. Inhabiting a strange new sexual body, adolescents start to feel awkward, anxious, and guilty (or afraid) of their repressed desires and feelings.

ADOLESCENCE

- 1904: Psychologist G. Stanley Hall declares adolescence to be a distinct period of development in the human lifecycle.
- 1938: The Fair Labor Standards Act in the United States sets 14 as the minimum age for employment outside of school hours.
- 1939: The word *teenager* appears in print for the first time, gaining instant currency in everyday vocabulary.
- 1944: *Seventeen* starts publication as the first magazine aimed exclusively at adolescents.
- 1951: J. D. Salinger's novel dealing with adolescent angst, *The Catcher in the Rye*, is published, becoming the first classic in the genre.
- 1950s–1960s: Rock and roll emerges as the musical voice of adolescence.
- 1970s–1990s: The adolescent market segment becomes an increasingly ascendant force in shaping social trends; puberty is documented as beginning several years earlier for females than it did in the early part of the twentieth century.
- 2000–: Incidents of violence in schools trigger a debate in the media and in society at large on why the adolescent period has become so troubling.

Consequently, they are besieged by a pervasive awareness of, and sensitivity to, what others think of them. Membership in a peer group is their way of gaining shelter from the ravaging effects of the coming-of-age stage. The peer group serves, therefore, as a kind of enclave sheltering adolescents from the burdens of puberty and allowing their repressions to be channeled through constructive social interaction.[6]

Why would Mother Nature have gone so far out of Her way to wreak such emotional havoc upon Her sexually maturing human progeny? The answer is, of course, that She has not. The experience of adolescence as a troubled, adaptive period is a direct consequence of a social experiment that was necessitated by a new economic reality nearly 150 years ago in Great Britain. Indeed, in societies around the globe that hold no such view of the coming-of-age period, no special "problems" associated with their pubescent members are reported. Only in ours does the bizarre perception exist that children reaching the age of puberty are *necessarily* inclined to undergo a difficult period of emotional adjustment.[7] The Hall-Freud theory is a classic example of a self-fulfilling prophecy. By having made high school obligatory for adolescents, by having passed specific kinds of labor and family laws for their protection, by targeting them primarily as consumers, by defining them as "half children, half adults," by pampering them as older children, and by expecting them to defer the responsibilities of social adulthood until after the high school years, we have created the social conditions that favor and sustain the peculiar (and often unwanted) emotional behaviors that we associate with adolescence.

Already in the 1930s, the great American anthropologist Margaret Mead (1901–1978) had assembled a large amount of data on Samoan society warning American society that the emotional traumas that our adolescents were purported to undergo were not reflexes of a "natural" adaptive stage in the human lifecycle. Mead reported that Samoan pubescent individuals experienced no drastic change in personality as they passed from childhood to adulthood, nor was the advent of puberty felt, in any way whatsoever, to be traumatic. This was because Samoan children were expected to take on the responsibilities of adulthood the instant they reached puberty. Simply put, Mead found that the traditional Samoan culture had young adults, but it did not have what we call adolescents![8] Culture, she maintained, had created the conditions that fostered "adolescent traumas," not nature.

Trauma theory came to be known more colloquially as "Sturm und Drang" theory (German for "storm and stress")—a term that comes from the play *Sturm und Drang* by Friedrich Maximilian von Klinger (1752–1831) in which passionate subjectivity is highlighted. But the original image of a highly sensitive young individual struggling against conventional society came from *Sorrows of Young Werther* (1774) by the great

German writer Johann Goethe (1749–1832). The work became a model for numerous tales of youthful subjectivity. One of these is J. D. Salinger's (1919–) *The Catcher in the Rye* (1951). The main character of that novel, Holden Caulfield, is a direct descendant of Goethe's Werther. In a sanitarium, the 16-year-old Holden, who was suspended from his preparatory school, recalls for a psychiatrist the events of the last few days before he suffers a nervous breakdown during Christmas vacation. Disgusted by the hypocrisy of adult society, Holden is especially repulsed by the "phoniness" and "dreariness" of people. In true romantic fashion, he desperately hopes to protect children, especially his sister Phoebe, from growing up and becoming just as phony and dreary as everyone else.

Throughout the twentieth century, the romantic view of adolescence has allowed the "problems of adolescence" to linger and to proliferate. In the 1950s, the publication of such unprecedented guidebooks for parents as *How to Live with Your Teenager* (1953) and *Understanding Teenagers* (1955) made that crystal clear. The number of organizations and agencies that have been established to deal with these problems since the 1950s is mindboggling. Their names are self-explanatory and tell a frightening story on their own—the National Youth Gang Center Institute for Intergovernmental Research, Students against Drunk Driving, the National Parents' Resource Institute on Drug Education, Teens Teaching AIDS Prevention, the National Youth Advocacy Coalition, Covenant House, the National Runaway Switchboard, the National Youth Crisis Hotline, the National Association of Anorexia Nervosa and Associated Disorders—and the list could go on and on!

TEENAGEHOOD AS A CREATION OF POP CULTURE

By the early 1940s, the term *teenagers* came into common usage. In hindsight, it is obvious that it was hardly just a colorful new way of referring to adolescents. Rather, it brought out the fact that adolescence had been appropriated as a market category by the ever-expanding pop culture world. This has been successful in carving out a different, more profitable image of the teenager, changing it from that of a young Werther to that of a rebel—but a "rebel without a cause," as the title of the 1955 movie so aptly phrased it. The fact that teenagers had become an important market segment of the pop culture economy was evidenced in the 1950s with the advent of movies and magazines directed specifically at teenagers (*Dig, Teen, Teen World, Sixteen, Teen Romances,* and so on) telling them how to become attractive and popular. The term *cool* became a shibboleth of an emerging teen lifestyle. *Being cool* meant hanging out with peers, going to parties, smoking cigarettes, consuming alcohol, engaging casually in sexual activities, and making one's physical appearance different from that of adults (by means of cosmetics, hairstyle, dress, and the like). A new music, *rock and roll*, crystallized as a music for and by teenagers. In 1956, with such number one hits as "All Shook Up" and "Don't Be Cruel," Elvis Presley emerged as the first teen rock idol. The new entertainment medium of television, with programs such as *American Bandstand*, turned aspiring

---

TEENAGEHOOD

- 1942: Frank Sinatra wows screaming "bobby-soxers" at the Paramount Theater in New York, giving America a foretaste of the kind of hysteria that will soon manifest itself typically at rock concerts.
- 1950s: The figure of the rebellious teenager is enshrined by the media into social consciousness. In 1955, the movies *Rebel without a Cause*, with James Dean as a teen idol, and *Blackboard Jungle*, with Marlon Brando as a motorcycle gang leader, make it obvious to one and all that teenagers had become a distinct social and, more important, market category. In the same year, Elvis Presley becomes the "king of rock," symbolizing teenage rebelliousness with his hip-swinging, brash attitude. The 1959 hit "Why Must I Be a Teenager in Love?" by Dion and the Belmonts encapsulates teenage angst—coping with romance in a society that views teenagers as children in adult bodies—perfectly.
- 1960s: Female rock groups such as the Ronettes, the Crystals, and the Shangri-Las, who are as tough looking as their motorcycle gang boyfriends, carve out a new "girl power" image for teenage females to emulate. Beatlemania sweeps the United States in 1964. The so-called generation gap widens as tensions between parents and teens become more intense and widespread. Around 1967, a counterculture movement originates in Berkeley, San Francisco, and New York, spearheaded by adolescents wearing long hair, bell-bottom jeans, and colorful shirts.
- 1970s: As the movement subsides, teen lifestyles become highly fragmented, as evidenced by the coexistence of heavy metal, punk, disco, and other lifestyles.
- 1980s: The cumulative economic clout of teenagers continues to increase. MTV (Music Television) is established as teenagehood's first own television channel. Rap goes mainstream around 1986, along with hip-hop lifestyle, characterized by a brash new rebellious attitude.
- 1990s: Gangsta rappers, with their violent lyrics, become popular. The MTV cartoon characters Beavis and Butthead make "grossness" a cool trait. Kurt Cobain, lead singer of the rock group Nirvana, commits suicide in 1994, spawning a movement among his followers to reject the superficiality of an entertainment-crazed society.
- 2000–: Constant change in teen lifestyle is the only "constant." Trends come and go virtually overnight, passing more and more from the teen world to the culture at large.

rock musicians into overnight successes. It also popularized the first family sitcoms, such as the *Adventures of Ozzie and Harriet,* which dealt with the problems of raising teenage children (two sons in this case).

An incident occurred in the winter of 1959 that emphasized to one and all that rock music was much more than dance music for teenagers. That year, three rock stars—Buddy Holly, Ritchie Valens, and the Big Bopper— were killed in an airplane crash on the way to a concert. Their death was treated by teen-directed media outlets as a tragedy of mythical proportions. Their songs, which would have faded away and been forgotten very quickly, became legendary classics. Movies and TV specials are still being made of Buddy Holly and Ritchie Valens! Posters and magazine photos of the three were transformed into icons of veneration and hung on bedroom walls throughout North America.

Teenagers in the 1950s also established their own implicit coming-of-age rites. As mentioned, traditional cultures have always marked the passage from childhood to adulthood with specific rites. City societies largely abandoned them centuries ago. But the need for them has never really disappeared. What occurred in the teenage world of the 1950s bears witness to this very fact. The "sixteenth birthday party" became an ersatz passage rite created by the teenagers themselves in partnership with the media—I mention, as cases in point, titles of songs such as *Sixteen Candles* and *Happy Birthday Sweet Sixteen,* which hit the top of the charts. The locus for the enactment of the rites was the high school, given that it provided the space and opportunity for teenagers to socialize and interact in a "tribal-like" fashion. To this day, the high school remains primarily a teen enclave, largely replacing the functions of the family in matters of maturation and courtship. As Lynd and Lynd observed already in the late 1920s, "The high school, with its athletics, clubs, sororities and fraternities, dances and parties, and other extracurricular activities is a fairly complete social cosmos in itself, and about this city within a city the social life of the intermediate generation centers."[9] Consequently, friendships forged in high school tend, often, to last beyond the high school years; they are rarely perfunctory and transitory.

The first true generation of teenagers were "rebels without a cause." Most adults expected the rebellion to fade quickly. But in the 1960s, something truly unexpected happened. The "second generation" of teenagers became real rebels, questioning the values of the society in which they were reared as never before. Known as "hippies," they denounced the adult "establishment," seeking inspiration from Eastern mystical traditions to fashion a new type of rock music, which spearheaded the clamor for social change. The rock concert became a "happening" of great political and ideological proportions, spurring on youths to social activism. Drugs were consumed at such concerts to induce or heighten the aesthetic experience of the whole event. Sexual activities were practiced openly, in obvious defiance of adult moralism. The new rock was ambitious. It was hardly just music for teen dancing. By the end of the decade, rock operas, such as *Tommy* (1969) by the Who, were being considered as serious musical works by mainstream music critics.

But, alas, the hippie movement did not last long. By the early 1970s it had virtually disappeared from the social radar screen. The hippies had, simply, become less inclined to revolt as they started to have children of their own. New musical trends emerged, as did new teen lifestyles. Ironically, as their own children grew into adolescence, the ex-hippies became terrified. The trend that worried them the most was so-called punk music. Alienating themselves visibly from mainstream culture, the punks were deliberately violent and confrontational. They spat on their audiences, mutilated themselves with knives, damaged the props on stage and in the hall, shouted, burped, urinated, and bellowed at will to a basic rhythmic pulsating beat, inciting their fans to follow suit. The fashion trends they introduced—chains, dog collars, army boots, and hairstyles that ranged from shaved heads to the wild-looking "Mohawk" hairdos of every color imaginable—communicated degradation, mockery, social caricature, and insubordination at once. The punks were antibourgeois and anticapitalist in ways that, ironically, the hippie parents of the 1970s teens found shocking and offensive. Their music was the rock equivalent of Andy Warhol's sculptures or of John Cage's compositions—it was sardonic, absurdist, preposterous, aleatory, and "do it yourself."

But the fears were unfounded. Indeed, the punk movement would recede from the mainstream. In the very same decade, teenagehood became a much more fragmented sector of the pop culture economy than anyone could possibly have foreseen. Other music-based lifestyles crystallized alongside the punk one. One of these involved makeup and cross-dressing. The rock band, Kiss, whose performances on stage were designed to shock adults, symbolized this new trend perfectly. Each musician assumed a mock comic-book role—a glamour boy, an alien from outer space, a kitty cat, and a sex-crazed Kabuki monster. Band members wore makeup and their stage act included fire-eating, smoke bombs, hydraulic lifts, and the smashing of instruments. *The Rocky Horror Picture Show* was another manifestation of this new trend. The movie became a cult phenomenon, with hordes of teenagers going to see it week after week, month after month, year after year. It was both a parody of 1950s rock and a paradigm of an emerging new lifestyle code. As Greenwald remarks, it was both an attempt "to shock by departing from the tradition of rock and roll machismo established by Elvis" and a new "grammar of cool" that favored "an overall smearing of the lines between the generations and the sexes."[10] Although it no longer inspires teen culture, there are some diehards who attend showings of the movie to this day.

Running totally against such trends was disco culture, epitomized by the 1978 movie *Saturday Night Fever*, starring John Travolta. Its popularity with hordes of teens was further evidence of teenagehood's fragmentation. Disco teens were vastly different from their punk and cross-dressing counterparts. Their lifestyle was a throwback to the days of swing and ballroom dancing. Punk teens rejected disco culture with the expression "Disco sucks!" So, too, did other teens who saw the disco scene as too superficial and much too acceptable to the adult world. But disco thrived nonetheless, because it was fun and sexy. But by the early 1980s, all such trends suddenly vanished, although snippets of the punk, cross-dressing, and disco cultures remained and are being recycled even today in movie remakes, TV nostalgia programs, and the like.

The teenagehood of the 1980s continued to split into more and more lifestyle factions. Two performers—Michael Jackson and Madonna—emerged to challenge traditional gender attitudes even more than had Kiss and Rocky Horror teens. Michael Jackson incorporated male and female sexual characteristics into his stage persona. His video album *Thriller* (1982) was a brilliant blend of Rocky Horror and Kiss-like gender bashing. It was obviously right for the times, earning an unprecedented eight Grammy Awards and becoming the best-selling album in pop culture history up to that time. Madonna's songs "Like a Virgin," "Material Girl," and "Dress You Up" satirized the traditional view of females as sexual objects. She adopted a Marilyn Monroe "sex-kitten" peepshow pose as one of her performance trademarks. Her songs topped the hit-parade charts, much to the chagrin and dismay of leading moral guardians of the day. She continues to reign as an icon of pop culture, constantly adapting her style to the ever-changing *Zeitgeist*. By the end of the decade, teenagehood continued to fragment, as hard rockers, mods, preps, and other teen cliques emerged with their own fashion, music, and lifestyles. This fragmentation became the defining feature of pop culture generally, spreading teen lifestyles to the culture at large. It is no exaggeration to claim that the foundation of our current economy is largely implanted in the terrain of teenagehood. Pop culture and teen culture have become virtual synonyms.

With the popularization of rap music in the late 1980s and its derivative hip-hop style in the 1990s, a fascination with African American youth lifestyles gained society-wide momentum, vindicating the often-ignored role played by black musicians in the birth of rock and pop music generally. Already in 1961, the rock group called the Tokens had recorded a highly popular song, *The Lion Sleeps Tonight*, which some critics consider to be a forerunner of rap style because of the fact that the lyrics were virtually "spoken," rather than intertwined with a melody line. The Beatles imitated the cognate Jamaican reggae style in their 1968 song "Ob-La-Di, Ob-La-Da." Reggae influenced the songs of Sting, The Police, Eric Clapton, and Led Zeppelin. The term *rap* was actually used for the first time in the mid-1970s to describe the eclectic mix of funk, soul, and hard rock played by disc jockeys in the dance halls of Harlem and South Bronx clubs. The more enthusiastic members of those audiences would sing-song rhymes, exhorting other teens to dance and "get into it." They were called "rapping" sessions. Shortly thereafter, these started cropping up all over the streets of New York, catching the ever-watchful eye of pop culture moguls.

SPREADING TEENAGEHOOD

The author and readers of this book are, by and large, "teenagers of yesterday." We made lifestyle choices that, in one way or other, were probably perceived by adults to be bizarre or unwise. As parents and even grandparents now, we sometimes tend to forget that we were once rebellious teenagers ourselves. Whether we were immersed in Elvis culture, disco scenes, punk culture, or hard rock lifestyles is irrelevant. The point is that we, too, were perceived as "difficult works in progress," rather than as "finished products," by our own parents and teachers. I can recall my late mother cringing at my tastes in clothing fashion and music when I reached the age of 13 in the late 1950s. I dismissed this at the time as "adult inanity." I now fully appreciate what she must have been going through. Most people alive today have grown up in a culture that has become accustomed to seeing teenagers as "alien" creatures, as the mother whom I mentioned in my preface so aptly phrased it.

The teenagers of today are no different from the teenagers of yesterday. They have their own fashions and music, and they continue to see themselves as distinct from adults. But there is one crucial difference. In no other era has the tendency for lifestyle fads to pass quickly from the teen culture to the adult one been so strong. In the late 1990s, the fashion trends and music of hip-hop artists, Latin American musicians, grunge groups, rappers, and "girl power" groups not only infiltrated teenagehood but also the world of adults. In a phrase, in our pop culture world, "Youth sells!" As a consequence, differences between young and old have become blurrier than ever before.

I will use the term *juvenilization* to refer to the inclination of people generally to perceive youth trends as the norm and, as a consequence, to adopt them outright. With an increase in life expectancy, juvenilization has become an all-pervasive process, inducing increasing numbers of people to think of themselves as "forever young." It can thus be defined as the bizarre inclination of society at large to take its lifestyle cues from the teenage sector. In the area of fashion, for example, teenage and tweenie females and their mothers now wear virtually the same kind of clothing. In the late 1990s, both donned belly shirts, frosted lipstick, wobbly footwear, and blue nail polish. Teen males wore baggy pants, sneakers, bandanas, and earrings in imitation of media-hyped rappers. The same fashion styles were adopted by their older siblings and even their fathers. Today one can walk into any clothing store and see virtually no difference among the clothing fashions intended for tweenies, teens, or adults. A mother could wear her 12-year-old daughter's clothes without getting a second look and vice versa: the daughter could wear her mother's clothes without appearing in any way precocious. As social critic Frank Thomas has skillfully argued,[11] having a "cool look," at any age, has become the defining Weltanschauung of the modern world.

The media-fashioned image of the teenager as a rebellious figure— sexually mature but emotionally and socially childish—has been a source of seemingly limitless capital for book and magazine publishers, recording companies, Hollywood, TV, and other media businesses since at least the 1950s. And because youth sells, trends in the adolescent world quickly become the cultural norm, dictating look, taste in music, and fashion. Teen aesthetics are now the aesthetics of all. As a consequence, the figure of the wise elder has faded away from communal consciousness. People now turn to the media, to psychologists, or to self-help books for advice. But these are hardly adequate replacements for the wisdom that comes from experience and maturity.

The roots of juvenilization are traceable to the truly amazing advances in medicine at the turn of the twentieth century that made it possible for

---

JUVENILIZATION

- Juvenilization can be defined as the media-conditioned inclination of adults living in consumerist societies to adopt youth-oriented lifestyle trends as their own. This tendency predisposes people to "hold on to youth," so to speak, longer and longer.
- Juvenilization traces its roots to an increase in average life expectancy. The prospect of living longer makes it possible to think of oneself as being "young" for a longer period of time. As a consequence, it is becoming commonplace to think of "old age" as something that can be postponed later and later.
- The result is an effacement of the traditional line between "young" and "old."
- It is now not uncommon for teens and adults to wear virtually the same types of clothes, to go to the same kinds of movies, and to listen to similar kinds of music.

people to live longer and, thus, to remain healthy for much longer than ever before. In the same era, more and more common folk started to have access to more personal wealth. They thus started to indulge more and more in the material accoutrements of the modern world, including fashion and cosmetics. Financial independence led, inevitably, to a disempowerment of the institution of the family and, thus, to its decreased role in matters of courtship and maturation (e.g., who and when to marry, what job or profession to pursue, and where to live). With more wealth and leisure time at their disposal, and without the strict controls of the family, common people became more inclined to live the good life, to decide whom to marry on their own whims, what jobs to pursue, and, most important, *when* to do so. Such "freedoms" were entrenched and nurtured by the messages that bombarded society from radio and print sources in the early part of the twentieth century—messages that became more persuasive and widespread with the advent of television in the early 1950s. By the 1960s, the desire to be young and free not only meant the desire to stay and look healthier for a longer period of life, but also to act and think differently from "older" people. Being old meant being a part of the corrupt and morally fossilized "establishment," as the consumerist way of life was called by the counterculture youths of the era. By the end of the decade, the process of juvenilization had reached a critical mass, on the verge of becoming *the* defining feature of Western groupthink. As the social critic Stuart Ewen has aptly put it, the business world discovered fortuitously in that era how to incorporate the powerful images of youth protest into "the most constantly available lexicon from which many of us draw the visual grammar of our lives."[12] What appealed to the young would shortly thereafter appeal as well to the old. It became a collective state of mind.

In a world where the marketplace and the media dictate lifestyle and even morality, it is little wonder that juvenilization has become so pervasive and forceful. The phenomenon surfaced, first, in the domain of music. In the 1920s, jazz music, once strictly the domain of the brothels in Kansas City and New Orleans, started to flourish across the United States as the musical idiom of young and sexually attractive people. In 1923, the Broadway musical, *Running Wild,* helped turn the Charleston into a dance craze for the young, a dance that brought out into the open the carefree sexuality of adolescence. There was, of course, a reaction against such trends from society's elders. Prohibition and a general censure of such musical trends were two consequences of the reaction. But juvenilization had started in full earnest and could not be curtailed. It was then, and is now, a two-edged sword. Although it challenged the stodgy puritanical status quo, it also induced people to believe that their youth was the only valuable thing to hold on to for the rest of their lives.

By the late 1920s, the cheapness and availability of mass-produced records led to a true shift in cultural aesthetics—the entrenchment of pop music as mainstream music. Despite its apparent lack of "classical good taste," people loved it, no matter how controversial or crass it appeared to music purists. Jazz and its derivative, swing, quickly evolved into a lifestyle "code" for the young and attractive. Band leaders such as Glenn Miller, with hits such as "Little Brown Jug," "Sunrise Serenade," "Moonlight Serenade," and "In the Mood," became the first icons of an ever-expanding pop culture. Miller disbanded his orchestra in 1942 and enlisted in the U.S. Army, where he formed the forty-two-piece, all-star Army Air Force Band, which entertained World War II service personnel with regular radio broadcasts. In 1944, Miller died when his small plane, headed to Paris, disappeared over the English Channel during bad weather. His influence on the spread of pop music became obvious to all. In the years subsequent to the war, Miller-style "swing" developed into a society-wide craze. In the same time frame, a so-called generation gap crystallized as the views of older adults on everything from politics to music came to be labeled as "old-fashioned" and "out of date."

Many blame juvenilization erroneously on the generation known as the "baby boomers." Between the years 1946 and 1964, a baby boom took place in North America whose magnitude had no precedents. During that period, 77 million babies were born. Already in 1957, the new boomer teen market was worth over $30 billion a year. The boomers were, in effect, the first true teenagers. And for their extravagant lifestyles they have been the targets of acerbic criticism ever since; they have become society's pariahs because of their ambivalence.[13] They spawned the counterculture revolution and the civil and women's rights movements; indeed, if gender and race discrimination have taken a beating since the 1960s, it is because of the efforts of the much-maligned boomers. However, it is true that they were also behind the popularity of such frivolous things as Barbie dolls and T-shirts. And what really annoys people today about them is the fact that they continue to see themselves as "hip," even more "than their own kids," as social critic Bruce Pollock puts it.[14] The reverence for Elvis Presley, for instance, that a large segment of the boomer generation continues to have is truly mind-boggling. Presley died on August 16, 1977. Since then, there have been constant pilgrimages to his home, his records and movies are being continually remade, and many fans even keep shrines to his memory and tokens from his life (vials of his sweat, scraps of carpet from his home, and so on) in their own homes. Elvis has even been immortalized on a 1993 U.S. stamp. Elvis's music was, and continues to be, fun. The fact that it has become the stuff of legend is the legacy of the boomers.

The ambivalence of the boomer generation has been captured ingeniously and profitably by *The Simpsons*, a cartoon sitcom that continues to be a huge success as I write. Homer Simpson, the father on the program, is the boomer antihero, who has all the wrong answers to family problems. But his views and those of other boomers on the show often reverberate with philosophical nuances. In an interesting collection of studies, put together by Irwin, Conrad, and Skoble in 2001, titled *The Simpsons and Philosophy*, the claim is made that the sitcom deals, in effect, with some of the greatest questions of philosophy and religion on a regular basis.[15] But I remain unconvinced. In my view, the sitcom is popular because of its biting satire of pop culture. It is a product of the ironic character of pop culture itself, where anything goes, including self-deprecation.

INSIGHTS

Of course, it is of little practical value to the parent of a troublesome teen to know that adolescence has been brought about by a social experiment and that, ever since its invention, it has been nurtured and sustained by economic and other kinds of modern institutions. A consideration of the history of adolescence, nevertheless, does afford several relevant insights that would explain why teens are the way they are. Knowledge of history is a necessary starting point for coming to grips with any situation initially. Otherwise, as the common saying goes, one is "condemned to repeating history."

In this, and in all subsequent "Insight" sections, I will use the words of teenagers themselves as they have been recorded by the research team assembled at the University of Toronto (see the introduction) as a basis for providing relevant insights.

"I am the way I am, no matter what my parents want. It's natural, isn't it?"

Perhaps the most significant insight to be gained from a historical analysis of the origin and evolution of adolescence is that our culture has now entrenched the conditions—social, legal, and institutional—that sustain a view of adolescent behaviors as rebellious and troublesome as natural outcomes of the maturation process itself. But as history makes clear, they have been brought about by culture, not nature.

The greatest lesson to be learned from studying adolescence in historical context is contained in a common English saying: "We have made our bed, now we must sleep in it." To complain today about teenagers as unruly, violent, confrontational, or rebellious is to ignore that they are products of the same social forces as their parents—who were also once tagged as unruly, rebellious, and the like. Perhaps the time has come to realize that the social experiment may have run its course, as I will discuss in the final chapter.

"Why is everybody always looking at me?"

By expecting pubescent individuals to put their sexual urges "on hold," that is, without providing them with a formal channel for their expression, we have, in effect, brought about the conditions that foster a state of excessive self-consciousness in adolescents related to the bodily changes that puberty brings about. This explains why teens may feel that they are being constantly observed, although the audience is more imaginary than real. One of the greatest fears of teenagers is to "stand out" with others watching and judging their appearance and behavior.

"Nobody really understands me. I'm not a kid anymore."

The separation of adolescents from children on the one side and adults on the other logically makes them feel that their own emotional problems are unique. I have interviewed teenagers who had just broken up with a girlfriend or boyfriend, and they have invariably attempted to impart to me that "no one else could possibly understand" what they are feeling, even though breaking up is a common experience. They also perceive their family-related problems as unique.

Adolescents are adults in every sense of that word, even though we do not perceive them as such. They cannot simply be told what is best for them and what to do. In effect, they want a relation with parents that is different from what it was when they were children. They "hate being called kids," as one informant emphatically put it to me.

"I can't live without my friends."

In the history of adolescence, one thing stands out saliently clear— teenagers form powerful bonds with peers because they find themselves in a situation that makes it virtually impossible for them to relate to anyone of any other age category. The peer group provides emotional shelter, allowing the teenager an opportunity to "blend in" socially with others who have the same pattern of feelings that he or she has. In turn, the peer group becomes all-encompassing, demanding unquestioning constant allegiance—a kind of "all for one, one for all" commitment, reflective of the musketeer motto in Alexandre Dumas's (1802–1870) 1844 novel, *The Three Musketeers*. Those who opt to remain individualistic are typically perceived as "outcasts" or "losers." The herd instinct among adolescents is very strong. In the now-forgotten 1958 teen movie called *The Snob*, teen protagonist Sarah encapsulates this with her penetrating observation: "They're so mean and hateful! They don't understand anybody who isn't one of their gang and who doesn't do the silly things they do!"

Peer pressure, as it is now called, can influence a young person to leave home, to join a gang or cult, to take drugs, or to take upon himself or herself some perilous risk. The good news is that it weakens considerably in

Table 1.2. How Important Are Your Friends in Comparison with Your Parents?

Early Teens (12–15) (Number of Subjects = 77)		Mid-Teens (16–18) (Number of Subjects = 72)		Late Teens (18–early 20s) (Number of Subjects = 51)	
Very	70 (90.9%)	Very	42 (58.3%)	Very	12 (23.5%)
Moderately	6 (7.8%)	Moderately	4 (5.55%)	Moderately	2 (3.9%)
Not at All	1 (1.3%)	Not at All	26 (36.1%)	Not at All	37 (72.5%)

the later stages of adolescence, as the research team found. When the 200 teenage informants interviewed for this book were asked to compare friends to parents, the responses revealed an age-related attrition pattern: that is, the older the teen, the less important the friends and the more important the parents. (See table 1.2.)

It is not typical for teens to change friends radically, especially in early adolescence. The decision to do so is usually brought about by some conflict in the teen's life, by the strong influence of certain individuals, or by some desire to escape the fold radically. Talking to the teen's previous friends and asking them why they think it has occurred is the best way to uncover the probable reason (as the research team discovered). Teens know these things better than anyone else, and they are usually willing to help out a friend who is in trouble.

I once interviewed a 13-year-old female who, at the beginning of our chats in 1989, belonged to a so-called hard rocker clique at her school. The members of her clique used light drugs and alcohol, smoked cigarettes, and engaged in aggressive behavior, but minimally on all counts. Their daughter's lifestyle clearly worried her parents, but apparently a "pact" had been worked out between them—the teen had to be home by a certain hour at night and the parents, in return, would cease to criticize her and her friends. Just before my interview sessions at the female's school came to a close one month later, I noticed several radical changes in her. She was starting to associate with older punk individuals. She shaved her head and started wearing "intimidating" punk clothing (a dog collar, nose rings, and army boots). She started to dislike talking to me. She did, however, answer one of my last questions rather revealingly. When I asked her why she had abandoned her previous friends, she answered abruptly: "They're a bunch of jerks." Soon after, she started missing classes and coming home later and later at night, and sometimes not at all. Serious trouble had entered the lives of both the teen and her parents. The unfortunate young female was jailed a few months later for committing a violent crime and for possession of drugs.

The parents were, needless to say, heartbroken. They had no idea that her personality change was triggered by a change in peer group—the hapless teen had been befriended by a punk female rather aggressively and was eventually persuaded to join the group. Although the unhappy daughter had abandoned the family, it was obvious to me after a brief visitation I had with her upon her release from jail that she was profoundly embarrassed and could not face her parents.

"I'm gonna get even with those guys; sooner or later those loudmouths will know what it feels like to be alone."

When a teen is ostracized by a peer group, a dangerous situation can emerge because exclusion can lead the teen to feel isolated, suicidal, or (as has been witnessed in recent cases of school violence) revengeful against peers. The typical signs associated with ostracism include an abrupt change in personality, an avoidance of family discussions, an increased need to be solitary, coming home later and later, skipping school, and appearing absentminded. Some erratic behavior in teens is commonplace. However, a dramatic increase in such behavior is cause for concern.

"Why are they always telling me what to do?"

The historical excursus undertaken in this chapter should make it obvious that virtually everyone alive today has been labeled an adolescent, unless he or she was reared in a vastly different culture. We all have had family arguments over such trite things as clothing fashion, friendships, musical tastes, and the like. Family arguments are, and have always been, particularly destructive events. What makes every teen's blood boil are expressions such as "When I was your age. . . ," "Young people today do not understand. . . ,"and the like. The moralizing tone in such discourse only increases the *emotional noise* in family communications, as it can be called, and this leads in turn to confrontational behavior. A physical noise is something unpleasant, unexpected, or undesired. It can affect someone in a negative way. Similarly, emotional noise can cause a negative reaction. Many teen behaviors are, and have always been, emotionally noisy. They are overtly confrontational. To counteract the effects of emotional noise, it is best to distance oneself from it. Reacting by shouting, screaming, and the like will not solve the problem at hand. All it will do is raise the emotional noise level even more.

STATEMENTS MADE BY TEENS DURING INTERVIEWS

- "I hate it, man, when my dad, like, always says, 'When I was your age.'"
- "Adults never let me finish talking; they think I dunno nothing."
- "My mom is a detective—'What party? Was there drugs?' I can't stand her!"

Table 1.3.   Examples of Antilanguage

Patronizing	Impersonal Reference	Name-Calling	Blaming
Dearie!	Are we having a bad day?	You're a moron.	You never get it, do you?
Sweetie!	The young man is out of it.	Stop being an idiot.	Can't you get this into your thick head?
Good girl!	Aren't we a bit too emotional?	You're as stubborn as a mule.	Today all you kids are disrespectful.
Poor you!	Who does the young lady think she is?	You're a jerk.	Kids aren't what they used to be.

There are two things that teens abhor the most. First, they detest the "pressure to succeed" that is put on them throughout the adolescent years. One teen expressed it this way to me: "I not only have to play for fun when I play hockey, I'm expected to win a Stanley Cup every time I'm out there." Second, teens dislike being talked down to. As one teen said to me: "Why is it that adults always give us a bad rap?" Even a book such as this one is suspect to teenagers, for it singles them out as "special cases." The difference, I hope, is that it will be perceived by teens as an attempt to portray them honestly and up front through their own words.[16]

In table 1.3 are examples of the kinds of communicative ploys that, as teenagers have indicated in the interviews, annoy them the most. They are examples of what can be called *antilanguage*.

Teens often do things that seem to be dangerous or silly. But reprimanding them is useless. If a teen gets caught speeding and under the influence of alcohol, the worst type of reaction would be "I told you so! You're incorrigible!" This is exactly what one teen told me a few years back. He also suggested to me that a better approach would be to counsel him as one would another adult: "You're OK; that's all that matters. Be careful next time." Simply put, if we are ever to grow up as a culture, then we must start treating teenagers like the adults that they are. Returning to Gramsci's remark, with which I started off this chapter, the time has come, in my view, to return to a simpler, more natural view of the lifecycle—one in which, as he put it, there are two "clear-cut phases, before and after puberty." This may require some radical adjustments in groupthink. But it will ultimately be worth it. Some of these will be discussed in the last chapter.

NOTES

1. Antonio Gramsci, *Letters from Prison* (New York: Columbia University Press, 1993), 162.
2. Gail Sheehy, *New Passages: Mapping Your Life across Time* (New York: Ballantine, 1995).

3. S. Shahar, *Childhood in the Middle Ages* (London: Routledge, 1992), 27.

4. Stanley G. Hall, *Adolescence* (New York: Appleton-Century-Crofts, 1904).

5. E. H. Erikson, *Childhood and Society* (New York: Norton, 1950); and E. H. Erikson, *Identity: Youth and Crisis* (New York: Norton, 1968).

6. For an overview of the main psychological findings and theories on adolescence, readers can consult the book by R. M. Lerner et al., eds., *Encyclopedia of Adolescence*, 2 vols. (New York: Garland, 1991); and the one by E. Atwater, *Adolescence*, 4th ed. (Englewood Cliffs, N.J.: Prentice Hall, 1996). The volume by G. J. Broude, *Growing Up: A Cross-Cultural Encyclopedia* (New York: ABC-Clio, 1995) provides a useful comparison of adolescence in different modern cultures. The facts and figures compiled by B. A. Chadwick and T. B. Heaton, eds., *Statistical Handbook on Adolescents in America* (New York: Onyx, 1996) provide quantitative detail to many of the trends that are discussed in this book.

7. Readers can consult the following books to get complementary perspectives and more detailed information on adolescence and teenagehood: J. E. Coté and A. L. Allahar, *Generation on Hold: Coming of Age in the Late 20th Century* (Toronto: Stoddart, 1994); H. J. Graff, *Conflicting Paths: Growing Up in America* (Cambridge, Mass.: Harvard University Press, 1995); G. Palladino, *Teenagers: An American History* (New York: Basic Books, 1996); P. Hersch, *A Tribe Apart: A Journey into the Heart of American Adolescence* (New York: Fawcett, 1998); W. Mueller, *Understanding Today's Youth Culture* (New York: Tyndale, 1999); and D. Pountain and D. Robins, *Cool Rules: Anatomy of an Attitude* (New York: Reaktion Books, 2000).

8. Margaret Mead, *Coming of Age in Samoa* (New York: North American Library, 1928); and Margaret Mead, *From the South Seas: Studies of Adolescence and Sex in Primitive Societies* (New York: Morrow, 1939).

9. R. S. Lynd and H. M. Lynd, *Middletown: A Study in Modern American Culture* (New York: Harcourt, Brace, and World, 1929).

10. T. Greenwald, *Rock & Roll* (New York: Friedman, 1992).

11. Frank Thomas, *The Conquest of Cool* (Chicago: University of Chicago Press, 1997).

12. Stuart Ewen, *All Consuming Images* (New York: Basic Books, 1988), 20.

13. Evenhanded assessments of the baby boomers can be found in Doug Owram, *Born at the Right Time: A History of the Baby Boom Generation* (Toronto: University of Toronto Press, 1996); and J. Queenan, *Balsamic Dreams: A Short but Self-Important History of the Baby Boomer Generation* (New York: Henry Holt, 2000).

14. Bruce Pollock, *Hipper than Our Kids: A Rock & Roll Journal of the Baby Boom Generation* (New York: Schirmer, 1993).

15. W. Irwin, M. T. Conrad, and A. J. Skoble, eds., *The Simpsons and Philosophy* (Chicago: Open Court, 2001).

16. Books written by experts to give advice to parents abound. Here are a few illustrative titles: L. Meyer, *Teenspeak! A Bewildered Parent's Guide to Teenagers* (New York: Peterson's, 1994); L. Kutner, *Making Sense of Your Teenager* (New York: Morrow, 1997); and L. Langford, *The Big Talk: Talking to Your Teens about Sex and Dating* (New York: John Wiley, 1998).

2

Sex

Interviewer	Have you ever had sex?
Teen Informant	A bit. All my friends have.
Interviewer	How old are they?
Teen Informant	Like me, 12.
Interviewer	What kind of sex?
Teen Informant	All kinds. I mean, it's unreal. Scary and fun! Just don't tell my folks!

BACKGROUND

In a 1962 media interview, the late German-born American actor Marlene Dietrich (1904–1992) quipped that sex in America "is an obsession; in other parts of the world a fact." This obsession is particularly noticeable in adolescents, who can be characterized as sexually maturing individuals living in a culture that expects them to put their sexual urges "on hold." Throughout North America, adolescents are discouraged and even prohibited from having sex, because they are defined legally as being "under age." This thrusts them into a bizarre state of existence. On the one hand, they experience natural sexual desires; on the other, they experience frustration because the society in which they live does not provide them with any formal outlet to channel or express them. The result is an obsession with sex, which they perceive as being both "scary and fun," as our 12-year-old informant so aptly put it.

The media picked up on this obsession opportunely in the 1950s when sex, romance, and courtship became the central themes around which teen-directed movies and magazines revolved (and continue to revolve). Since then, the obsession with sex has spread to our culture at large, not only because of a clash between its Puritan legacy and its progressive sexual openness, but also because of its unwitting endorsement of one of the most misguided social experiments of history—adolescence. The so-called psychological traumas that crystallize at adolescence are the result of this obsession, which cannot help but have an influence on the teenager's emotions and moods. Clearly, sex constitutes a critical feature in any portrait of contemporary adolescence.

SEX, SEXUALITY, AND GENDER

In order to discuss the question of adolescent sex in any meaningful way, three terms must be distinguished from the very outset—*sex, sexuality,* and *gender.* The term *sex* refers to the individual's role in biological reproduction, as either male or female. Colloquially, it is also used to refer to interest in activities such as kissing, genital touching, intercourse, and others that allow individuals to express or satisfy their reproductive urges in some way. *Sexuality* can be defined, instead, as engagement in sexual activities themselves in culture-specific ways. Note that what is considered sexual by one individual, group, or entire society is not considered so by another individual, group, or society. This is why there is so much variable opinion across the world, and even within a single society, as to what is sexual. The people of one culture may regard legs, earlobes, and the back of the neck as sexually attractive. But people of another culture may find nothing at all sexual about these body parts, preferring lips, buttocks, and breasts, for instance. Similarly, decorations such as tattoos or cosmetics

---

BIOLOGICAL AND CULTURAL DISTINCTIONS

- *Sex* refers to the anatomical and behavioral differences that distinguish an individual as *male* or *female.*
- *Sexuality* refers to the kinds of culture-specific sexual activities associated with amorous relationships, mate selection, and courtship.
- *Gender* refers to the sexual and social behaviors that are expected of an individual of either sex (male or female) by the culture in which he or she lives. The behaviors are defined as *masculine* or *feminine* accordingly. These vary widely from culture to culture and, even within one culture, from individual to individual.

that are designed to sexualize the body might be perceived as sexually stimulating in one culture, but not in another.

Sensing the other person's sex is a biological mechanism. Across species, the organism's sexual state is detected by another organism from the same species from the body signals it emits during estrus (going into heat). However, at some point in its evolutionary history the human species developed a sense and desire for sexuality independent of estrus. Other animals experience chemical and physical changes in the body during estrus that stimulate desire. People, however, normally experience desire first, which then produces changes in the body.

By the way, it is of little use to prohibit interest in sex, even in childhood, as some right-wing politicians are attempting to do as I write. Censorship and prohibition have never worked in regulating human interest in sexual matters. The assumption of these moral guardians is that children and adolescents must be protected from "indecent" information—whether in art, literature, or in daily life—that might harm their development. Where does the legitimacy for this assumption come from? Certainly not from nature. It comes from our romantic fantasyland view of children as "innocent" and "pure"—no more, no less.[1] When I was a child of barely 5, I remember being extremely interested in female sexual anatomy and found a willing partner to show it to me. Of course, my 5-year-old partner asked me to show her my own anatomy. Where did we get this "indecent" need from? Certainly not from the information present in the culture in which we grew up, which, at the time, strictly forbade any depictions of sexuality in the media. It may be hard for some politicians to believe, but interest in sex comes from Mother Nature.

Finally, the term *gender* refers to the sexual persona a male or a female is expected to assume in a specific culture. Characteristics and behavior associated with being a male are called *masculine*; those associated with being a female are called *feminine*. Gender roles mediate the relationship between the sexes in a society and are, therefore, directive of how we relate sexually with others. Until recently in Western society, men were expected to be the sex seekers, to initiate courtship, and to show an aggressive interest in sex. But it would be a mistake to assume that this is a universal pattern in males across the world. Among the Zuni Indians of New Mexico, these very same actions and passions have always been expected of the women. It is informative to note that the word *sex* comes from the Latin *secare* ("to section, divide"), suggesting that the traditional Western view was fashioned by the ancient myth of Hermaphrodite, the peculiar creature with two faces, two sets of limbs, and one large body. Hermaphrodite was resented by the gods, who ended up dividing her into two biologically separate sections—male and female. Western civilization has, in fact, always focused on differences between the sexes rather than on similarities, even though there are probably more of the latter. The 200 teens interviewed for this book were unanimous in pointing out that there is now little difference in how teen males and females seek sexual gratification. This response is symptomatic of what can be called a society-wide process of "degendering," that is, a tendency to blur and even eliminate traditional gender roles (as will be discussed in more detail in the next chapter).

We develop a concept of ourselves as either male or female early in life. We also learn early on how a person of our sex is expected to act. Parents, friends, teachers, television, religious teachings, and many other sources help shape our sense of gender and our perception of sexual matters. In adolescence, this concept is virtually turned on its head, at least for a while. When it comes to sex and romance in the pubescent period in our culture today, things are pretty well left up to the adolescents themselves. Sex in teen relations is something that "happens," as one informant aptly phrased it during an interview. It is something that everyone in the adult world knows goes on, but largely ignores. There are two main patterns that surfaced from the interview sessions connected with issues of sex and courtship. The content of the discussions on the tapes suggests that amorous relations in adolescence unfold casually and tend to involve specific peers (mainly school friends). Also, the research team found that most teens, of all age categories, engage in some form of consensual sex on a regular basis.

These findings stand in stark contrast to the traditions that our culture upheld as sacrosanct not so long ago. Courtship activities and marriages were arranged by families directly or were at least shaped by family input—traditions that continue on in many other cultures today. In our

---

SEXUALITY IN ADOLESCENCE

- As the research team discovered, a large percentage of younger adolescents engage in serious sexual activities. Of the 77 informants classified as early teens (ages 12–15), 69 (36 girls and 33 boys) admitted to having engaged in some form of sex (from oral sex to coitus) with a partner. Of these, 45 (20 girls and 25 boys) claimed to have engaged in sexual activities on a regular basis.
- Seventy-one of the 72 mid-teens (ages 16–18) interviewed, and all of the 51 late teens (18–early 20s), admitted to having engaged in consensual sex with a partner.
- Virtually all the informants (195) claimed that their sexual behavior was "typical" of all their friends and, probably, of "all teenagers."

society, courtship in adolescence is discouraged, and marriage either is prohibited or else is permitted only under strict conditions. In all except four states, marriage partners must be at least 18 years old to marry without parental consent. Nebraska and Wyoming require a couple to be at least 19. Mississippi and Rhode Island set the minimum age at 21. In some states, a person under age 16 needs a judge's permission to marry. These measures, however, have hardly blocked interest in sex and romance (as our interviews confirmed). All they have ended up doing is encouraging a gradual postponement of courtship and marriage to well beyond the pubescent years. In 1950, men married at an average age of 23, and women 20. By the mid-1990s, the average age was 27 for men and about 25 for women.[2] An increasing number of people today even choose not to marry.

The research team also found that adolescent romance is hardly devoid of formalism. Again, from the content of the interview sessions, the team was able to determine that a sui generis courtship goes on regularly among adolescents, involving coded signals, symbols, and rituals. One of the latter is smoking—a ritual rooted in a culture-specific form of sexual acting that is designed to keep the two sexes physically differentiated and highly interested in each other. As will be discussed in chapter 7, the particular enactment of the smoking ritual will vary in detail from situation to situation and from person to person, but its basic features and functions tend to remain the same. It is anchored in an unconscious repertoire of gestures and postures that reinforce gender-specific models of sexual attractiveness. Cigarette smoking in adolescence is, in a phrase, a ritualistic courtship display. This would explain why nearly all the 200 teenagers interviewed for this book (192) pointed out that they either smoke all the time or occasionally because it is "cool."

Another source of gender-specific modeling of sexual attractiveness is clothing. The original purpose of clothing and footwear was, no doubt, to protect the body and the feet. But that is hardly how they are perceived today. High-heeled shoes, for instance, are uncomfortable and awkward to wear; yet females wear them on certain occasions. Like cigarettes, they are largely unconscious accoutrements in sexual acting. They force the body to tilt, thus emphasizing the buttocks and breasts. Moreover, as the social historian William Rossi has written, they emphasize the fact that shoes and feet are perceived to be fetishes in our culture.[3] Even in fairy tales, the "lure of the shoe" undergirds such stories as *Cinderella* and *The Golden Slipper.*

In adolescence, the line between the "normal" and the "abnormal" in clothing styles is vague. Fashion trends are often taken directly from the fetishist's closet. The appropriation has been so complete that the teens wearing such garments and apparel are often unaware of their fetishist origins. All the teens interviewed evaluated clothing items for their "cool-ness" value. But in sexual acting, cool and sex are synonyms. This is why teens will go to great lengths in order to wear what is "in" with the peer group of the moment, even if it flies in the face of common sense—I have witnessed hordes of teenagers standing outside in below-zero weather barely clad, smoking happily, seemingly immune to the ravages of the weather. Clearly, sex in adolescence is more powerful a motivator of be-havior than is any inbuilt response system to weather, or to anything else for that matter.

MEDIA PORTRAYALS OF ADOLESCENT SEXUALITY

As mentioned in the previous chapter, although adolescence has turned out to be good for the modern economy, it has not been all that good for pubescent individuals in our culture since its invention as a social exper-iment. Adolescents are sexually mature individuals who are defined as children only by an accident of history. Left to their own whims, they will find ways to satisfy their sexual needs on their own terms. This is some-thing that our pop culture picked up on early in the experiment. Sex and romance have always made up the sum and substance of teen movies, from the silly beach movies of the 1950s and 1960s, such as *Muscle Beach Party* (1964), to the hilarious Ben Stiller films of the 1990s and 2000s, such as *Meet the Parents* (2000).

The movies have also provided the symbols and rituals for teens to adopt and adapt to their particular situations. Take, for instance, the role of cars and smoking in adolescent sexuality. Nicholas Ray's 1955 movie, *Rebel without a Cause*, constitutes a case in point. The "car chicken" scene in the movie is particularly memorable in this regard. Two male suitors are seen vying to "win over" a female paramour through this form of con-temporary tribal combat. Before the car battle, there is a ritualistic rubbing of the earth. Then the camera zeroes in on James Dean, one of the two combatants behind the wheel of his car, showing him with a cigarette hanging from the side of his mouth; his competitor is seen in his own car slicking down his hair. Cars, hairstyle, and cigarettes are, clearly, the pri-mary sexual props in this early depiction of teen sexual ritualizing.

Cigarettes are crucial sexual props also in Michelangelo Antonioni's 1966 movie, *Blow Up*. In one memorable scene, an adolescent Vanessa Redgrave is seen swerving her head excitedly to the rock music that David Hemmings, her boyfriend, has put on his record player. His objec-tive is to give her a lesson in female sexual foreplay, from his own per-spective. He tells her to keep still because her actions and gestures must be slow and deliberate. Then he gives her the cigarette he had in his mouth. She takes it quickly, eager to insert it into her own mouth. But, no, Hemmings instructs her, she must slow the whole performance down; she must go "against the beat," as he puts it. Leaning forward, Redgrave takes the cigarette and inserts it slowly and seductively into the middle of her mouth. She lies back salaciously, blowing the smoke upwards. She gives Hemmings back the cigarette, giggling suggestively. He takes it and inserts it into his own mouth, slightly to the side, visibly overcome by the power of her sexual performance.

Such images have become emblazoned in the collective memory of our culture. They undergird the unconscious association that teens make between smoking and sex. In effect, movies provide the fine details of what it means to be young and sexy. This is why, like the actors on the movie screen, teens act as if they were themselves characters in some imaginary movie, adopting the look, the talk, and the swagger of sexy actors to impress and attract each other. Incidentally, the Latin term for "cast of characters" is *dramatis personae*, which means literally, "the persons of the drama"—a term betraying the theatrical origin to the very concept of personhood. The sociologist Erving Goffman (1922–1982) drew attention to the idea that everyday life is, in fact, very much like the theater or the movies, because it involves a skillful staging of persona.[4] No wonder, then, that so many young males can be seen today looking like a Brad Pitt, an Eminem, or whoever is the sexy male *artist du moment*, and just as many young females can be seen looking like a Cameron Diaz, a Jennifer Lopez, a Britney Spears, or whoever is the sexy female *artiste du moment*.

Aware of the power of the movies to influence adolescents, a nonprofit advisory group, called Media Project, was established in 1984 to oversee the media's handling of teen sexuality. The very existence of such a body is testimony to the fact that we intuitively know that teens get their information about sexuality not from school, parents, or books, but from media representations. Wisely, the group has always taken a nonintrusive stance, providing mainly information on such crucial things as pregnancy, sexual diseases, and the like for media moguls to consider.

TEEN TRIBALISM

The term *tribalism* has been used several times previously in reference to teen social behavior. The subtext to its usage in this and other treatments of adolescence is that teens tend to form peer groups that assume a social structure that resembles that of tribal cultures.

In modern urban societies, where various cultures, subcultures, countercultures, and parallel cultures are in constant competition with each other, and where the shared territory is too large to allow for members to

---

TEEN TRIBES

- Traditionally, *tribe* refers to a group of people sharing customs, language, and territory. A tribe has a powerful leader who imposes his of her belief system on members.
- The word *tribe* is now applied to any group of individuals who bond together spontaneously for some specific reason.
- A teen clique is, in effect, a miniature tribe, with a strong leader and its own idiosyncratic lifestyle.
- As in traditional tribes, the belief system of the leader is directive of the behavior of clique members.

---

come together for basic ritualistic purposes, the tendency for individuals is to relate instinctively to smaller tribal-type groups (communities, clubs, and the like). This inclination toward tribalism, as the communications theorist Marshall McLuhan (1911–1980) emphasized, reverberates constantly within modern-day humans and may even be the source of the sense of alienation that many people who live in complex and impersonal social settings experience.

The first tribes were the first *cultures* of the human species because they organized their daily life on the basis of a system of symbols, rituals, and communal activities that gave stability and continuity to the life of the members. The tribal system also allowed the members to pass along what they acquired from one generation to the next. Archaeological evidence suggests that as the members of the early tribes became more and more culturally sophisticated, that is, as their cultures grew in complexity, they sought larger and larger territories in order to accommodate their concomitantly burgeoning social needs. In their new settings, diverse tribes developed a common, albeit complex, modus vivendi. The zoologist Desmond Morris aptly calls those settings "super-tribal."[5] The first super-tribes date back only 4,000 to 5,000 years. Out of these the first city-states evolved.

A modern society is a descendant of a super-tribe, a collectivity of individuals who do not necessarily trace their ancestral roots to a single founding tribe, but who nevertheless participate in a common cultural "amalgam" that has evolved over time. The amalgam allows individuals to interact in both spontaneous and ritualistic ways. Unlike tribes, however, the mode of interaction does not unfold on a personal level because it is impossible to know, or know about, everyone living in the same society. Moreover, a modern society often encompasses more than one cultural system. Consider what people living in the society known as the United States loosely call "American culture." This traces its origins to an amalgam of the cultures of the founding European societies that settled in the United States. Within contemporary American society, there are also aboriginal cultural systems with different ways of life, different languages, and different rituals. There are, moreover, many subcultures, with lifestyle and symbolic patterns of their own that set them apart from the larger American culture of which they are part. Subcultures may develop in businesses, ethnic groups, occupational groups, regional groups, religious groups, and other groups within the larger American culture. For example, Amish people in Pennsylvania and several Midwestern states make up a subculture, as do the members of a teenage street gang. Therefore, unlike his or her tribal ancestor, an American can live apart from the mainstream culture in a parallel one or can become a member of a subculture; he or she can also learn and utilize different languages and rituals, each with its own symbolism and meanings. But like tribal systems, American society still defines the "normal" through the primary cultural order; those living apart from this order will typically face risks, such as being subjected to various forms of ridicule, censure, and even ostracism.

Teen social life assumes a tribal structure for the simple reason that it is the default social structure of human groups. Nowhere is the inclination toward tribalism as noticeable as it is in hip-hop cliques. As will be discussed in subsequent chapters, those who join a hip-hop clique must go through a series of initiation rites that include a change in name and in clothing, complete with cap or tuque and jewelry. They must also adopt a brash swaggering demeanor and learn to utilize a repertoire of menacing hand gestures in imitation of rapper heroes.

Tribalism, however, is not unique to certain specific teen cliques. Sexually charged dancing, for instance, has always been a part of self-styled teen rites of passage. The movement of two sexually alert bodies in rhythmic coupling is a passionate act. Knowing the right dance moves is sexual savoir-faire. From the early *American Bandstand* shows of the 1950s to break dancers and rappers on MTV, the teen with the right moves has always been judged to be cool and desirable. Many media-hyped teen performers today, from Janet Jackson to Christine Aguilera, are essentially "sexual entertainers." The line between true erotic dancing and teen dancing has always been a blurry one. The sexuality of the dance may now be more explicit, but it has always been there.

Teenagers are sexually mature individuals. By defining them, legally and culturally, as "older children," we have put them into an emotionally and socially dangerous "holding pattern," as mentioned at the start of this chapter. It is no exaggeration to claim that all the lifestyle behaviors that are considered to develop "naturally" at puberty are, in fact, reflexes of this pattern. This topic will be taken up in more detail in the next chapter and revisited in the final one.

INSIGHTS

Sex, as Marlene Dietrich so keenly observed, is indeed an obsession in America. It is everywhere, from television and movies to advertising posters. In my view, much of this obsession has been brought about by the fact that we expect adolescents to put their sexual urges on hold. Some of the effects of this obsession can be extracted from the words of the teens themselves below.

"I don't care what my parents say; I'll wear what I want, and be who I want to be."
Sexual identity is built into what teens wear and in the look they fashion for themselves. This is, of course, true of anyone at any stage of the lifecycle. But it is particularly so at adolescence. The peer group provides a tribal context in which sexuality can be expressed ritualistically and symbolically. This is why adolescents wear clothing that they believe imparts a new identity to them that allows them to fit in sexually with the peer group.

Tribal cultures have always marked the coming of age event with elaborate rites involving cosmetic decorations, bodily alterations, and the like. For instance, the pubescent males of the Secoya people who live along the Río Santa Naría in Peru wear a sprig of grass through their nasal septum for the traditional passage rite. This allows them to keep their faces "poised," exuding confidence and sexual control. Among contemporary teens similar types of props, with virtually the same function, are the nose and the lip ring.

Cosmetics have a long and unbroken connection with tribal customs that go back considerably in time. As anthropologist Helen Fisher has observed, even in the prehistoric Cro-Magnon era, during the last glacial age, young humans spent hours decorating themselves, plaiting their hair, donning garlands of flowers, wearing bracelets and pendants, and decorating their tunics and leggings with multicolored fur, feathers, and beads.[6] Contemporary teen cosmetic, grooming, and clothing practices are really no more than modern versions of such ancient tribal customs. The colors used in lipsticks and eye decorations, as well as the rings put on ears, noses, lips, eyebrows, and tongues, are, in effect, tribal props in contemporary teen passage rites.

ORIGINS OF SEXUAL KISSING

- Representations of sexual kissing have been found on 2,000-year-old Peruvian pots and vases.
- Some argue that the origin of such kissing lies in the biological need to transfer sebum, the substance that lubricates our skin and hair, so that mating partners can achieve a form of chemical bonding.
- Others believe that we kiss because the lips, tongue, and interior of the mouth are highly sensitive erogenous zones connected to the limbic system, the oldest part of the brain and the source of sexual pleasure.

"Of course, I have sex. All the time, man. I mean, it's, like, natural, isn't it?"

The fact that teens have sex is, as our informant aptly put it, "natural." Reproductive urges at puberty are nature's way of ensuring species continuity. Even in childhood, some sexual behaviors are normal and natural.

Children as young as 4 and 5 may even engage in sexual kissing, unconsciously communicating awareness of gender differences and of incipient sexual feelings. In a sense, kissing is mock-suckling or mock-feeding, implying vulnerability, closeness, and romantic sensuality. But it is not universal. In many other cultures, it is felt to be a disgusting habit—as an "exchange of sputum." In our culture, the perception of kissing at adolescence as a sexual and romantic activity is, of course, reinforced by pop culture images in movies, advertisements, and the like.

Needless to say, the risks of engaging in sexual activities are very high in adolescence. Teens typically believe that they are immortal. For this reason, they become careless in the use of condoms, birth control devices, or other such measures, as the research team found. Although there is an increase in the use of precautionary measures in the later ado-

SEXUALLY TRANSMITTED DISEASES

- An estimated 10 to 12 million Americans develop a sexually transmitted disease every year, according to the Centers for Disease Control (CDC).
- The most common diseases include gonorrhea, syphilis, infections of the urethra not caused by gonorrhea, genital herpes, genital warts, scabies, urethral and vaginal infections of various sorts, and, of course, AIDS, now the most dangerous of all sexual diseases.

Chapter 2

Table 2.1.   Do You Use Condoms or Expect Your Partner to Use Them?

Early Teens (12–15) (Number of Subjects = 77)		Mid-Teens (16–18) (Number of Subjects = 72)		Late Teens (18–early 20s) (Number of Subjects = 51)	
Always	0 (0%)	Always	4 (5.5%)	Always	12 (23.5%)
Occasionally	6 (7.8%)	Occasionally	16 (22.2%)	Occasionally	20 (39.2%)
Never	71 (92.2%)	Never	52 (72.2%)	Never	19 (37.3%)

lescent years, as the figures above show, it is nevertheless frighteningly low for all categories of teens and, thus, is a major cause for concern (see table 2.1).

Teens do know a lot these days about sex. But the tendency is to ignore the use of precautions in the heat of the moment. The greatest risk is, of course, AIDS. Infection with HIV does not necessarily mean that a person has AIDS. People who are HIV-positive are often mistakenly said to have AIDS. A person can remain HIV-positive for more than ten years without developing any of the clinical illnesses that define and constitute a diagnosis of AIDS. The World Health Organization estimates that between 1981, when the first AIDS cases were reported, and the end of 1996, more than 8.4 million adults and children had developed AIDS. In this same period, there were 6.4 million deaths worldwide from AIDS. About 360,000 of these deaths occurred in the United States.

When our informants were asked specifically about AIDS, all indicated that they knew of it, but that they still would not necessarily take precautions. As one informant stated: "It's not cool to do so." Another pointed out, rather astutely, "Hey, in the heat of passion, what do you expect me to do, sanitize myself first?" (See table 2.2.)

AIDS

- AIDS is an acronym of acquired immune deficiency syndrome.
- It refers to a specific group of diseases or conditions that result from the suppression of the immune system by the human immunodeficiency virus (HIV).
- A person infected with HIV gradually becomes highly vulnerable to pneumonia, fungus infections, and other common ailments.
- With the loss of immune function, a clinical syndrome develops over time in the infected person and eventually results in the person's death from cancer or an opportunistic infection—an infection caused by an organism that does not normally cause disease except in people with very weak immune systems.

Table 2.2.   Do the Dangers of AIDS Stop You from Having Unprotected Sex?

Early Teens (12–15) (Number of Subjects = 77)		Mid-Teens (16–18) (Number of Subjects = 72)		Late Teens (18–early 20s) (Number of Subjects = 51)	
Always	2 (2.6%)	Always	6 (8.3%)	Always	15 (29.4%)
Occasionally	12 (15.6%)	Occasionally	19 (26.4%)	Occasionally	27 (52.9%)
Never	63 (81.8%)	Never	47 (65.2%)	Never	9 (17.6%)

"Of course, I watch videos; my girlfriend watches Christina Aguilera; she knows how to give it, eh?"

There is little doubt that the body language communicated by musicians and actors influences how teens perceive sexuality. Such language continues to be gendered to some degree. For girls, it varies from a tough girl look, such as that of girl punk musicians, to a Lolita-type sex kitten look, such as that of someone like a Britney Spears or her current outgrowths.[7] The informant was referring to the "Dirrty" look (spelled with two "rr's" to simulate the perceived feline nature of female sexuality) communicated by Christina Aguilera.

"Queers, man, they're weird!"

Sexual orientation may become a truly troublesome issue during adolescence. This term refers to a person's erotic, romantic, or emotional attraction to the other sex, the same sex, or both. As is well-known, a person who is attracted to the other sex is called a *heterosexual,* or sometimes *straight.* A person attracted to the same sex is called a *homosexual.* The colloquial word *gay* is often used in place of homosexual but is most often applied to men, whereas the term *lesbian* is applied to homosexual women. A person who is attracted to both men and women is called *bisexual.* A *transsexual* is a person whose sense of self is not consistent with his or her anatomical sex—for example, a person whose sense of self is female but who has male genitals. Homosexuality is not synonymous with transsexuality. Homosexual men's sense of self is male, and lesbian women's sense of self is female.

I have met a number of gay and lesbian teens who feel deeply alienated, no matter how open-minded society now seems to be vis-à-vis homosexuality. They pointed out to me that they are constantly ridiculed by peers and misunderstood by adults. Such teens are at risk. They need love and understanding, not confrontation and ridicule.

NOTES

1. On the topic of censorship, the reader can consult the excellent treatment by Marjorie Heins, *Not in Front of the Children: Indecency, Censorship and the Innocence of Youth* (New York: Hill and Wang, 2001).

2. These calculations are based on official U.S. and Canadian census surveys taken in the 1950s and in the 1990s.

3. William Rossi, *The Sex Lives of the Foot and Shoe* (New York: Dutton, 1976).

4. Erving Goffman, *The Presentation of Self in Everyday Life* (Garden City, N.Y.: Doubleday, 1959).

5. Desmond Morris, *The Human Zoo* (London: Cape, 1969).

6. Helen E. Fisher, *The Anatomy of Love* (New York: Norton, 1992), 252–53.

7. Different perspectives on the "girl power" image can be found in Simona Chiose, *Good Girls Do: Sex Chronicles of a Shameless Generation* (Toronto: ECW Press, 2001); and Catharine Driscoll, *Girls: Feminine Adolescence in Popular Culture and Cultural Theory* (New York: Columbia University Press, 2002).

3

Body Image

Interviewer	What is the most important thing for you at school?
Teen Informant	How I look! You know, you gotta' look cool or your friends will pick on ya.
Interviewer	What do you mean?
Teen Informant	Ya gotta look like your friends. Nobody wants to look like a loser.
Interviewer	What does a loser look like?
Teen Informant	Like a doorknob, out of it, uncool!

BACKGROUND

In his immortal play *Hamlet*, the great English playwright William Shakespeare (1564–1616) had his young hero decry the frivolity of "looks" with the following words: "God hath given you one face, and you make yourselves another" (Act 3, scene 1). Although written four centuries ago, Hamlet's admonition seems to resonate with particular relevance today. In our image-obsessed culture, having the right "look" has, in fact, become a widespread narcissistic fixation—a fixation that, as our 14-year-old informant astutely intimated, now largely shapes social relations among adolescents.

Known as *body image*, the subjective concept of one's physical appearance based on self-observation and the reactions of others emerges typically at puberty. In our culture, it tends to be a problem. This is why in the 1950s, psychologists started en masse to study body image as a defining feature of adolescent psychology. Erik Erikson (1902–1994), for instance,

saw it as the key to understanding most problematic behaviors.[1] He sin-
gled out peer pressure as the single most important factor conditioning
how teens come to view themselves and, thus, how they dress, how they
style their hair, and how they conduct themselves in the company of others. Erikson argued, further, that teens who were unsuccessful in constructing an appropriate body image to fulfill peer expectations would develop an *identity crisis,* which tended to bring about drastic consequences,
including withdrawal from most forms of social contact with others.[2]

BODY IMAGE IN ADOLESCENCE

Body image is a source of one's *sense of identity* at all ages. But, as the relevant research in psychology appears to suggest, it is particularly so during adolescence. Preoccupation over body image starts generally at puberty, but it may manifest itself even before that. It is not unusual, today,
to find tweenies who are as conscious about how they look as are their
older teenage counterparts. The difference, of course, is that tweenies are
essentially still children who are probably play-acting; teenagers, on the
other hand, are genuinely involved in constructing identity through body
image. However, I should add that play-acting is not an irrelevant matter.
It can become actual involvement if the obsession with body image becomes so profound and unconscious that it has drastic consequences involving eating disorders.

The association of slimness with attractiveness has always been a crucial one for most teens. Of course, this link has been forged by constant
exposure to images perpetrated by the media and lifestyle advertising.
The research team found that the fear of being "fat" is stronger than most
other fears during the earliest stages of adolescence. This is because teens
tend to ostracize "fat" peers from their social milieu and activities, not to
mention to ridicule and make fun of them in an abusive fashion. During
the fieldwork for this book, many examples of three main types of "small
cruelties" inflicted upon "fat" peers were noted and recorded: (1) name-
calling, (2) acts of physical aggression, and (3) ostracism. I refer to these as
"small" cruelties because that is what the English language calls them.
But they are hardly perceived as small by the teens themselves. The inability to present an appropriate slim body image to peers can have dire
consequences. The increase in eating disorders, such as *anorexia nervosa*
and *bulimia nervosa,* is one of these. Since the 1950s, the incidence of these
disorders has reached frightening proportions and is due, in my view at
least, partially to the fear of being perceived as obese by peers.[3] In *Fast
Girls: Teenage Tribes and the Myth of the Slut,* sociologist E. White has documented that girls as young as 8 years of age are worried about being fat.[4]

SMALL CRUELTIES

- Name-calling: "Hey, fatso!" "Looks like a tanker trailer rolled in today!"
- Acts of physical aggression: punching, shoving, kicking, and the like.
- Ostracism: excluding the teen from peer cliques and from socially meaningful peer events (parties, get-togethers, and so on)

"Appearance junkies," as White calls them, are made, not born. Our current image-obsessed pop culture has made body image the primary project in the lives of too many adolescents.

Perhaps in reaction to the ultraslim body image perpetrated by the media, in the 1980s female teens began adopting a "tough-looking" body image en masse. The first manifestations of this new trend crystallized in the fitness craze that played itself out not only in TV exercise programs and video products but also in movies such as *Physical* (1981) and *Flashdance* (1983). Known as a "girl power" movement, it was subsequently perpetrated by such pop music artists as the Spice Girls, Da Brat, Foxy Brown, L'il Kim, Courtney Love, Joan Jett, Patti Smith, and L7 and by media characters such as Buffy the Vampire Slayer, Xena, Charlie's Angels, and Lara Croft, among many others. As I write, clones of these stars are all over the media. The girl power look is no longer a fad. It seems to have become an unconscious pattern of feminine body image.

In the same time frame, males started becoming more concerned about aspects of body image that, in previous teen generations, would have been considered "girlish." *MH-18*, a male teen magazine that started publishing in the late 1990s, contained advice to males on how to bleach or dye their hair and on what kind of cologne and jewelry to wear in certain situations. The boom in unisex stores such as the Gap, Banana Republic, and Abercrombie & Fitch also made it obvious that differences in body image between males and females were becoming blurrier and blurrier. The popularity of boy bands such as NSYNC, 98 Degrees, and the Backstreet Boys, as well as Latino artists such as Ricky Martin and Enrique Iglesias, made it "cool" for male teens to worry openly about their looks. Clones of these stars now abound in all media.

In my view, the reason why body image is such a powerful factor in adolescence can be found in the artificial nature of adolescence itself. By having created an age category that separates adolescents from children on the one side and adults from the other, Western culture has unwittingly created the artificial conditions that lead to what can be called a "disconnection syndrome" in the personality of individuals reaching the age of puberty. In childhood, the individual's personality system—composed of emotional, social, and sexual components develops in an integrated fashion within the family, unless of course the family is dysfunctional. The family structure—nuclear, extended, single-parent, or whatever form it may assume—provides an affective context for the child to develop a sense of self that is meaningful to his or her situation. To put it more plainly, children who are cared for lovingly by those who constitute their family regularly develop a normal, healthy personality. At puberty, however, children are projected into an anomalous situation. Defined still as children, adolescents are forced to cope with incipient sexual feelings on their own terms. Consequently, the other components of personality—the emotional and the social—become "disconnected," so to speak, from the sexual.

The obsession over body image that emerges at puberty is, in my view, a direct consequence of the disconnection syndrome. Some of its most obvious manifestations are the awkward and smirky behaviors that are now so common in early teens. These do not show up in pubescent individuals in other cultures. As one informant put it during an interview: "I have a Middle Eastern friend who is so mature, even though he's just 13; I mean, he looks and acts like an adult; and yet he is just like us." Maturity can, in fact, be defined as the ability to maintain a balance between the emotional, social, and sexual components of personality at any age. Those who are incapable of doing so will, needless to say, undergo stress in some fashion. But no one would sensibly view the stress as a result of some necessary phase of nature. However, this is exactly how it is viewed by Western psychological theories of adolescence. But, as mentioned previously, such Sturm und Drang theories are really no more than rationalizations. In actual fact, teens desire emotional, social, and sexual stability. Not finding a society-wide context for it, they seek it in peer groups where it is everyone's concern.

Another consequence of the disconnection syndrome is a feeling of awkwardness that pubescent individuals typically feel in early adolescence. This may explain why adolescents resort typically to a series of "camouflage strategies." One of these is a deliberately slow and lackadaisical form of bodily locomotion, accompanied by a nonchalant and unflappable countenance. Their walk is typically laggard, to the point of being a drag or a stroll. Another is the girl power look mentioned above—a look that allows female teens to exude confidence and inner strength. But whatever look a teen adopts, it is clear that it constitutes a strategy that allows him or her to disguise the awkwardness he or she tends to feel. As one 13-year-old female informant put it: "You just gotta look cool, relaxed, and chilled out; otherwise you're dead meat, man."

The peer group that emerges in early adolescence is crucial because it provides a context in which teens can come to grips with the disconnection syndrome. In areas of the world where adolescence has never taken hold as a social experiment, there are no punks, hip-hoppers, or whatever name teens may use to refer to the peer groups they form. During the hippie era, some teens even went so far as to form peer groups, called "communes," that set themselves completely apart from others. The communes were formed primarily by adolescents, often in tandem with older individuals, who saw them as alternative social structures for living outside the mainstream social system.

DEGENDERING

As mentioned in the previous chapter, the trend toward the blurring of the traditional gender lines may be called *degendering*. The roots of this phenomenon can actually be traced to the first decades of the twentieth century when young women set themselves apart from their Victorian predecessors by openly displaying their sexuality through such dances as the Charleston, by smoking in public, and by becoming leading artists of the ever-expanding boundaries of pop culture (as singers, actresses, and the like). It developed into a full-blown movement in the hippie 1960s, when "unisex" became the operative shibboleth, not only in clothing but also in social activism. Before the degendering process, females in our culture rarely were perceived as physically, intellectually, and socially equivalent to males. Not only has this belief changed, but we also now even encourage females from childhood onward to outdo their male counterparts in all areas of human behavior.

Today, unisex trends are hardly perceived as radical or countercultural. They have, in effect, been enshrined into groupthink by media images. This is why the "gangsta" or some other "street-tough" look of the 1990s was adopted by both male and female teens. The primary features of this look were tattoos and various types of body piercings. In the 1990s, teen idols such as pop singer Janet Jackson wore jewelry on her nipples, tongue, and nose; and basketball and movie star Dennis Rodman wore rings on his nipples, ears, nostrils, navel, lip, and scrotum.

Tattooing in our culture was introduced by sailors (see box). It has always been a critical symbol of membership in motorcycle gangs. It has also been used by prisoners to convey toughness and identity. The adoption of tattooing as a fashion trend by teens began in the 1960s—a trend captured a little later by the Rolling Stones in their popular 1981 album *Tattoo You*. Tattooing and piercing reverberate with latent tribal overtones, allowing teens to convey a street-tough look. The degendering subtext in such trends is, clearly, the perception that human skin is an extension of self—a theme that was captured rather effectively by Melissa Etheridge in her 2001 album, named appropriately *Skin*.

TATTOOING

- Tattooing is the technique of decorating the skin by inserting colored substances under its surface. The skin is punctured with a sharp instrument, usually an electric needle.
- Tribal people used (and continue to use) tattooing to indicate social rank.
- Rank-significant tattooing was also practiced by the Egyptians around 2000 B.C. (and possibly long before that).
- Sailors introduced tattooing into Europe during the sixteenth and seventeenth centuries. They used it initially to set themselves apart from other members of society.
- In the 1960s and 1970s, tattooing starting gaining popularity with counterculture youths, gangs, and prison inmates.
- In the 1980s, tattooing among teens increased considerably.
- Because of complaints by health authorities that contaminated needles spread infectious diseases, particularly hepatitis, by the mid-1990s tattooing was outlawed in some American communities and restricted to persons over 18 years of age in others.
- In place of tattoos, body paints and pictured adhesives, called *skin transfers* or *decal tattoos,* became popular in the early 2000s.

Today, tattooing and piercing have evolved into society-wide trends, having lost most, if not all, of the tribal symbolism with which they originally resonated among teens. They have become mere "cosmetic practices" used by media icons and common folk alike, with no distinction as to age, gender, or social class.[5]

Paradoxically, despite the degendering forces at work in society, the awareness and display of sexual difference have hardly disappeared from the peer tribe. As they say in French, the *vive la différence* perception of gender is alive and well among adolescents. For example, the "display of the bust" through tight and revealing clothing by teen females to emphasize sexuality and girl power made a "comeback" in the late 1990s—I characterize it as a "comeback" because this fashion trend is not unlike the one of wearing "cleavage-showing" corsets in the eighteenth and nineteenth centuries. Actually, this bust-focused image of "feral womanhood" has an ancient history, from ancient myths to early pop culture representations. It was perpetrated and rendered mainstream by early 1960s female teen-rock groups such the Ronettes, the Crystals, and the Shangri-Las. It was cloned in the 1970s by TV characters such as Wonder Woman and Charlie's Angels. Today, it is an unconscious pattern of female sexuality. It is found everywhere in the media and on the streets—in movies such as *La Femme Nikita* (1991), *Lara Croft: Tomb Raider* (2000), and *Charlie's*

Angels (2000). It is a look designed to convey physical prowess, intellectual deftness, and breathtaking sexuality.[6]

But nothing endures in pop culture—a form of culture that thrives on constantly changing images and representations. In contrast to the girl power image, the media introduced a counterpart image in the 1990s through a genre known generally as "Chick Lit," after the 1997 novel *Bridget Jones's Diary* by Helen Fielding. The plots of the genre revolve around 20- and 30-year-old females starting out on the career track in big cities, who search for, but rarely get, the "perfect guy." The general message is that "it's OK to be female and on one's own." The subtext of the genre also constitutes a condemnation of traditional courtship practices. TV programs such as *Sex and the City* are products of the genre. As I write, however, I notice a decline in its popularity. Perhaps people have become tired of seeing weary self-absorbed characters who rarely have solutions to the relationship problems they raise.

COOLNESS

One of the most visible strategies adopted by teens to counteract the disconnection syndrome is known colloquially as *coolness*. Simply put, it means knowing how to look, walk, and talk in peer-appropriate ways. The fear of not being perceived as cool is why camouflaging body image features perceived to be awkward is of paramount importance to

---

ORIGIN OF COOLNESS

- In order to set themselves apart from older adults, many young men and women of the Roaring Twenties adopted a lifestyle that earned them the nickname "Flaming Youth." They frequented secret nightclubs called "speakeasies," where they drank bootleg liquor, smoked cigarettes, and enjoyed jazz music.
- The expression *being cool* originated in the context of the speakeasies, where a distinction was made between the swinging "hot jazz" style and the more relaxed, behind-the-beat style known as "cool jazz."
- By extension, *being cool* crystallized as an expression describing any sexually attractive young man who frequented the nightclub scene.
- The "sexual cool" of the nightclub scene was captured for the first time in film by the classic movie *Casablanca* (1942).
- Teen coolness was portrayed for the first time in 1950s movies such as *Rebel without a Cause* (1955) and *Blackboard Jungle* (1955).

teenagers. As our informant above so aptly put it: "Nobody wants to look like a loser . . . uncool."

Coolness may vary in detail from situation to situation, from clique to clique, and from teen generation to teen generation, but it retains a common essence that can be called simply *bodily aplomb*. Needless to say, the main source of coolness models is pop culture. In the 1950s, cool male teens modeled themselves after Elvis Presley—a paragon of coolness revived by the television character known as "The Fonz" on the 1970s sitcom *Happy Days*. In the 1960s, the male cool look was revamped by the media after the way the Beatles dressed, talked, and styled their hair and, a little later, after the fashion styles adopted by the hippies. Females in the 1950s modeled themselves after teen idols such as Annette Funicello and her lookalikes. It consisted of ponytails, bobby socks, and kilt-type skirts. In the hippie 1960s, females dressed like their male peers—hence the crystallization of the term "unisex" to describe the new look. In the 1970s, coolness varied from a disco to a punk look for both males and females; in the 1980s, a number of coolness models emerged in tandem, varying from the "surf" and "preppie" look to hard rock, mod, and various other kinds of "hard cool" looks. In the 1990s, hip-hop became the norm, competing toward the end of the decade with a Latino look exemplified by stars such as Ricky Martin, Enrique Iglesias, and Christina Aguilera and a resurgent grunge look exemplified by Pink and Avril Lavigne. Without pop culture, coolness would become much less variable and, indeed, might even disappear.

Coolness ranges from a "soft" form to an extreme "hard" type. The lifestyles of punks and gangstas, for instance, would be located at the "hard" end of the coolness spectrum, where aggressive behavior, the use of vulgar language, and the wearing of intimidating clothes are central components of the cool look. The girl power look would be located instead near the "soft" end, providing females simply a body image with which they can assert themselves physically. But no matter where one falls on the spectrum, the aspiration to look cool in peer settings has been a fact of life since the fabrication of teenagehood by pop culture in the 1950s. The choices teens have today are much more eclectic than in the past, but the underlying motivating force is the same—a desire to look, act, and talk in ways that will meet with peer approval.

I admit that the above portrait of coolness is perhaps a little overdrawn. Not all teenagers aspire to look cool. During the research phase for this book, I myself met some who showed no desire whatsoever to conform to any existing model of coolness. There are, despite the portrait being drawn here, many studious and individualistic adolescents who are unaffected by peer pressure. But, by and large, it is accurate to say that coolness is a general trait that manifests itself in adolescence. And, because it has been appropriated almost totally by pop culture, it has become highly variable and subject to rapid change. Incidentally, as irksome as coolness attitudes may be for parents and teachers, the best strategy is to ignore them completely. Unnoticed coolness has no value whatsoever. Coolness is meant to be observed, admired, and (in some cases) feared. It is part of staging persona; without an audience, the staging is purposeless. That is why, when out of the company of peers, teenagers seem to be different.

To conclude the discussion of coolness, I would like to suggest that, as a symptom of the general process of juvenilization, coolness has become an unconscious pattern of general lifestyle in the culture at large, perpetrated and reinforced by media images.[7] As Canadian social activist Naomi Klein has emphasized, the latter are intended to turn people into appearance junkies, reducing daily life aspirations to superficial matters of look and fashion; the modern-day consumerist economic system depends, Klein claims, almost entirely on the partnership that has been forged conveniently among the previously autonomous worlds of business, media, and entertainment.[8]

CLOTHING

Clothing is the material means through which body image becomes body language. Like the costumes worn by actors, clothing is an intrinsic prop in the staging of a cool character in front of peer audiences. During the 1950s, the clothing styles worn by the first rock stars and by media personages, such as the teen dancers on *American Bandstand*, spread quickly to the teen population at large. It became obvious that teens wanted to dress alike. Cool females wore pleated skirts, dressed their hair in "ponytail"

TEEN CLOTHING

- Teens tend to model their dress and hairstyles after teen media icons and especially pop musicians.
- The most common function of clothing in adolescence is to allow teens to fit in with peers.
- Some teens adopt bizarre nonconformist clothing styles to make a counterculture statement, to shock adults, to look tough, or to mock the styles of other teens. For example, the hippies of the 1960s donned clothing designed to symbolize love, freedom, and antiestablishment values; the early punks donned clothing designed to convey subversiveness and anarchy; and so on.

style, and donned bobby socks—a fashion style, incidentally, that actually originated in the 1930s. Cool males wore leather jackets and slicked their hair in imitation of such media personages as Elvis Presley and Marlon Brando (who wore a leather jacket as a motorcycle gang leader in the 1955 movie *Blackboard Jungle*).

Today, teen clothing is no longer homogeneous. It varies from clique to clique and from lifestyle to lifestyle. But the basic function of clothing in adolescence has not changed one iota. When teens put clothes on their bodies, they are, as just mentioned, primarily engaged in play-acting. The "script," however, will vary considerably today. Teens may, for example, intentionally wear provocative clothes and use unusual props (jewelry stuck through their nostrils, for example) to make an antisocial statement. Often, this is no more than a temporary behavior, a means of attracting attention and provoking adults. But at times it represents something much more, as it did during the counterculture era. Some teens may also use clothing as a means to intimidate peers. This came out during an interview session I had a few years ago with a teen who defined himself as a *neopunk*. He indicated to me that the way he dressed (with army pants and boots) and looked (with many piercings, tattoos, and a shaved head) made him feel powerful. "Ya, I walk down the school corridor, man, and all the shits get outta my f—— way" was his blunt manner of making sure I understood this. Intimidation dressing is not, however, the privilege of punks. The leather jackets of the 1950s were perceived to have the same kind of effect that our punk teen wanted to have on his peers. In the 1990s, male hip-hop teens achieved it by wearing baggy pants backward, ultra long-sleeved shirts and jackets, unlaced sneakers, and tuques.

The heterogeneity of current fashion trends is a noticeable feature of contemporary adolescence. Alongside hip-hop fashion, many male teens now wear tight-fitting pants, colorful shirts (or blouses), and hair cream that keeps their short hair spiked. Alongside tight-fitting leather suits à la Janet Jackson, a Lolita-like skirt à la Britney Spears, or "bust-showing" blouses used by girl power groups, female teens also don disco-type clothing that conveys elegance and high fashion. The "Britney Spears look," consisting of midriffs, embroidered jeans, sequins, ruffles, glitter purses, sneakers, and skate shoes is also in competition with a "neo-grunge look" consisting of shaggy unkempt hair, worn-out T-shirts, 1970s-style plaid Western shirts, low-rise blue jeans, baggy pants, undershirts, and chain wallets—a look exemplified by such media icons as Pink, Avril Lavigne, the Strokes, the Vines, the White Stripes, and Audioslave.

Needless to say, alongside such trends, punk and hip-hop continue to hold great appeal among teens. More often than not, however, teens today are unaware of the symbolism that their clothing items have. As the research team discovered, few contemporary punk teens know the story

---

HIP-HOP CLOTHING

- The clothing worn by hip-hop teens is part of a lifestyle code that is designed to set them apart from adults and other teens.
- The basic message of the code is street toughness.
- This is manifest, for example, in the wearing of pants with the crotch near the knees—a style that is imitative of prison dress (for safety reasons, prisoners are not allowed to wear belts, forcing them to wear their pants in this way).
- The jewelry worn by hip-hop teens (neck chains, earrings, and so on) is similarly intended to send out signals of toughness and intimidation.
- However, as hip-hop clothing styles came to be adopted by the mainstream fashion industry in the early twenty-first century, the "gangsta" symbolism of such styles started to lose its impact and meaning.

---

behind the wearing of leather collars with sharp spikes protruding from them. Originally, such collars were designed for dog training. The spikes protruded inward. The reason for this was negative conditioning—if a command was disobeyed, the dog's leash, attached to its collar, would be pulled, thus punishing the dog by driving the spikes into its neck. Being against all forms of authority and social conditioning, the early punks reversed the dog collar in parody of such obedience training. The protruding spikes, therefore, symbolized a reversal of power alignments, signaling that the wearer would never be controlled by society.

Such items of clothing are elements in what may be called a *confrontation dress code*—a subversive code that is designed to transform everyday clothing props, such as collars, into bizarre fashion items that subvert their original social meanings. The use of razor blades, tampons, and clothespins as "jewelry" by some contemporary followers of punk culture are other examples of confrontational clothing props.

I should mention, however, that as such fashion trends become mainstream, they quickly lose their symbolic force and become highly popular. One well-known fashion guru to recognize this was Karl Lagerfeld. As design consultant for Chanel, he was among the first to send models swaying down the runway in 1991 in hip-hop clothing, with sneakers and chunky gold chains that had Chanel nameplates engraved on them. Versace, Gucci, Prada, Tommy Hilfiger, and others followed quickly behind, openly embracing hip-hop fashion and, thus, spreading it to other age groups.

Undoubtedly, as readers are going through this book, the styles described above will have become passé. But whatever the clothing craze *du moment* may be, there is no doubt in my mind that it will continue to be used by teens to set themselves apart from adults and to look cool—however that look is defined. All this would likely not have come to be if, as discussed in the opening chapter, adolescents were to be viewed as adults rather than as "adults in waiting." More will be said about this in the final chapter.

INSIGHTS

The all-encompassing concern over body image in early adolescence is due, in my view, to the self-consciousness that crystallizes from the disconnection syndrome. It is little wonder that the concern has clearly become an obsession. According to a 2001 survey by Teen Research Unlimited, a Chicago-based marketing company, in 2000 American teens spent an astronomical $155 billion for cosmetics and various other personal maintenance props. And they persuaded their parents to spend another $100 billion. Teen "beauty inflation" crosses all social boundaries, involving teens of all ethnic and socioeconomic stripes. And for the first time in the history of teenagehood, the trend is now as much a consequence of a shift in parental attitudes as it is of media influence. Many of today's parents act more like friends than custodians, eager to share lifestyle preferences with their teen sons and daughters. Not only do they act like pals to their teens, but they also often look like them, pursuing virtually the same beauty ideals.

But how is this relational pattern really perceived by the teens themselves? In early 2002, the research team asked the question "If your parent(s) were to dress in a very young style, similar to how you and your friends dress, how would you rate it?" to the 200 subjects (see table 3.1). Their responses are truly revealing.

These results bring out rather forcefully that teens do not see this juvenilization trend as "cool." Only mid-teens gave it a somewhat cool rating (33.33 percent). Teenagers seem to feel that differences between young and old are relevant and should be kept distinct through lifestyle fashions and practices.

Table 3.1.   "If your parent(s) were to dress in a very young style, similar to how you and your friends dress, how would you rate it?"

Early Teens (12–15) (Number of Subjects = 77)		Mid-Teens (16–18) (Number of Subjects = 72)		Late Teens (18–early 20s) (Number of Subjects = 51)	
Cool	8 (10.39%)	Cool	24 (33.33%)	Cool	2 (3.92%)
OK	21 (27.27%)	OK	11 (15.28%)	OK	2 (3.92%)
Silly	48 (62.34%)	Silly	37 (51.39%)	Silly	47 (92.16%)

For most teens, body image is not just a matter of staying in tune with pop culture trends. It is a crucial part of how they construct their social persona. Interestingly, like Hamlet (with whose words I started off this chapter), teens are aware, by and large, of the frivolity of fashioning a cool appearance. They see it as a two-edged sword. As one 13-year-old female teen remarked during an interview: "Cosmetics for women are, like, both good and bad." Her comment was uncannily discerning in sociological terms. Many condemn the use of cosmetics as a narcissistic disease spread by the beauty industry and the media working in tandem. But the use of cosmetics has also been useful socially, as Kathy Peiss has recently argued in her book on the cosmetic industry.[9] Simply put, cosmetics have liberated women to express their sexuality—something that traditional cultures have always tended to strictly forbid (and continue to do so). The founders and early leaders of the "cosmetic movement" were simple women—Elizabeth Arden (1884–1966), a Canadian, was the daughter of poor tenant farmers; Helena Rubinstein (1870–1965) was born of poor Jewish parents in Poland; and Madam C. J. Walker (1867–1919) was born to former slaves in Louisiana. Although it is true that our media culture preys on social fears associated with "bad complexions," "aging," and so on, it has at the same time allowed women to assert their right to emphasize their sexuality, not conceal it.

In some of our interviews with parents, concerns were expressed about the use of cosmetics and clothing by girls to emphasize the sexuality of the female form, suggesting to us that measures to censor or repress media representations to "protect teenagers" should be taken by those in government. Although their concern is certainly understandable, history teaches us that the censorship route has always proven to be a misguided one. For one thing, media messages are truly effective only if individuals are already predisposed toward their content; and for another, media moguls will find ways around such measures. A case in point is the 1998 strategy adopted by the makers of Camel and Marlboro cigarettes. Early in that year, the U.S. Congress banned the Joe Camel and Marlboro Man figures from cigarette advertising, claiming that they influenced teenagers as role models. In response, ad creators came up with truly ingenious, and more effective, alternatives. Later in that year, Salem cigarettes used a pair of peppers curled together to look like a pair of lips, with a cigarette dangling from them. It became one of the most effective ad campaigns ever recorded by the manufacturer. Benson and Hedges ads in the same year portrayed cigarettes as people floating in swimming pools, lounging in armchairs, and the like. As it turned out, this new "government-permissible" form of advertising was even more persuasive in suggesting the glamour and pleasure of smoking than were the figures of Joe Camel and the Marlboro Man, as witnessed by the fact that smoking among teenagers went up significantly from 1999 to 2000 (according to national surveys published at the time by agencies such as the Centers for Disease Control).

"I don't care what my parents say; I just wanna be like my friends."

The disconnection syndrome induces a heightened sensitivity to the views and opinions of others, and this leads teens, in turn, to engage in *self-watching*. Conformity in dress, hairstyle, and overall look to peer expectations is a defensive strategy that teens employ to divert critical attention away from themselves. Although human beings of all ages are influenced by the opinions of others and tend to conform to lifestyle models that are acceptable to their own peer groups, teenagers are particularly susceptible to such influence because of the syndrome.

"I wish I was taller!"

Concerns over body image can be agonizing. This is why one constantly hears teens utter such things as: "I wish I was taller!" "Why are my breasts so small?" "I hate zits!" "His nose is too big!" and so on.

A teen who is worried about height, nose size, obesity, and so on will tend to adopt a *protective persona* designed to masquerade the feature that he or she detests. Sometimes, this involves not only clothing and cosmetics but also the use of verbal humor. Many jokes, cracks, witticisms, quips, and the like are designed to deflect attention away from oneself. The same strategy is also used to cover up, or minimize, things that weigh heavily on the teen's mind. Jokes bragging about failure at school may reflect an anxiety over academic performance, cracks about the appearance of others may indicate insecurity about one's own appearance, and so on. Irony in particular emerges at puberty as a powerful defensive verbal strategy. It allows the adolescent to interact with peers in tactful ways. This topic will be taken up further in the next chapter.

The quest to present the "right look" to peer audiences has reached such extremes among some (perhaps many) teens that, I believe, it is cause for serious concern. The number of teenage females who are having implants to increase the size of their breasts is alarming, to my mind at least. And it seems to come, more often than not, with parental approval—as our interviews revealed! Have we as a society created notions of beauty that leave young females with little choice other than to alter their bodies drastically? Our research team found that virtually all of the females interviewed had at the very least thought about changing the shape and size of their breasts. A few had undergone breast surgery. What really surprised us was that in those cases, the parents had knowledge of the surgery and, except in one single case, approved of it.

"I hate anybody criticizing me and especially invading my space."

Fearful of how they will be perceived and accepted by peers, adolescents will go to great lengths to adopt hairstyles, clothing fashions, and any accoutrement that will allow them to "blend in" with the peer group of choice (punks, ravers, hip-hoppers, and so on). This is why they are oversensitive to criticisms by parents about how they look. Such criticism is useless. It has the same effect as calling a soldier weird for wearing combat gear, or a priest bizarre for putting on vestments to say Mass. In a sense, the clothing and bodily decorations that teens adopt make up the bodily armor that they need in the peer battlefield.

Teens will "let their guard down" and "remove their armor," to extend the metaphor, in their "own space," as one informant described her bedroom. Adolescents not only unwind and relax in such spaces, away from the peer spotlight, but they also fashion their own "private identity" through personal objects (posters, photos, compact disks, letters, and the like). In the private space, the true self comes out. This is why unwanted visitations in this space are felt to be intrusions, including those made by parents to clean the room themselves or to instruct their adolescents to tidy it. Of course, not all teens have a private bedroom. In many households the bedroom is shared, by necessity, with siblings. And many poorer youths have essentially nowhere to stay but on the streets. But it is accurate to say that most teens desire their own private space, whether or not it is available. And even on the streets, they mark self-space by declaring a portion of the street as "personalized." As one street teen told the research team: "On this side of the street, I'm king, man."

"I'm not gloomy, man. That's, like, the way I am."

Two sure signs of the onset of the disconnection syndrome at adolescence are awkwardness and moodiness. Most of the teens interviewed saw themselves, in fact, as "awkward" and as constantly feeling "excitable," as one teen so cleverly put it.

For many years, psychology has tended to attribute feelings of awkwardness and of "angst," as adolescent moodiness is commonly called, to the effects of hormonal changes. But in my view, most emotional disturbances in adolescence have little to do with biological processes. They derive from the social experiment of adolescence itself. This is why adolescents go through periods when they genuinely wonder what their "real" personality is. As mentioned at the start of this chapter, the psychologist Erik Erikson called this an identity crisis. Ironically, adolescents who have gone through a prolonged identity crisis may actually end up feeling a stronger sense of identity as a result of taking the time to examine who they are and where they are headed.

"I'm not sure who I really am sexually, sometimes."

Maturity involves not only a physical capacity to reproduce but also the ability to deal with sexual feelings, to negotiate intimacy with another person, and to establish a sexual orientation. At some time, incidentally, almost all adolescents worry about their orientation.

Unfavorable attitudes toward homosexuality may cause significant distress for adolescents who experience gay and lesbian feelings, especially if they encounter hostility from those around them. Teenagers attracted to members of the same sex face many challenges. Unfortunately, they often have to overcome these challenges without the support available to their heterosexual peers. This situation is changing, but it remains a major concern of those subjects interviewed who have a homosexual orientation.

"My parents just don't understand why I look the way I do."

Fitting in with peers entails donning the appropriate "battle gear." Within the peer group, such things as hairstyle and clothing are of great concern, as I have attempted to drive home throughout this chapter. No wonder, then, that teens spend so much time on their looks. As bizarre as they may seem to a parent who is accustomed to deciding what his or her child would wear not so long ago, the adolescent must cope with problems of body image for the reasons discussed in this chapter. That is the main insight that can be gleaned from any study of body image. This has always been the case, from the 1950s on. For example, in the 1960s, hippie teens wore ripped jeans, long hair, and sandals; disco teens in the 1970s wore bell-bottom slacks and other clothing accoutrements associated with the disco scene; hard rock teens wore their hair long after the hairstyles of hard rock or heavy metal musicians in the 1980s; punks shaved their heads in imitation of their punk rock heroes; hip-hop teens wore baggy pants in emulation of hip-hop recording artists in the 1990s; and so on.

"She knew she had anorexia, but she did nothing about it!"

These words were relayed to me by the relatives of a student of mine who passed away, tragically, from complications related to anorexia during a school term several years ago. I was shocked to find that she had the disease and deeply aggrieved by the whole incident. It took me a considerable period of time to regain the necessary composure I needed to carry out my pedagogical duties in that class.

The fixation with body image is no laughing matter. If it becomes inordinately obsessive, it may lead to a serious situation, as I found out firsthand. Some adolescents become so concerned about it that they take drastic measures, even literally starving themselves to death. Anorexia nervosa was virtually nonexistent in other cultures until recently. And even in ours, it did not occur before the age of 10 until a few years ago. I read with frightful consternation that it has been spreading throughout the global village and that it is starting to crop up in children as young as 5 or 6![10]

It was once believed that such disorders were more common in North America and Western Europe than in other parts of the world, and that they were more prevalent among the prosperous and well educated. However, research in the late 1990s found them to have spread among all social and economic levels and to have cropped up in countries throughout the world. Through media images, the juvenilization of the globe has brought about a concomitant spread of "teen disorders" as well. In effect, in the global village teenagehood knows no boundaries or social situations. It also is beginning not to know any age difference.

"I'm no different from anyone else!"

As the mother I met several years ago emphasized to me (see the introduction), teens sometimes look like "aliens" to adults. She was referring to the way her son dressed, to the kinds of things he put on (e.g., earrings and a tongue ring), and to the insouciant and apathetic facial expressions that he often wore on his face. But as alien as they may appear, they really are no more than temporary peer-socialization strategies.

What teenagers hate the most without exception is being centered out and critiqued constantly about the body image choices they make, as the statements recorded by various members of the research team make abundantly clear (see box). Above all else, the use of antilanguage to critique the teen's choices is not only useless but is also often counterproductive (see chapter 1). One teen told me that her father would always say such things as "You look like a goof!" and "Stop wearing those idiotic clothes!" This only clogged the lines of communication between them more than they would have been otherwise. Children take what an adult has to offer as authoritative and as the "final word." Teenagers, on the other hand, will turn the tables around and challenge virtually everything adults have to say. Teens want a reason for doing things according to a prescribed way, not

---

STATEMENTS MADE BY TEENS TO THE RESEARCH TEAM

- "My parents don't get it. I'm just like my friends. No big deal. They dressed weird when they were young. Weird!"
- "I hate being told what to wear. I'm, like, not a kid anymore."
- "I don't care what they say, I'll wear whatever I want. It's what I am."
- "My parents are not cool. They dress like goofs. I'll never do that."
- "My parents try to look like teenagers. They're funny, man. They should dress their age."

just an order to do so. This is because they are adults, not "older children," as our culture so wrongly categorized them 150 years ago.

NOTES

1. Erik H. Erikson, *Childhood and Society* (New York: Norton, 1950).
2. Readers interested in a psychological discussion of body image and related issues can consult, for instance, David Elkind, *All Grown Up and No Place to Go* (Reading, Mass.: Addison-Wesley, 1984) and David Elkind, *The Hurried Child: Growing Up Too Fast Too Soon* (Reading, Mass.: Addison-Wesley, 1988).
3. Readers wanting to know more about anorexia nervosa and its causes can consult the books by H. Bruch, *The Golden Cage: The Enigma of Anorexia Nervosa* (Cambridge, Mass.: Harvard University Press, 1978); J. J. Brumberg, *Fasting Girls: The Emergence of Anorexia Nervosa as a Modern Disease* (Cambridge, Mass.: Harvard University Press, 1988); and M. Hornbacher, *Wasted: A Memoir of Anorexia and Bulimia* (New York: Harper Flamingo, 1998).
4. E. White, *Fast Girls: Teenage Tribes and the Myth of the Slut* (New York: Scribner, 2001).
5. Insights on teen tattooing and piercing trends can be found in L. Reybold, *Everything You Need to Know about the Dangers of Tattooing and Body Piercing* (New York: Rosen Publishing Group, 1996); J. Lopiano-Misdom and J. De Luca, *Street Trends: How Today's Alternative Youth Cultures Are Creating Tomorrow's Mainstream Markets* (New York: Harper Business, 1997); and B. Wilkinson, *Coping with the Dangers of Tattooing, Body Piercing, and Branding* (New York: Rosen Publishing Group, 1998).
6. On the topic of girl power images in the media, see Sherrie Inness, *Tough Girls: Women Warriors and Wonder Women in Popular Culture* (Philadelphia: University of Pennsylvania Press, 1999).
7. The relation between advertising and lifestyle was examined critically by Bryan Wilson Key in a series of attention-grabbing books in the 1970s and 1980s: *Subliminal Seduction* (New York: Signet, 1972), *Media Sexploitation* (New York: Signet, 1976), *The Clam-Plate Orgy* (New York: Signet, 1980), and *The Age of Manipulation* (New York: Holt, 1989).
8. Naomi Klein, *No Logo: Taking Aim at the Brand Bullies* (Toronto: Alfred A. Knopf, 2000).
9. K. Peiss, *Hope in a Jar: The Making of America's Beauty Culture* (New York: Metropolitan Books, 1998).
10. Mary Pipher, *Reviving Ophelia: Saving the Selves of Adolescent Girls* (New York: Ballantine, 1995), has become a widely read work on how adolescent girls have been manipulated psychologically by our beauty-obsessed culture. S. Azam, *Rebel, Rogue, Mischievous Babe: Stories about Being a Powerful Girl* (Toronto: HarperCollins, 2001), looks at body image questions from the perspective of a contemporary female teen (the author herself).

4

Language

Interviewer	What word did you use to describe that boy over there?
Teen Informant	He's a quid, man.
Interviewer	How would you define a quid?
Teen Informant	There ain't nobody worse. He's a real creep-o; someone who wastes life.

BACKGROUND

An article published by the *Washington Post* on March 15, 1987, offered an insight into adolescence that is as penetrating today as it was then: "In the halls of schools across the land, wild-eyed youths are flinging freshly invented words and newly coined phrases at one another with the hope of including a Few and, at the same time, excluding Us." Freshly invented words, such as the form of *quid* used by our informant, are so typical of how teenagers communicate with each other that we hardly ever take notice of what they mean, how they are coined, and what they reveal about adolescence. But taking notice of them is, in fact, the goal of this chapter.

Most people would refer to words such as *quid* as slang. But this term gives the wrong impression. They are, more accurately, verbal forms created by teens that allow them to refer effectively to things that matter to them and to them alone. Incredibly, such forms have been making their way more and more into the linguistic mainstream. Words and expressions such as *loony, chick, dude, sloshed, chill out*, and *24/7*, among many others, have become so much a part of our everyday vocabulary that we no longer remember that they originated in teen discourse. In all previous eras, the speech mannerisms manifested by young people were hardly considered to be worthy of emulation. Indeed, the contrary was true. Young people were expected to learn and use adult forms of grammar and vocabulary. But today, proper usage seems to have gone out the window with the fashions of the old. Like never before, language is being shaped by the ever-changing categories of adolescent discourse, not because the latter is better than the standard language but because it is everywhere.[1]

EMOTIVITY

Teens speak in distinct and easily recognizable ways that they acquire un- consciously by communicating with peers. As mentioned, many refer to teen talk as slang. But this is wrong, in my view. It is really a social dialect. In previous publications, I referred to it as *pubilect* (the dialect of puberty), since it constitutes a variety of the spoken language that is peculiar to teens. It differs from the standard language mainly in its distinctive stock of words and phrases that teens coin typically to refer to things, events, and people that make up their particular social world. Predictably, it is highly variable, continually changing from one teen generation to the next, from one clique to another, and so on.

By recording and analyzing the conversations of adolescents over the years, I have found that two main features surface constantly in pubilect. They can be called *emotivity* and *figuration*. The former refers to the fact that the ways in which teenagers construct and deliver their verbal mes- sages are governed primarily by emotional needs and by moods of vari- ous kinds. When teenagers utter such highly charged expressions as "Awesome!" "Yuck!" "Neat-oh!" "Ohmygod!" and the like with pro- longed stress, accompanying gesticulations, facial contortions, and the like, they are drawing attention to their feelings and moods.

There are four main manifestations of emotivity in teen discourse: (1) *tagging,* which is marked by a tone of voice in the communication of statements that is indistinguishable from that used in interrogatives; (2) *vocalism,* which is marked by the use of highly charged expressions; (3) *hesitancy,* which is characterized by the use of *fillers* and *hedges* (words and expressions that allow teens to keep their turn in a conversation as they formulate their thoughts); and (4) *profanity,* which is characterized by the use of vulgarisms and swear words of various kinds. (See table 4.1.)

Called *uptalk* colloquially by the media, tagging can be characterized as the tendency to utter sentences as if they were interrogatives, even though a question is not intended. For example, an utterance such as "We, like, studied (?) (intonation like a question) . . . but couldn't get anywhere (?)

Table 4.1. Manifestations of Emotivity

Tagging	Vocalism	Hesitancy	Profanity and Vulgarity
We, like, called her up (?) (intonation like a question) . . . but she wasn't there (?) . . . so we, like, hung up (?).	Ugh! Yesssss! Ohmygaaad.	Like, I called him up, but, like, he wasn't sure, if he, like, could come.	This sucks! I'm pissed off! What a shithead! I'm all f—ed up.
Tagging reveals that the teens feel a strong need to ensure the full participation of their interlocutors in what they are saying.	Vocalized expressions allow teens to draw attention to their feelings, opinions, and moods in an emphatic way.	Fillers and hedges are gambits that allow teens to maintain their turn in a conversation with limited interruption as they gather their thoughts or search for words.	Profane and vulgar expressions are used typically by teens as verbal weapons, but because they have become so common they have probably lost much of their intended forcefulness.

(same intonation) . . . so we, like, quit and took off (?)" (same intonation), with its rising tones, makes it appear as though the teen is asking questions. And, in an implicit way, he or she is. A *tag* is a word, phrase, or clause added to a sentence in a rhetorical fashion: "She's coming tomorrow, isn't she?" "That's a good course, right?" and so on. The uptalk pattern that occurs in adolescent discourse is essentially an implicit tag pattern—a tag sentence without the tag. It highlights the need of teenagers to ensure the full participation of their speakers in what they are saying. As I write, this feature is starting to recede from pubilect, being replaced by what can be called a kind of *laggardness* in speech delivery, for lack of a better term. This consists of slowing down the rate of speech to a drawl or nasal drone, conveying aplomb and savvy. It is noticeable throughout the media—for example, in teen sitcoms or dramas such as *Buffy the Vampire Slayer,* where female characters exude great composure through the nasal delivery of sarcastic messages.

Hesitancy devices such as *duh, like,* and *man* have very important functions in pubilect. *Duh* is a word that, when it resurfaced in the 1980s, was much maligned by parents, educators, and language purists. But like the hedges in adult language—*yeah, uh-huh, well,* and the like—*duh* is really no more than a useful conversational gambit. With its perfectly paired linguistic partner, *yeah right,* it is, above all else, a versatile discourse tool for conveying savvy and sarcasm. During an interview, I once asked a 15-year-old boy, "Don't you think it's a great day today?" His answer was a wry "Duh," indicating to me in a truly artful way the futility of my comment. It was equivalent to saying, "Tell me something I don't know." *Duh* is assertive, a perfect tool for undercutting mindless chatter or insulting repetition.

Like surfaced in the 1980s at first as a simple hesitancy device, giving teen speakers time to put words to ideas without losing input in a communicative situation: "I, like, wanna come but, like, I'm a little busy now."[2] It continues to have this function today, carrying the implicit meanings: "Are you listening to me?" and "Don't you agree?" But *like* now has many other functions. One of these is providing teens with a means to soften the negative impact of a statement. Saying that a "song is, like, bad" is much less harsh and confrontational than saying flatly that the "song stinks." Another function of *like* is indirect citation. It is thus used as a *quotative*—an expression, such as "she said" or "he repeated," followed by a quotation. For example, in place of "Sherry said: 'What are you doing?'" teens will typically say instead "Sherry was like: 'What are you doing?'" A third common function of *like* is as a *quantifier*. In place of a word or expression such as *nearly, approximately, very,* and so on, or a structure such as *It must be,* teens regularly use *like* as follows: "The CD's, like, 20 dollars"; "It's, like, late, ya know"; and so on.

Incidentally, some of these functions predate current pubilect. A 1954 *Time* magazine article—"You wanna hear some jazz, like?"—described it as a mannerism of the teenagers of that era. And, incredibly, the *Oxford English Dictionary* reports that the use of *like* meaning "in a way, so to speak," as in "I'm, like, so in the mood," goes back to 1778! The use of *like* as a quotative was satirized in 1982 by the late Frank Zappa with his song "Valley Girl," in which he parodied the "Valley Girl" slang that was in

---

DISCOURSE FUNCTIONS OF "LIKE"

- As a hesitation device: "I, like, wanna tell you that she, like, also wants to . . . you know what I mean?"
- To maintain conversational contact: "Like, you know what I mean? It's, like, even you said."
- To soften criticism: "I think the song is, like, bad."
- For satirical purposes: "He was, like, a real loser, like a freak!"
- As a quotative: "Sherry was like: 'What are you doing?' And I'm like: 'Nothing.'"
- As a quantifier: "It's like a hundred dollars."

vogue at the time among female teens with such lyrics as "Your toenails are like so grody" and "She's like, oh my God." Recently, I discovered the use of *like* as a hesitancy device in the Scooby-Doo comics and cartoons of the late 1960s.

Finally, the interjection of *man* in various kinds of utterances—"That guy's a loser, man"; "I'm so hammered, man, I think I'm going to heave"; "He's seriously wasted, man"—emerged in the hippie era as a kind of "code word" for male teens to express camaraderie. Today, it has gained currency with both genders and, significantly, with speakers of all ages. A comparable word is *guys,* which is now used by both males and females to refer to peers. For example, "Hey, guys, let's get goin'," was uttered by a female teen to her female peers on the interview tapes, and "C'mon guys, it's time to go," was uttered by a male teen to his male peers.

FIGURATION

The second main feature of pubilect is, as mentioned above, *figuration.* This refers to the fact that teenagers use words and phrases, and invent many new ones, not only to convey their feelings but also to *figurate* ("draw pictures of") the people and events in their immediate social world in graphic fashion. I came to understand this in the early 1990s, when I recall asking a teenager what the word *dork* meant. At the time, *dork* had not gained the currency that it enjoys today. She defined a dork as "a greasy male teen, who studies chemistry all night." I had certainly seen such boys, but I had not thought of them as belonging to a seman-tic category as such. I simply viewed them as studious, but unpopular, teens. I knew of no word in the English language, previous to hearing *dork,* that called attention to them in a specific way. But after learning the word *dork,* I suddenly started seeing *dorks* everywhere, eventually be-lieving that the "dork" category did indeed have a raison d'être. I even started using the word to describe people in my own social environ-ment!

Many of the figurative devices used by teenagers in actual conversa-tions are self-explanatory (such as the ones in the conversation repro-duced in the box). Essentially, they are coded forms that allow students to convey opinions in a dramatic way—much like theatrical language.

A few years ago, I collected relevant data in a Toronto high school. I asked a group of female teens what specific words they would use to de-scribe males in their school whom they found to be attractive. Accord-ingly, they were asked to complete the phrase *He's* _____. The words they came up with reveal rather clearly how figuration undergirds the

CONVERSATION BETWEEN TWO MALE TEENS
RECORDED IN SAN DIEGO, 2001

—Yo ("hi").
—Yeah, whassup ("what's up")?
—Not much.
—Did you, like, talk to that hotty ("good-looking girl")?
—Yeah, but she gave me headbubbles ("a headache").
—Like, why are you still really dealing with ("going out with") that mint chick ("good-looking girl")? There are others, ya know?
—Yeah, I know, shithead.
—Straight up ("really"), duh? I'm trying to help, and you're always like: "F—— you!"
—I know, but I can't help it. She plays with ("fools around with") this homie guy ("loser") too much, so I chilled out ("cooled off"). That dude sure ain't no player ("cool guy"). She can have him.
—Yeah, man, that's nasty ("an awful thing").
—Listen, nobody plays with me ("fools around with me").

Vocabulary Creation Techniques

- Abbreviating words:
  delish ("delicious"), bro ("brother, friend"), bod ("body"), rad ("radical")
- Combining words or parts of words:
  megabitch ("very troublesome female"), vomatose ("vomit" + "comatose"), chill out ("relax, do nothing"), diss on ("criticize, belittle")
- Composing acronymic phrases:
  MLA ("massive lip action" = "passionate kissing"), GMO ("get me out"), BTW ("by the way"), TSH ("that shit happens"), DL ("down low" = "secret"), L ("liquor store")
- Coining graphic expressions:
  jonesing ("craving"), ralph ("vomit"), skank ("promiscuous female")
- Composing rhyming word pairs:
  sight delight ("good-looking male"), bad rad ("good party person")
- Borrowing from pop culture:
  Yo! Whassup? (greeting expressions from hip-hop culture)
- Changing the meaning of words:
  radical ("wild at a party"), bad ("good"), mint ("cool, good-looking"), bones ("money"), millers ("earrings"), wicked ("excellent")

teenager's train of thought. The "attractive male teen" was characterized by the subjects as being dangerous or untrustworthy ("He's bad," "He's nasty"), a type of animal ("He's a stag," "He's a stud," "He's a fly," "He's a catch"), a desirous object or place ("He's a Ferrari," "He's a diamond," "He's chiseled," "He's Park Avenue"), something tasty or edible ("He's yummy," "He's a stud muffin," "He's a burger"), and as a hot (sexual) substance ("He sizzles," "He's hot").

The research team recorded many instances of figurative language use during the interviews. It also solicited language data directly ("What words do you and your friends use?"). The data collected in this way have made it possible to develop a typology of vocabulary creation techniques that teens use commonly to make up their word forms. The main ones are abbreviating words *(delish, bro, rad)*, combining words and affixes *(megabitch, chill out, diss on, vomatose)*, composing acronymic phrases *(MLA, GMO, BTW, TSH)*, coining graphic (largely onomatopoeic) expressions *(barf, jonesing, ralph, skank)*, composing rhyming couplets *(sight delight, bad rad)*, adopting words from pop culture *(yo, whassup)*, and injecting different meanings into ordinary words *(radical, bad, wicked, random)*.

Each coinage is comparable, in a fundamental sense, to a one-word or one-phrase poem, since it is designed to convey an experience, an idea, or an emotion in a way that is more concentrated, imaginative, and powerful than ordinary words and expressions. But the poetry is, more often than not, of an ironic nature. Most coinages seem to be designed to parody and satirize or, simply, to evoke a humorous response. As a discourse strategy, irony is absent in childhood conversation.[3] However, at puberty it seems to crystallize as a dominant strategy. Indeed, most of the forms compiled by the research team seem to have been designed on purpose to mock, deride, or satirize. Words and phrases such as *biffed* ("crashed"), *epic* ("a long ride"), *burbulating* ("relaxing"), *fly girl* ("party girl"), and *sperm donor* ("a father who's never around") are really one- and two-word ironic jokes, allowing teens to poke fun at specific aspects of everyday life in much the same way that a satirist would. As the American poet Carl Sandburg (1878–1967) once put it, pubilect "is a language that rolls up its sleeves, spits on its hands and goes to work."[4]

Children learn to use language as a means to understand the world and the people in it, not to critique it. At puberty, however, adolescents start realizing that language can be used as another kind of tool—as a "weapon" that can be deployed for defensive or aggressive reasons. This can be seen in words such as *megabitch, geek, party animal, dog* ("unattractive person"), and *wimp dog* ("male with little personality"), to mention but a few. The weaponry can, of course, involve a strategic use of humor. Expressions such as *MLA* ("massive lip action," or passionate kissing), *barf* ("vomit"), and *blimp boat* ("obese person"), which were in vogue in the early 1990s, never fail to evoke the kind of sardonic chortle or snicker that only irony can summon forth. As the American author and critic Elizabeth Hardwick so astutely observed a few years ago: "The language of the younger generation has the brutality of the city and an assertion of threatening power at hand. It is military, theatrical, and at its most coherent probably a lasting repudiation of empty courtesy and bureaucratic euphemism."[5]

The research compiled by the research team also shows that, as in other areas of adolescence, degendering has become noticeable in the domain of language as well. However, a hypocritical "double standard" still seems to persist to this day, albeit to an increasingly limited extent. Females who are aggressive in dating were called *sluts* by the interviewees, whereas males were called *studs* or *players*. As one female teen said despondently during an interview, "I change boyfriends a lot; everyone at school calls me a whore, a slut. But guys get away with it. They're called players or studs instead. You know what I mean?" For some reason, females continue to be held more accountable than males for their sexual activities, even though we live in an openly sexual culture. The reasons for this would require a treatise of their own and are therefore well beyond the scope of the present book. Having said this, I noticed in a large number of the interview tapes that derogatory terms such as *slut* are starting to lose their negative connotations. Indeed, the epithet *slut* is being used more and more to convey something positive about females, namely, attractiveness and sensuality. For example, one male informant called his girlfriend "my beautiful slut, who is faithful only to me," either unaware of, or oblivious to, the traditional meaning of that word.

The words reproduced here (see box) have been selected from the database put together by the research team to give the reader an idea of the basically ironic and "world savvy" nature of pubilectal vocabulary. The items tell a truly revealing story by themselves, without any need for an explanatory intervention on my part. Some seem to have been invented simply to provide color or add a humorous touch to discourse—for example, 24/7 ("all the time," short for "24 hours a day, seven days a week"), 5-0 ("police," derived probably from the reruns of the TV program *Hawaii Five-0*), *I'm ghost* ("I'm leaving"), and *whassup?* Other coinages show a "coded savvy" about certain topics—for example, *chick flick* ("sentimental movie," indicating that it is a genre watched by female teens), *crib* ("home," emphasizing the childish treatment teens receive at home), *issues* ("personal problems"), and *run* ("liquor," suggesting that liquor is to be obtained illegally, as if on the run).

Some coinages are indirect ironic assessments of common things and people, spotlighting specific features for the listener to notice without elaboration or justification—for example, *busted* ("ugly female"), *butt* ("ugly"), *chunk* ("obese"), *dick* ("unfair"), *grille* ("face"), *nasty* ("unattractive"), *peeps* ("friends"), and *stain* ("useless person"). A large number of the coinages are graphic metaphors depicting sexual matters, desires, organs, or activities—for example, *bombs* ("female breasts"), *booty* ("rugged"), *dip* ("girlfriend"), *gettin' nice* ("going steady"), *hittin' it* ("having sex"), *player* ("promiscuous male"), and *skank* ("promiscuous female").

VOCABULARY RECORDED IN 2001–2002 BY THE RESEARCH TEAM

- 24/7 ("all the time")
- 5-0 ("police")
- all about that ("in favor of that")
- anyway ("goodbye")
- babe ("good-looking guy")
- bag it ("forget about it")
- ballin' ("flaunt money")
- beats ("music")
- benjamins ("dollars")
- bitch out ("yell at")
- blower ("telephone")
- bombs ("female breasts")
- booty ("butt," "rugged")
- bud, chronic, herbals, ish, nuggets, trees issues ("marijuana")
- busted ("ugly female")
- butt ("ugly")
- cannons ("female breasts")
- cheddar, flow ("money")
- chick flick ("sentimental movie")
- chill ("relax")
- chunk ("obese person")
- crib ("home")
- dick ("unfair")
- digits ("phone number")
- dip ("girlfriend")
- ditz ("good-looking girl but clumsy")
- dog ("loyal friend")
- dope ("excellent")
- Flintstones ("older people, parents")
- fly, killer, lethal, gone, hammered, wasted ("drunk")
- fresh ("cool")
- gank ("break up")
- gettin' nice ("going steady")
- gnarly ("gross/cool")
- grille ("face")
- grub ("food")
- hardcore ("extreme")
- heated ("angry")
- hittin' it, rukin', slammin', blessin' it, stylin' it, taggin' it ("having sex")
- hot box ("stolen car," "cool car")
- issues ("personal problems")
- it's all good ("it's cool")

(*continued*)

VOCABULARY RECORDED IN 2001–2002
BY THE RESEARCH TEAM (*continued*)

- jacked, buff, cut, diesel, deeze, ripped ("muscular")
- jawsin' ("talking")
- jet, bounce, flex, outee, I'm ghost ("I'm leaving")
- kiss-up ("opportunist")
- later, peace out ("goodbye")
- lit, baked, blazed, blitted, blunted, fried, lifted ("inebriated, drugged out")
- lynched ("falsely blamed")
- mad ("a lot, much") ("He's making mad loot at that job")
- minute ("a long while") ("Where you been? I haven't seen you in a minute")
- nasty ("attractive/unattractive")
- peep this ("listen to this")
- peeps, crew ("friends")
- phat, sweet, nice, ill ("superb")
- played ("used, dumped") ("She really got played by her man")
- player ("promiscuous male")
- popo ("police")
- props ("respect") ("You get props for that")
- rad ("cool")
- rag on ("make fun of")
- random ("odd") ("There were some random guys at that party")
- run ("buy liquor")
- scrub ("ill-mannered")
- shotgun ("front passenger seat")
- skank ("promiscuous female")
- skater ("rock aficionado")
- sketch out ("act strangely")
- sketchy ("weird, shady")
- stain ("useless, annoying person")
- step to ("challenge")
- stoner ("druggie")
- sucks ("unpleasant, awful")
- sweat ("desire") ("She sweats me")
- tenda ("girlfriend")
- tool ("someone trying hard to belong")
- tooled on ("roughed up")
- whack ("screwed up") ("That was whack")
- whip, ride ("car")

Overall, such coinages provide a snapshot, so to speak, of how the teen brain thinks. Needless to say, adult language is also highly emotive and figurative, but not to the extent that pubilect is. However, adult language itself is becoming increasingly more juvenilized. Adults can be heard using fillers such as *like* and *man*, and a host of words derived directly from the lexicon of pubilect, such as *cool, chill out, 24/7,* and *dude*. These have even been listed in standard dictionaries of the English language. Even such recent expressions as *easy* ("see you later"), *floss* ("to show off, brag"), *ice* ("diamonds set in platinum"), *mad* ("anything to its extreme"), and *tight* ("to be broke") have been added to no less an authoritative dictionary than *Random House.*

The spread of pubilect to society at large is no doubt due to the media culture in which we live and that we cannot avoid. On television sitcoms and talk shows, in movies and ads, and in pop music lyrics, forms and mannerisms taken directly from pubilect abound. The juvenilization of language, like the juvenilization of fashion, has become a widespread phenomenon indeed.

It is not a recent phenomenon, however, although it never has been as widespread as it is today. The youth-based jazz subculture of the 1930s and 1940s, for instance, was responsible for introducing words such as *hip, stylin', cool,* and *groovy* into mainstream vocabulary. The words *pot* and *marijuana*, which were part of a secret criminal jargon in the 1940s, became common everyday words in the 1960s when the hippies adopted them. In the 1990s, hip-hop culture supplanted jazz culture as a source for new vocabulary. Expressions such as *bad, chill,* and *nasty* come from that culture. In a phrase, the teen words that make it into the mainstream tend to have a pop culture history behind them. Take *bad* as another example. The trend today of using the word *bad* in a nonliteral way (meaning "attractive") was probably initiated by Michael Jackson with his album titled *Bad* in 1987. Then, in 1989, hip-hop artist LL Cool J introduced the phrase *not bad* "meaning bad, but bad meaning good," as he defined it in his song *I'm Bad.*

In sum, pubilect has so many sides to it that it would require a treatment that is well beyond the scope of the present chapter.[6] Suffice it to say that it is a powerful verbal code that allows teens to imprint attitudes and values directly into the structure, meaning, and mode of delivery of words and phrases.

In the past, its primary conduits of new vocabulary were writers. Shakespeare, for instance, brought into acceptable usage such slang terms as *hubbub, to bump,* and *to dwindle*. But not before the second half of the twentieth century did it become routine for the conduit to be teenagers. As mentioned, the words *pot* and *marijuana* became common words in the 1960s after they were adopted by the counterculture youth of the era. The number of such words that have entered the communal lexicon since the 1960s is truly mind-boggling, constituting strong evidence that juvenilization in all domains of modern-day life has become a major social force. In a postscript to the published version of his play _Amadeus_—which became a 1984 movie—British playwright Peter Shaffer (1926–) makes the following insightful comment on this subject:[7]

> Cinema is a worrying medium for the stage playwright to work in. Its universal essence offers difficulties to anyone living largely by the spoken word. Increasingly, as American films grow ever more popular around the world, it is apparent that the most successful are being spoken in Screenspeak, a kind of cinematic esperanto equally comprehensible in Bogotá and Bulaway. For example, dialogue in heavy-action pictures, horrific or intergalactic, now consists almost entirely of the alternation of two single words—a cry and a whisper—needing translation nowhere on the planet: _Lessgidowaheer_ ["Let's get out of here"] and _Omygaad_ ["Oh my God"].

Shaffer's statement rings true as I write. Cinema continues to be a source of Screenspeak.[8] The way actors speak on screen seems to constitute a model of how to speak on the streets. Screenspeak and pubilect have become virtual synonyms. On TV sitcoms today, it is rare to hear anything other than a form of pubilect. Needless to say, this is especially true of teen-directed sitcoms, which may themselves constitute sources of new vocabulary. On _Buffy the Vampire Slayer_, which went off the air in 2003, new terms and phrases were coined on nearly every episode. Known as "slayer slang," that program constituted a veritable "field laboratory" of trends in teen language. And, far from being ephemeral vocabulary, slayer slang has left its mark on everyday speech. Expressions such as "My egg went postal on me," "What's up with that?" "Wow, you're a dish," and "Doesn't Owen realize he's hitting a major backspace by hanging out with that loser?" have come from slayer slang.

SUBDIALECTS

Predictably, there is no one single form of pubilect. It tends to vary according to the specific clique or teen subculture to which an adolescent belongs or aspires to belong. In a phrase, the teen will speak in ways that are appropriate to the peer group in which he or she gains membership or whose lifestyle he or she desires to emulate. This produces versions or "subdialects" of pubilect. For example, 1980s members of hard rocker cliques used profane language (obscenities, vulgarisms, and the like) to convey toughness; in the 1990s, many teens adopted hip-hop style in order to convey street toughness and savvy (real or implied); and so on and so forth.

HIP-HOP EXPRESSIONS

- 411 ("information") ("What's the 411 on him?")
- all that ("in possession of all good qualities")
- B-Boy (from "break boy," meaning "one who breakdances")
- baller ("basketball player," "successful person")
- battle ("to compete")
- being down with ("favoring someone")
- boo ("term of endearment") ("She leaves school early to see her boo")
- butter ("smooth, nice") ("That's a butter jacket")
- come correct ("to be genuine")
- digits ("phone number")
- dis (short for "disrespect")
- diva ("with style")
- dog ("buddy")
- down low ("quiet, secret") ("They kept their plans on the down low for months")
- down with ("to be sympathetic toward someone")
- flavor ("style") ("He has mad flavor")
- fly ("attractive")
- front ("pretending") ("He's unpopular 'cause he's always frontin'")
- gangsta ("gang member," "violent rapper")
- get on ("to do something well")
- homeboy/homegirl ("close friend")
- hyped ("cute")
- ill ("to be obnoxious")
- jiggy ("to be rich")
- keepin' it real ("staying cool")
- mack ("pimp")
- mad ("beautiful, good, very")
- peep ("look at") ("Did you peep the Knicks game last night?")
- peeps, posse ("friends, people")
- phat ("rich, really good, attractive")
- player ("promiscuous male")
- recognize ("take notice of") ("You'd better recognize, or you're history")
- represent ("do something well") ("Shaq O'Neill represents on the basketball court")
- shorty ("girlfriend")
- slamming ("attractive")
- tag ("a person's graffiti nickname")
- word ("truth")
- yo ("hello")

The ability to utilize the appropriate subdialect effectively is, in fact, as important to clique membership as is clothing. Indeed, those with ineffectual verbal skills risk being outcast or else compelled to accept marginal status within the clique.

The most common subdialect of the early twenty-first century was hip-hop (see box). No doubt, its pervasiveness throughout the teen world was due to the prominence accorded to hip-hop music and lifestyle trends by the media (especially by music channels and movies). However, as I write I am beginning to notice that it, too, is becoming less and less popular as new linguistic trends emerge on an almost daily basis.

Interestingly, the research team found that the parents interviewed were still quite fond of using words and mannerisms that belonged to their own teen years. Holding on to the speech patterns of one's youth is something that is probably inevitable. As the American behavioral psychologist William James (1842–1910) so aptly put it: "Hardly ever can a youth transferred to the society of his betters unlearn the nasality and other vices of speech bred in him by the associations of his growing years."[9] However, at no other time in history, it would seem, have adults become so mesmerized by how young people speak. The witty and acerbic British writer Oscar Wilde (1854–1900) saw this as a basic flaw in the American character. He put it ironically as follows: "In America the young are always ready to give to those who are older than themselves the full benefits of their inexperience."[10]

INSIGHTS

A simple listing of pubilectal words and expressions provides, in itself, many insights that are largely self-explanatory. Above all else, the forms allow us to see "what's in the minds" of teens "through their own words." It is nevertheless useful to discuss some insights in a general way here, again using the words of teens themselves as convenient points of departure. I should also emphasize that the lifespan of pubilectal vocabulary is, generally, quite limited. By the time this book goes to press, in fact, most of the words and expressions reported here will likely have disappeared. However, the vocabulary-creation mechanisms described in this chapter will be the same.

"Man, I'm grossed, f——ed, pissed, and puked out."

The way teenagers speak is often emotionally noisy (a term that was coined in the opening chapter) and, as such, can often be annoying to adults. Derogatory remarks and profane expressions are particularly irksome. But one should always remember that, most of the time, they are used by teens to deflect attention away from the self by putting the verbal spotlight on others.

Perhaps the most emotionally noisy words used by teens are the "four-letter" ones they tend to sputter out so matter-of-factly. No doubt, profanity is meant to be offensive and injurious. Very little can be done about it. Shouting back will only raise the emotional noise level. Some teens consistently use extremely vulgar and menacing language when discussing troublesome issues. Often, this is a short-lived phase or even a put-on. Other teens might use a similar kind of language to intimidate peers. This came out during an interview session I had a few years ago with a teen who defined himself as a "gangsta hip-hopper." He pointed out emphatically to me that speaking the "gangsta talk" made him feel powerful. The best response is, needless to say, for adults not to use such language. Moreover, one can simply tell a teen that vulgar language is not appropriate, simply as a matter of courtesy.

As an aside, I mention that such language is probably now more a part of Screenspeak than we might realize. In a recent interesting study, Robert Wachal found that four-letter words are now common in all types of media.[11] In a single two-hour episode of the HBO series *The Sopranos* alone, Wachal recorded 100 uses of "f——"!

"I, like, don't know, what he's, like, going to do!"

As discussed above, those annoying fillers and hedges (*like, duh,* and so on) are intrinsic features of adolescent conversational style. They allow teens to maintain the attention of their listeners, to convey their feelings, to lighten up a situation, to gain time in collecting their thoughts during discourse, and so on. I have noticed that these fillers and hedges, like teen clothing fashions, now tend to pass quickly into adult language. They are akin to computer viruses; once they enter a culture's verbal "hard drive," they are extremely difficult to eradicate.

"I hate those chick flicks, man; they're hardcore."

When teens speak to each other, parents might think that they are listening to veritable "aliens" speak in a strange tongue. As the *Washington Post* article cited at the beginning of this chapter perceptively remarked, this allows them to "exclude adults" from listening in on their conversations. Certain terms are recognized and used universally by teens; others are more restricted. For instance, a term such as *cool* or *whassup* is recognized by virtually everyone, whereas others, such as *cheddar* and *crib*, have a very restricted usage and are much less known. Interestingly, some words have more staying power than others—for example, *cool* ("nice"), *jock* ("athletic type"), and *chick* ("female teen") go back to the 1950s; *stoned* ("inebriated, drugged out") and *hip* to the 1960s; and *wheels* ("car") and *bummer* ("unpleasant experience") to the 1970s.

"Don't f—— with me, or I'll f—— with you!"
In the same way that a dangerous situation could develop when a teenager changes body image, lifestyle, or friends abruptly and radically, so too an extreme change in language could be worrisome. One of the most obvious verbal danger signs is an increase in the use of profanities as routine features of discourse. Another one is a noticeable increase in aggressive language (threats, vulgarities, and the like). A third is frequent reference to macabre themes (e.g., death wishes and Satanism). Finally, recurrent expressions of severe hatred toward other teens might indicate that there is trouble brewing in the teen's life.

In all cases, it is a matter of degree rather than of substance. Profanities, aggressiveness, gruesomeness, and expressions of hatred are present in the talk of everyone, teens and adults alike. But if they become conspicuous, regular, and increasingly overdrawn, it is an indication that something is amiss. It might indicate that a teen has joined a gang or a dangerous clique, or is undergoing serious personal difficulties. One teen expressed this as follows: "My friend was a nice guy once; now he swears all the time; that's because he joined those holy terrors."

"I talk like my friends. It's the only language that makes sense to me."
Words such as those listed here (see box) show that pubilect is a means by which teens fit in with their peers. They provide details of the mental images that go through the adolescent's mind on a day-to-day basis. They tell the story of teenagehood in vivid ways.

Many of these have gone, or are about to go, out of style as I write. Ephemerality is the defining feature of pubilect. As mentioned, the coinages that do survive are those that are adopted by the adult world: for example, *24/7* and *Ohmygod* are now used by people of all ages commonly, being piped into society on a daily basis through movies, TV pro-

---

VERBAL DANGER SIGNS

- An increase in the use of profane and vulgar language, for no apparent reason
- An increase in the use of aggressive discourse
- An increase in the macabre content of conversations
- An increase in the use of hate expressions aimed at other teens

---

**2002 TEEN VOCABULARY RECORDED
BY A MEMBER OF THE RESEARCH TEAM**

- bender ("someone who is sad")
- bent ("upset")
- blaze ("smoke up")
- bo ("girlfriend")
- book it ("let's go")
- bottled ("drunk")
- bredgrin ("a friend")
- bucket-o-solid ("you are ugly")
- chillax ("chill out + relax")
- chopping ("flirting")
- dime ("a joint")
- facing ("kissing")
- floater ("someone who listens to all types of music")
- fun bags ("breasts")
- ghetto clothes ("stylish clothes")
- ho ("loose girl")
- hotty ("cute guy/cute girl")
- ill ("cool, good, stupid")
- peaked ("ugly")
- purple monkey ("sex")
- sick ("cool/good")
- skater ("someone who wears baggy clothes and has many piercings")
- wigger ("wannabe thug")

---

grams, advertisements and commercials, and other channels of pop culture. As a result, adult language is becoming increasingly more juvenilized, changing and adapting in response to adolescent categories of talk. Teen words are, as mentioned earlier, being increasingly listed in standard dictionaries of the English language, such as the *Oxford English Dictionary* and *Webster's.*

"Why are my parents always bugging me about how I talk?"

Like body image and clothing, language allows teens to play a role on the stage of peerdom. Words such as those listed in this chapter are keys to understanding the nature of that role. They also provide insights into the kinds of thoughts that the disconnection syndrome (as it has been called in this book) generates during adolescence.

Using a moralizing or judgmental approach toward teens will lead nowhere. Moreover, one must never forget that teens may have an awful

---

DEFENSIVENESS TRIGGERS

A teen will tend to become defensive and may use profane or vulgar language in response to triggers such as the following.

- Criticism: "That language is despicable!"
- Control: "You can't say that around here!"
- Coyness: "I really wouldn't say that."
- Pseudoneutrality: "I don't care what you say; it is irrelevant to me."
- Superiority: "When I was your age, I spoke correctly."
- Certainty: "I know for sure that you are wrong."

---

lot of things to say that are meaningful and even profound, no matter what subdialect they may use to express them. One should always listen to them with an open mind, especially since, as mentioned above, it is the very language of teens that is making its way to the mainstream through Screenspeak—a trend that reflects the current "global ethos." In his great novel *1984* (1949), the British writer George Orwell (1903–1950) saw language as the key for unlocking the ethos of a society. The worst world in which one could possibly live, he emphasized, is one in which people turn instinctively to "exhausted idioms" and trendy new words, yet end up saying virtually nothing of value. Only language that ennobles the human spirit will persist. In my view, Screenspeak will not persist because it does not ennoble the spirit, as Orwell put it.

NOTES

1. The actual words, phrases, and statements cited in this chapter were compiled by the University of Toronto research team. Some of the items were taken from interview sessions on various topics, where they occurred spontaneously. Most of them, however, were elicited directly by members of the research team by asking the informants questions such as: "What words or expressions do you and your friends use that are different from those of adults?" "Can you tell me what these words mean?" "How many such words do you know?" and so on.

2. For the use of *like* as a hesitancy device, readers can consult Gisle Andersen, *Pragmatic Markers and Sociolinguistic Variation: A Relevance-Theoretic Approach to the Language of Adolescents* (Amsterdam: John Benjamins, 2001); and Muffy Siegel, "Like: The Discourse Particle and Semantics," *Journal of Semantics* 19 (2002): 35–71.

3. On the topic of irony in childhood language, see the excellent book by Ellen Winner, *The Point of Words: Children's Understanding of Metaphor and Irony* (Cambridge, Mass.: Harvard University Press, 1988).

4. Carl Sandburgh, letter, *New York Times*, February 13, 1959, 25.

5. Elizabeth Hardwick, *Bartleby in Manhattan and Other Essays* (New York: Random House, 1968), 46.

6. For an in-depth study of adolescent language, readers can consult Connie C. Eble, *Slang and Sociability* (Chapel Hill: University of North Carolina Press, 1996). The articles in M. A. Nippold, ed., *Later Language Development: Ages Nine through Nineteen* (Boston: Little, Brown, 1988), offer scientific insights into the social role of speech during adolescence. The recent guide by M. Ellis, *Slanguage: A Cool, Fresh, Phat, and Shagadelic Guide to All Kinds of Slang* (New York: Hyperion, 2000), constitutes a lighthearted look at regional slang throughout the United States.

7. Peter Shaffer, *Amadeus* (London: Penguin, 1993), 109.

8. Since the 1960s, there has been a considerable amount of research conducted by linguists on adolescent language. I indicate some of the more interesting studies here as cases in point: C. Adelman, "The Language of Teenage Groups," in S. Rogers, ed., *They Don't Speak Our Language* (London: Edward Arnold, 1976), 80–105; M. H. Leona, "An Examination of Adolescent Clique Language in a Suburban Secondary School," *Adolescence* 13 (1978): 495–502; W. Labov, "Social Structure and Peer Terminology in a Black Adolescent Gang," *Language in Society* 11 (1982): 391–413; P. Eckert, "Adolescent Social Structure and the Spread of Linguistic Change," *Language in Society* 17 (1988): 183–207; D. Eder, "Serious and Playful Disputes: Variation on Conflict Talk among Female Adolescents," in D. Grimshaw, ed., *Conflict Talk* (Cambridge: Cambridge University Press, 1990): 67–84; T. Labov, "Social Language Boundaries among Adolescents," *American Speech* 67 (1992): 339–66; D. Cameron, "Naming of Parts: Gender, Culture, and Terms for the Penis among American College Students," *American Speech* 67 (1992): 367–82; Cecilia A. Cutler, "Yorkville Crossing: White Teens, Hip Hop and African American English," *Journal of Sociolinguistics* 3 (1999): 428–42; Mary Bucholtz, "Language and Youth Culture," *American Speech* 75 (2000): 280–83; Thomas C. Cooper, "Does It Suck? Or Is It for the Birds? Native Speaker Judgment of Slang Expressions," *American Speech* 76 (2001): 62–78; Andersen, *Pragmatic Markers and Sociolinguistic Variation*; and James Paul Gee, Anna-Ruth Allen, and Katherine Clinton, "Language, Class, and Identity: Teenagers Fashioning Themselves through Language," *Linguistics and Education* 12 (2001): 175–94.

9. William James, *Principles of Psychology*, vol. 1 (New York: Holt, 1890), 331.

10. Oscar Wilde, "The American Invasion," *Court and Society Review* (London), March 23, 1887, 11.

11. Robert S. Wachal, "Taboo or not Taboo: That Is the Question," *American Speech* 77 (2002): 195–206.

5

Music

Interviewer	What kind of music do you like?
Teen Informant	What else, hip-hop, rap, it's, like, mad, bad, the best. It's music to move to.
Interview	What about the music your parents listen to?
Teen Informant	Boring. History. It's weird, man.

BACKGROUND

In 1979, Keith Richards (1943–), a member of the Rolling Stones, quipped that rock and roll was music "for the neck downwards."[1] In a similar vein, our informant characterized hip-hop as music to "move to." And indeed, from the "swing" dancing of the 1950s "sock hop" to the "moshing" scenes of the 1990s, where teens were hurled from the stage into the crowd and passed hand over hand, the purpose of adolescent music seems to have always been electrifying the body from the neck downwards, as Richards so aptly put it.

Whatever musical style is fashionable with a teen generation, there is little doubt in my mind that it constitutes a means that teens utilize to release sexual energy and to simulate corporeally the diverse moods that such energy engenders. It has always been, and continues to be, music for "raging hormones." Needless to say, some rock compositions have risen (and continue to rise) to the level of what we traditionally call "musical art." To coin a counterpart expression to the one used by Richards, it can be said that certain rock songs constitute music "for the neck upwards"—

that is, music that stimulates the cerebral, rather than hormonal, part of human anatomy. But, by and large, rock (or whatever it is called) is music that allows teens to engage in a kind of hedonistic tribal dancing through which they can put their bodies on display, release sexual energy, and transmit flirtation and seduction signals.

Rock and hip-hop constitute the subject matter of this chapter. I will not deal with country music here because it seems to have a low popularity index among teens. Of the 200 subjects interviewed, in fact, only five claimed to listen to country music. And only one of these indicated any serious interest in such music.

A HISTORICAL SKETCH

The seeds of rock were planted between 1935 and 1945 when the swing dancing of the 1920s became a craze among American youths. In part, the lifestyle associated with the music probably provided a means to cope with the stark economic realities of the post-Depression era and the moral ravages of world war. But, in larger part, it crystallized as a way that

---

THE EARLY HISTORY OF ROCK

- 1947: Wynonie Harris records "Good Rockin' Tonight," an up-tempo blues number in which the word *rock* signals an emerging new trend.
- 1948–1952: The following recordings set the stage for rock and roll: Rosetta Sharpe's "Up above My Head" (1948), Pee Wee Cayton's "Blues after Hours" (1948), James Moody's "The Fuller Bop Man" (1949), the Delmore Brothers' "Pan American Boogie" (1949), Hank Williams's "Mind Your Own Business" (1949), Wild Bill Moore's "Neck Bones and Collard Greens" (1951), Jackie Bernston and His Delta Cats' "Rocket 88" (1951), and Lloyd Price's "Lawdy Miss Clawdy" (1952).
- 1952: Sam Phillips starts the Sun Label in Memphis; WFIL-TV starts a new dance show in Philadelphia for young people called *Bandstand*; and DJ Alan Freed holds a "proto-rock" stage show in Cleveland on March 21.
- 1954: Elvis Presley's version of "Good Rockin' Tonight" and Johnny Watson's "Space Guitar" establish rock and roll as an autonomous new musical style.
- 1955: Bill Haley and the Comets record "Rock around the Clock," which becomes the first commercially successful rock song.
- 1956: Rock and roll develops into the musical voice of teenagehood; Elvis emerges as the "king of rock"; and *Bandstand* is renamed *American Bandstand*.

young people saw as effective for socializing among themselves and for expressing their sexuality in public ways.

The first true rock songs were composed in the late 1940s and early 1950s, reflecting a blend of popular musical forms—the *blues*, the gospel-based vocal-group style known as *doo wop*, the piano-based rhythmic style known as *boogie woogie*, and the country music style known as *honky tonk* (made popular by Hank Williams). They were recorded and released by small, independent record companies and promoted by controversial radio disc jockeys such as Alan Freed, who coined the term *rock and roll* to help attract white audiences unfamiliar with African American music styles. By the time Elvis Presley recorded "Good Rockin' Tonight" in 1954, which was a remake of Wynonie Harris's 1947 rendition of the song, rock had established itself as a powerful new trend in pop culture. After Bill Haley and the Comets recorded "Rock around the Clock" in 1955, it was appropriated by the first generation of true teenagers as music they could call theirs and theirs alone. The song was the theme music for *The Blackboard Jungle,* a 1955 motion picture about teenagers and coming of age in the 1950s.

The link between rock and roll and teenagehood was visible from the outset. Changes in the world of rock music became sources of change in teen lifestyle. The two went hand in hand. Indeed, to understand what is going on in teen culture to this day, the best place to start is with the music of that culture.[2]

The success of rock caught the attention of media moguls. Hollywood jumped on the teen bandwagon, producing, in addition to *The Blackboard Jungle* and *Rebel without a Cause,* a slew of rock movies that were, in effect, forerunners of the rock video. The 1956 movie *Rock, Rock, Rock,* for instance, included acts by the Moonglows, among many others. It also featured an appearance by Alan Freed. Similarly, in *Rock, Baby, Rock It* (1957) and *Go, Johnny, Go!* (1958), the finest rock musical talent of the so-called golden age of rock was featured. The rock stars of the era—Chuck Berry, Elvis Presley, Little Richard, and Buddy Holly, to mention but a few— have become emblazoned in the annals of pop culture history as "pioneers." Presley's "Hound Dog" (1956) and "All Shook Up" (1956), Little Richard's "Tutti Frutti" (1955) and "Lucille" (1957), Chuck Berry's "Maybellene" (1955) and "Johnny B. Goode" (1958), and Buddy Holly's "Peggy Sue" (1957) catapulted rock music to the forefront of American pop culture. It was music "in your face." Teens loved it; parents hated it. But, as the 1958 song by Danny and the Juniors put it rather prophetically, rock and roll was "here to stay."

In the 1960s, rock changed its complexion, fragmenting into diverse styles—Motown, California surfer rock, folk rock, and so on. The so-called British Invasion began in 1964 with the arrival of the Beatles in

New York City—a key moment in the history of teenagehood since, arguably, it gave momentum to a then-fledgling counterculture movement.[3] By 1967, with the album *Sgt. Pepper's Lonely Hearts Club Band,* which was the first "rock concept album," the Beatles established new standards for studio recording and carved out the image of the rock musician as a creative artist, an image that remains intact to this day.

The most famous style came to be known as counterculture rock. It emerged in San Francisco around 1966 and was associated with the use of hallucinogenic drugs, psychedelic art, light shows, peace, free love, and universal brotherhood. Counterculture musicians such as Jerry Garcia and the Grateful Dead experimented with long, improvised stretches of music called "jams." It was obvious that this new type of rock was vastly different from golden-era rock, spearheading and sustaining a nonpolitical youth movement, whose objectives were to reject the traditional bourgeois goals of consumerist society. It also reflected how much teens had changed in a decade. They were "rebels with a cause," denouncing the corrupt "business and political establishment" as the cause of all social ills. They even turned away from the aesthetic traditions of the West, seeking inspiration from Eastern customs. Musicians and musical groups such as the Who, Jim Morrison and the Doors, Frank Zappa, and Jimi Hendrix, among many others, were known not only for their music but also for their political views. The rock concert became a "happening" of great ideological impact, spurring on youths to social activism and to engage in subversive acts. At concerts such as Monterey Pop (1967) and Woodstock (1969), drugs were consumed to induce or heighten the aesthetic experience of the music, and sexual intercourse was practiced openly, in obvious defiance of adult moralism. In a bizarre way, what Plato (c. 427–347 B.C.) feared most about music millennia ago had come about in the adolescent counterculture world of the 1960s. As the Greek philosopher astutely pointed out: "For the introduction of a new kind of music must be shunned as imperiling the whole state; since styles of music are never disturbed without affecting the most important political institutions."[4] Counterculture rock certainly seemed to imperil the modern state.[5]

But the counterculture movement faded by the early 1970s. Various analyses have been put forth to explain its demise—the end of the Vietnam War (a major reason for youth protest), effective social changes brought about by the movement itself, and the like. But, in my view, this "second period of adolescent rebellion" faded because the adolescents became older and because the adult establishment itself forged a tacit merger with the rock stars who, despite their antiestablishment attitudes, nevertheless signed lucrative contracts with major recording companies. This set the stage for the music to be perceived as a "thing of the past" for the next generation of teens.

By the mid-1970s, a number of distinctive new styles appeared—disco, glam rock, punk rock, new wave, reggae, and funk—showing that teenage-hood was fragmenting more and more into distinctive subcultures. Initially associated with the gay lifestyle of New York City, disco drew upon black popular music, attracting a large teen following. Although despised by many other teens, disco had a substantial impact on rock music, especially after the release of the motion picture *Saturday Night Fever* (1977) and its hugely successful soundtrack featuring the Bee Gees. Around 1976, punk rock originated in London and New York as a reaction against the com-mercialism of disco and the "artistic pretentiousness" of 1960s rock. Punk rock was raw, abrasive, and rude. In a sense, it was a throwback to the golden-era sound of a "Hound Dog" or a "Tutti Frutti." But, unlike early rockers, punk bands such as the Sex Pistols and the Clash eliminated melody and harmony from their music, transforming it into an angry, shrill, brutal style. Eventually, with such bands as Blondie and Talking Heads, it evolved into a softer form, called *new wave*, which has modern-day de-scendants. Also in the mid-1970s, reggae music—developed by musicians in Jamaica—began to attract attention among a sizable number of teens, es-pecially after the release of the 1973 film *The Harder They Come*, which starred reggae singer Jimmy Cliff in the role of an underclass gangster. The superstar of reggae was, however, Bob Marley, who by the time of his death in 1981 had become one of the most popular musicians in the world.

By the end of the 1970s, rock music sales plummeted and it appeared, for a little while at least, that the final chapter on rock history had been written. It was technology that came to the rescue. The advent of the music video, the debut in 1981 of Music Television (MTV), and the introduction onto the market of the digitally recorded compact disc in 1983 revived interest in rock music. A new generation of "video rock stars," such as Michael Jack-son, Bruce Springsteen, Prince, and Madonna, became the new icons of "TV teens"—a name assigned to them by the media in that era because they were the first generation to have grown up in front of a television. The as-tronomical success of Michael Jackson's 1982 *Thriller* album contributed greatly to demonstrating the promotional value of video rock, as did the videos of heavy metal bands, such as Van Halen, AC/DC, and Metallica.

The success of video rock highlights the role that television has always played in the propagation of rock (and more recently hip-hop). Rock and roll become popular across the teen world after Elvis Presley appeared on *The Ed Sullivan Show* in 1956. The same program catapulted the Beatles to fame in 1964. An estimated 73 million people watched the Beatles' first appearance on the show. The list given here was adapted from a list com-piled by VH1 and *Entertainment Weekly* magazine (see box). It shows the top moments that link TV with the diffusion and promotion of rock throughout society.

CRITICAL ROCK TV MOMENTS IN
CHRONOLOGICAL ORDER, 1956–1985

- 1956: Elvis Presley debuts on *The Ed Sullivan Show,* emphasizing to all of America that rock and roll had become the musical idiom of teenagers.
- 1956–1960: Dick Clark's *American Bandstand* both mirrors and sets teen trends in music, fashion, and dance.
- 1964: The Beatles' debut on *The Ed Sullivan Show* showcases the "Beatle-mania" that was starting to grip the United States.
- 1967: The Who include explosives in their musical act on the *Smothers Brothers Comedy Hour,* transforming rock performances into clamorous, violent spectacles.
- 1968: Elvis Presley makes a legendary comeback with his special on NBC.
- 1975: *Saturday Night Live* introduces rock acts into its weekly program, entrenching rock as mainstream music in American culture at large.
- 1981: MTV is launched with the video, "Video Killed the Radio Star," by the Buggies.
- 1983: The *Motown 25* special features Michael Jackson's first "moon-walk," signaling a new trend in teen music.
- 1984: Madonna shocks the adult world by appearing in a wedding gown singing "Like a Virgin" on the MTV Video Awards.
- 1985: The Live Aid concert is aired by ABC and MTV, rekindling interest in rock as a vehicle for expressing political and social sentiments.

Arguably, without television, rock would have remained confined to the teen world. Its crossover to the musical mainstream was fostered and nurtured by television. Television continues to be a major player in the spread of teen music. Only specialty channels play classical music, jazz, or other types of music. Teen music reigns supreme virtually everywhere else on TV (and on radio, for that matter). In a recent book titled *If It Ain't Got that Swing* (2000), Mark Gauvreau Judge argues that "adult pop music" has been gradually marginalized since the advent of rock in the 1950s.[6] He suggests, however, that the "rock experiment" may have run its course. Judge may be right. Rock appears to be increasingly an object of nostalgia. In 1995, for instance, the Rock and Roll Hall of Fame opened in Cleveland, Ohio—a sure sign that rock may have become "museum music." Also in the 1990s, several major television documentaries were produced on the history of rock and roll, and historical box-set recordings were reissued featuring rock artists from the past—further signs that rock music may have indeed become more a part of pop culture history than anything else.

Since the mid-1980s, in fact, the word *rock* started being used less and less to refer to teen music. Actually, it was rock superstars, such as Peter

Gabriel, David Byrne, and Paul Simon, whose 1985 album *Graceland* featured musicians from Africa and Latin America, who played an unwitting role in bringing this about by exposing the works of different musical styles to audiences in the United States and Europe. At about the same time, a new style, called *rap*, seemed to come out of nowhere to attract the attention of the new generation of teens. Rap is a genre in which vocalists perform rhythmic speech, usually accompanied by music snippets, called samples, from prerecorded material or from music created on purpose. The first rap records were made in the late 1970s by small, independent record companies. Although rapper groups such as Sugarhill Gang had national hits during the late 1970s and early 1980s, the musical style did not enter the pop culture mainstream until 1986, when rappers Run-D.M.C. and the hard-rock band Aerosmith collaborated on the song "Walk This Way," creating a new audience for rap among white, middle-class teens. By the end of the 1980s, MTV had established a program dedicated solely to rap, and the records of rap artists such as M.C. Hammer and the Beastie Boys achieved multiplatinum status.[7]

RAP AND HIP-HOP

Rap and hip-hop are now used interchangeably. But the former, which derives from the seminal recording by Sugarhill Gang called *Rapper's Delight* (1979), refers to the musical style itself, whereas the latter refers to the attendant lifestyle that those who listen to rap tend to adopt. The word *hop*, actually, has been around since the 1920s, when so-called Lindy hop dancing, also known as *jitterbugging*, was popular in Harlem. The word was also used to describe 1950s rock dancing, as captured by Danny and the Juniors in their 1958 hit "At the Hop."

The rise of hip-hop in many ways parallels the birth of rock and roll in the 1950s. Both originated in African American culture and both were initially aimed at black audiences. In both cases, the new style gradually attracted white musicians, who made it popular to white audiences. For rock and roll, the musician was Elvis Presley; for rap it was, as mentioned above, Aerosmith. In the same year, a white group from New York City called the Beastie Boys released the rap song "Fight for Your Right to Party" (1986), which quickly reached the *Billboard* top-ten list of popular hits.

Rap vocals typically emphasize lyrics and wordplay over melody and harmony, achieving interest through rhythm and variations in the timing of the lyrics. Rap is not unlike the musical form of the late medieval era known as the *madrigal*—a composition for two or three voices in simple harmony, following a strict poetic form, developed in Italy in the late thirteenth and early fourteenth centuries. Rap is pop culture's version of the madrigal. Its lyric themes can be broadly categorized under three headings: those that are blatantly sexual, those that chronicle and often embrace the so-called gangsta lifestyle of youths who live in inner cities, and those that address contemporary political issues or aspects of black history. By the mid-1990s, rap developed into a more eclectic musical form, as rap artists borrowed from folk music, jazz, and other music styles. Consequently, it became more melodious and traditional in its use of instrumentation.

In 1988, the first major album of gangsta rap was released, *Straight Outta Compton*, by the rap group NWA (Niggers with Attitude). Songs from the album generated an extraordinary amount of controversy for their violent attitudes and inspired protests from a number of organizations, including the FBI. So, too, did the early music of Ice-T, Dr. Dre, and Snoop Doggy Dogg. However, attempts to censor gangsta rap only served to publicize the music more widely and, thus, to make it even more attractive to youths generally. The "in-your-face" sexual attitude noticeable in hip-hop videos today, some of which appear to be little more than erotic videos, continues to be worrisome to parents at the same time that it is highly attractive to teens.

The lifestyle associated with rap music is called, as mentioned, hip-hop. It became popular in the mid-1990s. Among the salient features of hip-hop lifestyle, I mention the practice of assuming a new name, known as a "tag," along with the related practice of etching the tag on the urban landscape—on bus shelters, buses, subways, signs, walls, freeway overpasses, mailboxes, and so on—with markers, spray paint, or shoe polish. There are two main forms of tagging, known as "throw-ups" and "pieces." Hip-hop teens also tend to spell their new names in phonic imitation of Black English. No doubt, this is intended to convey to others that they belong to a subculture that intentionally sets itself apart from the mainstream. They thus spell the English language on their own terms—*boyz* instead of *boys*, *dogg* instead of *dog*, and the like. But, as the research team found out, such teens are generally unaware of the fact that such a practice originated in 1952, when the African American musician Lloyd Price spelled his hit song "Lawdy Miss Clawdy," in obvious imitation of Black English pronunciation. The hippies, too, intentionally referred to themselves as *freeks* (rather than *freaks*) and spelled *Amerika* with a "k" as a political statement.

So interesting had tagging art become by the late 1990s that some traditional art galleries even started putting it on display. In December 2000, the Brooklyn Museum of Art organized an exposition of 400 pieces of urban street art, called *Hip-Hop Nation: Roots, Rhymes & Rage*, reflecting several decades of hip-hop tagging art. In a city where nearly 2,000 arrests for graffiti offenses were carried out in the same year, the art gallery had taken on the role previously confined to the streets.

Much like the hippies of the 1960s, teens who become involved in hip-hop culture tend to become less attached to the family. In my view, what probably makes hip-hop lifestyle attractive to some youths is, paradoxically, its highly organized structure. Hip-hop culture is subdivided into classes, subgroups (networks of friends), and mentor–protégé relationships. The tag name, for instance, is negotiated with peers—a ritual acknowledging that one is noticed, included, and individualized all at once within the structure of the hip-hop tribe. As one interviewee told a member of the research team, "To be accepted is what every hip-hop person is out to do." Pretenders—individuals who dress, talk, and act as if they were the genuine article, but are not—are intensely disliked. However, I must admit that both the research team members and I had difficulty distinguishing between "who is" and "who is not" a genuine hip-hopper. Given the diversity of backgrounds of those who espouse hip-hop culture, distinguishing "who is who" is becoming increasingly difficult and, probably, useless.

This became especially evident during the interviews when the topic of rap-metal music came up, a style directed at first at male teens known in the late 1990s as "mooks." The subtext of that music, which has fewer and fewer followers as I write, is a combination of rage and profanity. Groups such as Korn and Limp Bizkit, as well as the controversial rapper Eminem, symbolize that style perfectly. Female rap-metal bands came into the spotlight in the early twenty-first century, showing as much rage and profanity as their male counterparts.

Why all the rage? Is it a legitimate response to a commercially crazed world gone amok through its extravagant materialism? Is it a way to let off steam, safer than walking through a high school corridor with a weapon under one's coat? Is it rage against family breakups and divorce? These questions were put to our teen informants. Most of them told us that, by and large, mooks were mainly "fakes," as one 15-year-old labeled them. Most interviewees hardly perceived the fascination with rage music as legitimately arising from individuals caught in an underclass situation or from teens who felt oppressed and victimized. Rather, they perceived it as a mere ploy of bored, middle-class youths who espoused rage music as a veiled attempt to eschew the responsibilities of growing up. Being rude and expressing rage for its own sake constituted "a trick to be bratty kids again," as one teen interviewee sagaciously put it to me; "It's a way of being lazy and nothing more," she continued. This is perhaps why all the rage gets channeled fairly quickly into marketable niches where it can be appreciated without any undue impact on the larger society.

In December 2002, I asked one teen informant why she thought that Eminem had become so popular. She put it this way to me: "He knows how to appeal to wannabes. He looks, acts, and talks tough, but everyone knows he's fakin' it. It's easier to fake it than to do it." Her astute comment was borne out, somewhat, by the fact that in early 2003 Eminem signed an ex-crack dealer who had been wounded by gunshot many times, called 50 Cent (Curtis Jackson), to his Shady/Aftermath label. As Eminem obviously knows, the combination of wordplay and gunplay is rap's most potent marketing strategy.

As I write, change is occurring all over the pop music world as the hegemony of rap gives way to competing styles. Latino rock, grunge, jazz, techno, soul, a return of swing music, folk styles, and many more trends are now competing for the teen's attention and, more important, for his or her dollar.[8] Hip-hop continues to have appeal, but it now has many competitors, ready and able to depose it as the leading style in pop music.

MUSIC AND ADOLESCENCE

As the French-born American critic and novelist George Steiner (1929–) stated in 1971, 1950s and 1960s rock and roll emerged as the universal language of teens throughout the world because it cut "across languages, ideologies, frontiers and races." Is teen-directed music still relevant to teens? Is it still a "universal language," as Steiner characterizes it?

The interview sessions revealed that teens continue to perceive the music they like as very important. But few now see it as a universal language, that is, as a single language for all teens—as it was in the early period of rock. Most see it as a means to relate with peers.

A look at the lyrics and forms of current musical styles actually reveals that certain things never seem to change. Sexuality still dominates the basic thrust of teen music, as can be seen in hip-hop and Latino music videos. And, as in the hippie 1960s, protest and a general critique of society still can be found somewhat in hip-hop, grunge, rave, and techno music. Late 1990s groups such as Rage Against the Machine attempted to continue the tradition of Bob Dylan and Crosby, Stills, Nash, and Young, expressing rage against the "system." But although such musical voices remain an important way to convey and debate ideas, like all other things in teenagehood they seem either to pass much too quickly from the public eye or else tend to have very little effect other than to get teens to buy CDs and DVDs.

Ultimately, when one stands back and takes a dispassionate look at teen music, from rock, disco, and punk to rap, grunge, and techno, one reaches the same inescapable conclusion reached by Keith Richards, which was cited at the beginning of this chapter. It is, in the final analysis, essentially "music for the neck downwards."[9] Sexuality and rebellion are the heart and soul of teen music. The ten songs identified by *USA Today* (November 20, 2000) as the all-time greatest rock songs bring this out perfectly. The theme of romance and sex is communicated in a straightforward manner in the Beatles' early hit "I Want to Hold Your Hand" and the Jackson Five's "I Want You Back." In Madonna's "Like a Virgin" and Michael Jackson's "Billie Jean," this theme is given a different twist—the former is a parody of traditional female sexuality, the latter a caricature of sex and romance. Rebellion, defiance, and individualism are the themes that can be found, to greater or lesser degrees, in "Satisfaction" by the Rolling Stones, "Smells like Teen Spirit" by Nirvana, "I Want It that Way" by the Backstreet Boys, "Respect" by Aretha Franklin, and "One" by U2. The number one rock song of all time, according to the *USA Today* survey, is the Beatles' song "Yesterday"—a truly exceptional song in the history of rock. During one of the interviews, an informant mentioned to me that the reason why he loves the music of the Beatles is because "it speaks to the heart" and because "it understands how *nostalgic* I often feel."

So emotionally powerful is rock music, both for the listeners and the performers, that once the period of adolescence is over, in fact, it is becoming increasingly difficult to let go of the excitement. This is especially evident in the continual recycling of previous music and in the glorification of rock artists from the past. Some seem to refuse to let go of their adolescence, aspiring to remain forever young along with their legions of fans. The stars of yesteryear, such as Cher and Michael Jackson, are continually undergoing cosmetic surgery in order to maintain a youthful appearance. In 1998, Cher recorded an album, *Believe,* that sold more than 10 million copies worldwide, and the similarly named single became her biggest hit ever. Michael Jackson has been dressing as ghoulishly as he did in his *Thriller* video and undergoing plastic surgery that seems designed to transform him permanently into the character he played in that video.

And then there are the Rolling Stones, those ageless rockers who, at the start of the twenty-first century, were still rocking away, even though each of the members was either in his sixties or approaching them. As Stephen Davis labeled them, they are "old gods almost dead."[10] I suppose that once a rock-and-roller, always a rock-and-roller. Incidentally, Mick Jagger, the lead singer of the Stones, received a British knighthood in 2002 at the age of 58—an event that was particularly ironic, since "the Mick" was viewed, in his heyday, as the epitome of the dangerous street punk. The Rolling Stones are 1960s rebellious teens trapped in aging adult bodies, attempting to cling to the excitement that their music once generated.[11]

Life magazine's March 11, 2002, issue—devoted to "Rock & Roll at 50"—bears out that rock is becoming more and more a matter of nostalgia. In its survey of the top ten rock stars of all time, the stars—Elvis Presley, The Beatles, Bob Dylan, James Brown, The Rolling Stones, Madonna, Stevie Wonder, Chuck Berry, Michael Jackson, and Kurt Cobain—are either dead or long past their prime. The "fade-out" has started. Even the resounding success of the 2000 CD of the Beatles' greatest hits was successful not because teenagers listened to it but because they bought it as a gift to their parents. Less than half of 1 percent of people aged 8 to 24 years old named the Beatles as their favorite performers, according to a 2001 Zandl survey. Similar percentages were registered for Bob Marley and Jimi Hendrix. Rock icons resonate mainly with the generation that knew them as performers.

Since the mid-1950s, teenagers have been seen as the tastemakers by the pop culture world, given their buying power and demographic clout. They have shaped trends in every corner of society, from music and movies to fashion and cell-phone technology. Adolescence has been good for business because the only constant with teens is inconstancy. They tend to be different almost every six months, and this allows businesses to turn their products over rapidly and profitably. It is no exaggeration to say that the entire economic system in which we live seems to have become completely dependent upon ensuring an incessant craving for anything new—new music, new fashion, new everything. The French culture critic Roland Barthes (1915–1980) called this paranoid affliction *neomania*.[12] However, as Bob Dylan so aptly put it in one of his songs, the times may be "a-changing" now more than ever. Bored with the onslaught of new musical fads, new musical icons, and simply bad music, many teens told the research team that pop music and its stars have become annoying. Particularly upsetting is the fact that hip-hop artists have shown themselves to be just like their rock counterparts. Hip-hop, like the hippie and punk subcultures before it, started out as rebellion.[13] But it is becoming more and more about gold rings, gold chains, and brand-name sneakers.

INSIGHTS

The most important insight to be gleaned from the discussion of music is that, along with body image and language, it provides a very important detail for completing the portrait of adolescence. Pop music styles come and go and are significant only to a specific generation of teens or even, more narrowly, to a specific teen clique. Teenagers rarely read novels, anthologies of poetry, or (certainly) books of philosophy to gain in-

Table 5.1. **"What do you read, watch, or listen to in order to gain meaning to your life?"**

Early Teens (12–15) (Number of Subjects = 77)		Mid-Teens (16–18) (Number of Subjects = 72)		Late Teens (18–early 20s) (Number of Subjects = 51)	
Music	70 (90.9%)	Music	51 (70.8%)	Music	18 (35.3%)
Novels	1 (1.3%)	Novels	4 (5.6%)	Novels	2 (3.9%)
Philosophy	0 (0%)	Philosophy	0 (0%)	Philosophy	2 (3.9%)
Television	1 (1.3%)	Television	7 (9.7%)	Television	10 (19.6%)
Movies	5 (6.5%)	Movies	10 (13.9%)	Movies	19 (37.3%)

sight into life. They get it from the music they listen to, as the research team found out, although the older they become, the more they start turning to other sources.

The subjects were asked to choose one or more of the given sources—music, novels, philosophy works, television, and movies—as those that they turn to for "gaining meaning" to their lives. The informants were also asked to identify any other source as meaningful. Only a couple of subjects identified magazines and comics as other sources. The pattern of responses is given in table 5.1.

"My parents don't get the music I love, 'cause they're old-fashioned and have weird musical tastes."
As argued in this chapter, the history of teenagehood is intertwined with the history of pop music. Rock was forged in the 1950s as the musical voice of the emerging teen culture. The fragmentation of this culture during the 1960s was mirrored in a concomitant differentiation in musical styles. Since the 1970s, the music of teenagehood has become more and more diverse.

The musical tastes of one teen generation are not those of subsequent ones. This is why a teen is likely to characterize the musical tastes of older people as "weird," as our informant so graphically put it.

"My music means a lot to me."
As in the case of body image and language, the most commonsense approach to understanding musical preferences is simply to ask what the music means, as the research team did. As Roberts and Christenson[14] and Holloway,[15] among many other cultural analysts, have aptly written, pop music has always played, and will probably continue to play, a central role in the life of adolescents as long as adolescence is around.

Over the history of teenagehood, music preferences have become increasingly eclectic. Whatever the style, music has great significance to adolescents, because it speaks to them emotionally. One can gain significant insights into what a teen thinks about and values most by learning to "read the meanings" of the music to which he or she listens. Music preferences, in fact, are intrinsically intertwined with whatever clique the teen joins and what "general philosophy" of life he or she will tend to espouse.

The ancient philosophers of classical Greece believed that music originated with the gods Apollo and Orpheus, and that it reflected in its melodic and harmonic structure the laws of harmony that rule the universe. They also believed that music influences human thoughts and actions, because each melody possesses an emotional quality that listeners experience directly. In some African societies, music is considered to be the faculty that sets humans apart from other species. Among some Native American cultures, it is thought to have originated as a way for spirits to communicate with human beings.

The question of what constitutes musical art is not an easy one to answer, because music appeals to our feelings more than it does to our intellect. But one thing is for certain—only those works that are genuinely meaningful to one and all will remain. Beethoven's *Missa Solemnis* and his last four string quartets, to mention but a few examples, will remain because they convey, through sound, a profound inner quest for meaning to life. Rummaging through the pop music experiment of the last fifty years does not produce anything that comes close to the Beethovenian standard. As Greil Marcus put it in 1976, in the end rock will fade away because it "is a combination of good ideas dried up by fads, terrible junk, hideous failings in taste and judgment, gullibility and manipulation, moments of unbelievable clarity and invention, pleasure, fun, vulgarity, excess, novelty and utter enervation."[16]

All this might sound élitist to the reader. But it is not. Mozart wrote music that he intended for the enjoyment of common folk—not just the cognoscenti. The operas of Verdi and Rossini, too, were "populist" forms. The idea of "classical music" as an élitist form of art is a modern one. And it is a myth that simply needs to be dispelled once and for all. We are lucky to live in an era where the music of a Mozart or a Beethoven need not lie dormant. It can be heard for the price of a CD. Their musical art cannot be so easily managed by the entrepreneurs of taste. It will exist regardless of the economic system in place in a given society in a given era.

It is also ironic to reflect on the fact that the greatest composers of all time were barely "teenagers" (as they would be called today) when they composed some of their greatest works. And they died at ages that would be considered way too young. To wit: Mozart died at the age of 35, Chopin at 39, and Schubert at 31. But their music was and continues to be "ageless" and "timeless."

"Sex is what it's all about, man!"

From a primal, pagan-like form of frenzy (as in some heavy metal songs) to a subdued, romanticized form of swooning (as in early rock love ballads), teen music is essentially about romance and sex, as our informant so aptly put it. The lyrics of the 1950s ranged from love as infatuation—"puppy love" à la Paul Anka—to explicit sex—"breathless" à la Jerry Lee Lewis. In the 1960s, the lyrics of rock stars urged sweeping social changes, turning it temporarily into music for the "neck upwards." But love and sex did not disappear from the rock scene. Indeed, sex was practiced openly at rock concerts. Gone from mainstream rock was the puppy love theme, probably once and for all, although it occasionally resurfaces in tweenie-directed music (as it did, for example, in the early music of the rock ensemble Wham! in the 1980s and in 1990s performers such as the Backstreet Boys, the Spice Girls, Britney Spears, and a host of their clones).

"Hip-hop, man, it's becoming history."

This statement was uttered to me by a teen who had joined a hip-hop clique a few years earlier, taken on a new identity, and lived out his life as a member of his hip-hop "family." It is testimony that nothing lasts in pop culture. I also sense a decrease in the hegemony of hip-hop culture in contemporary teenagehood. The signs of this are unmistakable. Many hip-hop artists now taunt each other in their songs and on TV directly, rather than decry social inequalities. Some of these taunts have led to violent deaths, such as those of Tupac Shakur, the Notorious B.I.G., and Jam Master Jay (of the group Run-DMC). Significantly, a *New York Times* 2002 survey found that most of the top rap artists at the time were "historical figures" in the rap movement—Dr. Dre, Warren G, Puff Daddy, Shaggy, SMX, Nelly, Ludacris, Coolio, Salt-N-Pepa, and Snoop Doggy Dogg.[17]

A *Rolling Stone* poll taken in the same year asked its readers to choose their 100 all-time favorite albums. The top ten chosen, which include *Revolver* by the Beatles (1965)—the number one album of all time—*Nevermind* by Nirvana (1991), and *Appetite for Destruction* (1987) by Guns n' Roses, does not contain a single rap album. Although the age demographic of *Rolling Stone's* readership has been inching upward for years, it is nevertheless surprising to find that rap has made few inroads.

As a final word on the topic of rap, and on pop music generally, I cannot help but mention the phenomenon of the "white rapper" Eminem (born Marshall Mathers). In 2002, he eclipsed even the African American rapper Ja Rule. His widely acclaimed movie, *8 Mile*, raised Eminem to the level of a mythic hero, at least according to the reviews. The movie got its name from an east-west road in Detroit that once divided city from suburb, blacks from whites, and lower class from middle class. Directed by Curtis

Hanson, the film was essentially a semibiographical drama featuring sub-urbia's angriest white rapper. It recreated 1995 Detroit when the hip-hop movement was at its peak. But despite the great press it received, the objective of the movie was, to my mind at least, to refashion Eminem into an Elvis Presley in rap clothing—a white man making a black man's art his own. Once denounced as a threat to America's moral fiber, Eminem transformed himself through the movie into an icon of pop culture. His shows subsequently started to draw little kids and their parents! But how genuine is the art of Eminem? As one rapper teen put it to a member of the research team: "Eminem's a white man pretending to be black, and everyone can see through it; he's hip now; but he won't last long." To paraphrase: Eminem is all about rap gesture and rap culture without rap substance.

NOTES

1. Cited in Simon Frith, *Sound Effects: Youth, Leisure and the Politics of Rock* (London: Constable, 1983), 77.

2. The topic of rock and roll and youth music generally has received extensive attention from all kinds of quarters—from the music industry, from academia, from parents' groups, and from pop culture historians, among others. This indicates rather conspicuously how important people think it has become in shaping modern-day youth values and belief systems. I cite here a number of volumes that I consulted for this book and that, in my view, provide interesting insights on various aspects of pop music: R. Palmer, *Rock & Roll: An Unruly History* (New York: Harmony Books, 1995); D. Szatmary, *A Time to Rock: A Social History of Rock 'n' Roll* (New York: Schirmer Books, 1996); J. A. Jackson, *American Bandstand: Dick Clark and the Making of a Rock 'n' Roll Empire* (Oxford: Oxford University Press, 1998); D. Roberts and P. Christenson, *It's Not Only Rock and Roll: Popular Music in the Lives of Adolescents* (New York: Hampton Press, 1998); J. Miller, *Flowers in the Dustbin: The Rise of Rock and Roll, 1947–1977* (New York: Simon and Schuster, 1999); and R. Padel, *I'm a Man: Sex, Gods and Rock 'N' Roll* (London: Faber and Faber, 2000).

3. A good treatment of the role of the Beatles in shaping the counterculture movement is the one by Ian MacDonald, *Revolution in the Head: The Beatles' Records and the Sixties* (London: Pimlico, 1995).

4. *The Republic*, ed. C. M. Blackwell (New York: Charles Scribner's Sons, 1956), 234.

5. A good treatment of counterculture rock is the book by Sheila Whiteley, *The Space between the Notes: Rock and the Counterculture* (London: Routledge, 1992).

6. Mark Gauvreau Judge, *If It Ain't Got that Swing: The Rebirth of Grown-Up Culture* (New York: Spence, 2000). A similar kind of point was made by Martha Bayles a few years earlier in *Hole in Our Soul: The Loss of Beauty and Meaning in American Popular Music* (New York: The Free Press, 1994).

7. See N. George, *Hip-Hop America* (New York: Viking, 1998); and A. Light, ed., *The Vibe History of Hip-Hop* (New York: Three Rivers Press, 1999) for overviews of the hip-hop movement.

8. See S. Reynolds, *Generation Ecstasy: Into the World of Techno and Rave Culture* (London: Routledge, 1999).

9. See, in particular, Sheila Whiteley, ed., *Sexing the Groove: Popular Music and Gender* (London: Routledge, 1997); Simon Reynolds and Joy Press, *The Sex Revolts: Gender, Rebellion, and Rock 'n' Roll* (Cambridge, Mass.: Harvard University Press, 1995), and Ruth Padel, *I'm a Man: Sex, Gods and Rock 'n' Roll* (London: Faber and Faber, 2000).

10. Stephen Davis, *Old Gods Almost Dead: The 40-Year Odyssey of the Rolling Stones* (New York: Broadway, 2001).

11. On this point, see John Strausbaugh, *Rock Till You Drop* (London: Verso, 2001).

12. Roland Barthes, *Mythologies* (Paris: Seuil, 1957).

13. See, on this point, Russell A. Potter, *Spectacular Vernaculars: Hip-Hop and the Politics of Postmodernism* (Albany: State University of New York Press, 1995).

14. Donald Roberts and Peter Christenson, *It's Not Only Rock and Roll: Popular Music in the Lives of Adolescents* (New York: Hampton Press, 1998).

15. R. Holloway, *All Shook Up* (New York: Spence, 2001).

16. Greil Marcus, *Mystery Train* (New York: E. P. Dutton, 1976), 18.

17. *New York Times,* November 3, 2002, 27.

6

Cliques, Gangs, and Cults

Interviewer	Do you often go out after school?
Teen Informant	Yeah, all the time.
Interviewer	Why?
Teen Informant	So I can be with my friends.
Interviewer	Is that important to you?
Teen Informant	Sure is. My friends are, like, everything to me.

BACKGROUND

In her widely read, albeit highly controversial 1992 book *Sex, Art, and American Culture,* the social critic Camille Paglia (1947–) made a comment that merits repeating here, because it so vividly encapsulates what this chapter is all about: "Teenage boys, goaded by their surging hormones, run in packs like the primal horde."[1] As our teen informant (who was actually a female) put it, such packs "are everything" to a teen, especially during the early phases of adolescence.

The primal "herd instinct" is certainly powerful in adolescence, as Paglia quips. But it is so for *both* boys and girls. Understanding what motivates teens of both genders to band together, to become members of this or that clique, gang, or cult, is the aim of this chapter.

CLIQUES

During childhood, parents generally have a say into the friendships that their children contract. Adolescents, on the other hand, tend to choose their own friends, no matter what their parents may think of them. Typically, the friends bond together and become congregations of various kinds that, as discussed in previous chapters, constitute miniature tribes. It is within these tribal aggregates that social life in adolescence unfolds.

The research team found that peer congregations are now forged in the tweenie years in junior high school. The need to maintain peer friendships during the early teen years is so powerful that it tends to overshadow most other interpersonal relations, activities, and interests, including scholastic ones. For this reason, the school context is perceived as a locus for socialization. School chums are, in fact, the peers with whom a teen tends to hang out, as the expression goes, and share experiences.

To be sure, this assessment is somewhat overdrawn, although of the 200 informants interviewed, 169 claimed that school-based friendships were of high to moderate importance to them. Although most of these were in the early teen and mid-teen categories (104 in total), their response nevertheless stands out as a significant pattern of social behavior among teens generally. But this does not mean that peer groupings are homogeneous or even similar. The ways in which adolescents relate to each other cannot help but be highly diversified today, given the high degree of variability that now characterizes the onset of teenagehood, the presence of ethnically diverse teens in many schools, and the differing socioeconomic backgrounds of teens. Moreover, not every adolescent feels the pressure to be part of a peer clique. Indeed, the high schools are filled with adolescents studying hard, striving to achieve well-defined goals, and immune, by and large, to peer pressure. But it is also true to say that contracting peer friendships by becoming part of a specific clique has been "symptomatic" of how adolescents have developed socially over at least the last five decades.

In most surveys, teens continue to rate peer friendships as crucial. In 2000, the sociologists Bibby and Posterski asked over 3,500 teens the three questions listed in table 6.1.[2] The answers of their subjects, in percentage figures, are self-explanatory.

Table 6.1.

What do you enjoy the most?				When something big goes wrong, whom do you want to tell?		When something great happens, whom do you tell?	
Friends	26%	Partying	3%	Friends	61%	Friends	47%
Sports	19%	Reading	2%	Family	22%	Everyone	35%
Sex	7%	Family	1%	God	2%	Family	15%
Music	6%	Other	36%	Teacher	1%	Other	3%
				Other	14%		

The research team also found that most early and mid-teens rate peer-related events as critical to their self-esteem. For example, when asked what kinds of things worried them most in their relations with friends, virtually all the early teens (75 of the 77) and most of the mid-teens (60 of the 72) indicated ostracism from social events such as parties. Those who are not invited to a party, or who may have actually preferred not to go to one, are often ostracized, derided, and sometimes confronted physically by other teens. In later adolescence, the pressure to be popular and to belong to peer groupings becomes greatly attenuated. Indeed, the transition from early teenagehood to late adolescence is marked by a decrease of interest on the part of the individual to be part of a clique or teen "party scene."[3]

As mentioned, cliques constitute miniature tribal systems. Within them, there typically emerges an implicit set of attitudes, beliefs, values, and principles among the individuals, and this set defines the clique's *groupthink*. The main "symptoms" of this groupthink are the illusion of invulnerability, the rationalization of warnings, agreement on issues, a view of other teens as outsiders, and a tendency to shield clique members from adverse information. If disagreements or conflicts are not resolved within the clique, ostracism from the clique generally ensues. This is a major cause of concern, as mentioned above, given that friendships are so important emotionally and socially at adolescence.

Social activities are decided during clique congregations, usually under the guidance of a leader. This may include which parties to go to, where to hang out, which movies to see, and the like. The teen party, in particular, constitutes a pivotal event given its function as a kind of implicit sexual and courtship ritual—a ritual that has been parodied in movies such

---

"SYMPTOMS" OF TEEN GROUPTHINK

The members of a clique may tend to:

- Share the illusion of invulnerability, which provides them with the impetus to take extraordinary risks
- Rationalize warnings and potential danger signs
- Assume that agreement on issues is unanimous among all members
- Ignore the broader ethical implications of what they do
- Consider some other teens corrupt or hostile and therefore exclude them from social events organized by the clique
- Put pressure on those members who stray from the clique's belief system to conform, marginalizing or ostracizing those who do not comply
- Avoid speaking out when they are not in favor of the clique's actions
- Screen the clique, and especially the leader, from adverse information

as *Animal House* (1978) and, more recently, the *American Pie* movies (2000, 2001). The party is a structured performance. Acting silly and rude is expected of some participants, whose roles are perceived to be similar to those of clowns. Others, on the other hand, are expected to provide sexual flirtation signals provoking the comical and exaggerated behaviors that get the "party animals" to act out their roles.

One of the most prestigious qualities a teenager is expected to possess is, in fact, the ability to entertain clique members. Anyone acclaimed as the *clown prince* of the clique is always accorded ample talk time in all kinds of situations. Clown prince status is achieved by those teens who are adept at telling funny, sarcastic stories and jokes. To maintain his or her status, the clown prince must, however, also be able to face and defeat any taunting verbal challenges that the peer group puts forward. The strategic use of humor, especially of a sexual nature, is thus a way of negotiating status within the clique. Although the open telling of obscene jokes referring to sexual anatomy is largely a taboo in the adult culture, such jokes are staples at teen gatherings—a fact that shows that teens tend to ignore politically correct trends in the adult culture.

Recordings by the research team of spontaneous conversations within clique settings contained numerous instances of "clowning" and, in all cases, this role was either assumed by a specific member or else assigned to him or her directly: "Hey, man, when are you goin' to make us laugh?" "Whassup, Billy, lost your sense of humor?" The clown prince is rarely challenged. He or she is accorded all the necessary time required to make the others laugh.

Cliques are directive of the lifestyle choices that teens make. Those choices are typically assigned names. The most common clique names documented by the research team (up to December 2002) are provided here (see box). Ravers, for instance, are teens who engage in raves—concerts that focus on dancing, in which occasional drugs are consumed. Hip-hoppers and gangstas look, dress, talk, and act like rap and hip-hop artists. Skaters, skiers, and snowboarders are teens who value skateboarding and other similar physical activities. Industrialists, metalheads, and grunophiles are teens who embrace certain types of music and their accompanying lifestyles. And, of course, punks and skinheads are teens who fashion their lifestyles after punk and other "radical" musicians. The difference between the two is that skinhead groups and their followers tend to espouse racial prejudice, whereas punks do not.

Readers of this book may have belonged to cliques during their school years. Some of the names of 1980s and early 1990s cliques are provided here as reminders of this fact (boxes). Cliques are often named after music styles, genres, or bands. But this is not the only source of naming. One of the oldest clique names is jocks. Although coined in the 1950s,

CLIQUE NAMES USED IN 2002

- gangstas
- goths
- grunophiles
- hip-hoppers/rappers
- industrialists
- metalheads
- punks
- ravers
- skaters
- skiers
- skinheads
- snowboarders
- surfers

1980s and 1990s Cliques

- housers: teens who assigned great value to dance music and especially to the whole club scene connected with it
- rockers (also called hard rockers, metalloyds, or metallurgists): teens who identified with hard rock bands and who wore leather boots, ripped jeans, and leather jackets
- mods/goths: teens who listened to the new wave music of the mid-1980s, and who wore black clothes and dyed their hair pitch black.
- Ginos/Guidos and Ginas: teens of Italian or Latino background who wore stylish clothing and listened to disco-type music
- deadheads: teens who listened to 1960s music and wore hippie-style clothing; their name was derived from the 1960s rock group The Grateful Dead
- B-boys: teens who wore basketball jackets and caps, and who listened to rap music; they are now called hip-hoppers

Coolness Traits (Identified by the University of Toronto Research Team)

1. cigarette smoking
2. sexual promiscuity and prowess
3. alcohol consumption
4. physical appearance
5. music preferences
6. clothing
7. drugs
8. dance-related activities
9. automobile ownership
10. academic achievement
11. physical aggression
12. individuality or "weirdness"

it continues to be used to this day to characterize teenagers actively involved in sports. The clique name Ginos (or Guidos)/Ginas refers not to
rock stars but to teens who have an ethnic background, generally Italian
or Latino, or who fashion their look and lifestyle after Latino musicians.

But whatever their name, all cliques espouse specific kinds of activities
as highly meaningful, and others as less so or even totally meaningless. To
uncover what these were, the research team asked the 200 subjects the following question: "What things do you think are cool for guys and girls
within your own group of friends?" To ensure that their answers were not
influenced in any way by the preconceptions of the research team, no
prompts were used. The answers given to this question provide a cata-
logue of critical *coolness* traits that define clique interests and activities.
The box lists the traits in order of frequency.

Smoking, engaging in sex, and drinking alcohol were mentioned by virtually everyone (187 of the 200). Only members of certain cliques mentioned other traits as desirable—for example, for some automobile ownership was considered a highly desirable trait, but for others individuality
or "weirdness" were instead considered highly desirable. The former was
seen as critical by Ginos/Ginas, the latter by goths. Overall, however,
these fared fairly low in the taxonomy of choices made. Significantly, academic achievement was considered to be valuable primarily by the late
teens (39 in total), only slightly above physical aggression (34) and individuality or weirdness (29).

As mentioned, virtually every interviewee identified the smoking of
cigarettes as a critical behavior for defining coolness. The consumption of
alcohol, too, emerged as a desirable cross-clique trait. These findings
show once again that the measures taken by the adult world to protect
teens from themselves tend to be fruitless and may be even counterproductive. Teens feel a strong desire to think for themselves, not according
to the categories and dictates that come down to them from the adult
world.

Knowing the "right" music—whatever it may be—was also perceived
to be a critical trait and an important one for status achievement across the
board. However, also knowing the "right" dance moves was identified as
desirable by hip-hoppers and Ginos/Ginas (42 in total). Conformity in
dress was also identified as a critical attribute by many teens (145 in total). Prowess in fighting and doing drugs were seen as important primarily by punks and hip-hoppers.

Sexual prowess was felt to be a critical trait for males by virtually all the
interviewees. A large number (146), however, considered it also to be a
positive attribute for females. This shows, once again, that gender roles
are being constantly redefined by the teens themselves. Christina Hoff
Sommers argued in her insightful book, titled *The War against Boys* (2000),

that the "boys will be boys" attitude has been extremely harmful to male adolescents over the years, since they have borne the brunt of the criticism from social activists.[4] However, if the results of our survey are indicative of a larger trend, then it appears that there has been considerable change within the contemporary adolescent world. Sex-seeking is no longer the privilege of males; it is now a largely genderless act among teens. Males and females alike, not just males alone, are expected to search out sexual partners. Females also can flaunt their sexuality openly with nary a notice from peers. This paradigm shift in gender roles is still in its early stages, and it remains to be seen how it will unfold in the future.

One of the more important functions of cliques is, as mentioned, to provide a context for sexuality and courtship to unfold.[5] Dating outside the immediate peer configuration is rare. Dating can mean a variety of situations and activities from gatherings that bring males and females together to group dates in which a group of boys and girls goes out jointly. There can be casual dating in couples or serious involvement with a boyfriend or girlfriend. The "stages" reported here were provided by a 15-year-old informant to a member of the research team in 2001 (see box). The descriptors used constitute the informant's way of describing how courtship unfolds in his peer world. But, as his "four-stage model" shows, there is really nothing new here, since most dating practices unfold more or less in similar ways. The first stage is making contact. Our informant called it *kickin' it* (a hip-hop term). The second stage involves a lot of talking and, for this reason, the interviewee called it *rappin'*. It also involves identifying the dating partner to clique members or, if the partner is from a different circle of friends, introducing him or her to the inner circle of friends. The third stage is the one during which sexual activities become frequent—hence the informant's euphemism of *seeing each other*. If a romantic bond ensues between the partners, it may lead to a pact of faithfulness and commitment—hence the informant's term *going out*. The teens may even feel compelled to introduce each other to their respective families during this fourth stage.

Dating has always been a major preoccupation in adolescence, given the lack of formal courtship rituals in our society that are similar to the formal communal rituals of tribal and religious societies. In our culture, dating is pretty much left up to the adolescents themselves. In the late 1940s and early 1950s, concern over this very fact was evidenced by the widespread use of classroom guidance films with titles such as *Dating: Do's and Don'ts* (1949), *What to Do on a Date* (1951), and *More Dates for Kay* (1952)—movies that attempted to provide some structure to dating practices among adolescents by emphasizing certain aspects of the "dating game." They typically urged teens to stand up straight, groom themselves appropriately, stay clear of the wrong crowd, be polite to parents, avoid alcohol and

---

**STAGES IN DATING CIRCA 2001
(AS IDENTIFIED BY ONE INFORMANT)**

Stage 1: *Kickin' it*—The potential courtship partners make initial contact in a peer setting; rejection by one of the partners is called *kickin' it back*.

Stage 2: *Rappin'*—The partners enter into a communicative relation characterized by phone-calling and e-mailing, chatting in places with friends around, and sending messages to each other through friends.

Stage 3: *Seeing each other*—The partners start hanging out with each other more frequently, without making a definite commitment; this stage of the relationship generally involves sexual relations.

Stage 4: *Going out*—The partners develop a tacit agreement of faithfulness, and may even introduce each other to their respective families.

---

cigarettes, and desist from sexual activities of any kind. With their simple-minded scripts, the films were intended to be doses of "mental hygiene" for the new hordes of teens, as a retrospective anthology of these films by film historian Ken Smith, titled *Mental Hygiene: Classroom Films 1945–1970* (2002), recently emphasized. I am absolutely sure that readers of this book who grew up during that era and who may have been exposed to the films considered them to be greatly "out of touch" with reality.

The dating game, like sex itself, has become an obsession. Television has always capitalized on this obsession. Programs such as *The Dating Game* have always been extremely popular. These are, in effect, bizarre and often grotesque events emphasizing instant fame, near-instant sex, and a little money on the side. In a society that has eliminated formal courtship rituals, it should come as no surprise to find that the appurtenant rituals are showcased on TV with such programs as the 2002 *Meet My Folks*, where suitors are grilled by Mom and Dad using a lie detector. As I write, the obsession with dating shows on TV has, in fact, reached astronomical proportions, with names such as *Blind Date, Change of Heart, Date Plate, A Dating Story, Dismissed, Elimidate, Extreme Dating, The 5th Wheel, Love by Design,* and *Shipmates*.

GANGS

There is probably nothing more alarming to a parent than to learn that his or her teen has joined a gang or is involved in some form of criminal activity. The concern is a real one. Official U.S. crime reports in the 1980s showed that about one fifth of all persons arrested for crimes were under

---

GANG MEMBERSHIP RITUALS

A new member must:

- Pledge permanent allegiance to the gang and its leader by donning body symbols (tattoos, scars, and so on)
- Assume a given gang nickname
- Show physical prowess or endurance in some brutal initiation rite (such as being kicked repeatedly by other members)
- Assume the duty of patrolling a dangerous territory determined to be a turf
- Learn to use hand signs so as to be able to communicate furtively with other members in the presence of outsiders

---

18 years of age. During the five-year period 1995–2000, juvenile arrests decreased slightly each year. However, it is likely that a higher percentage of juveniles was involved in minor criminal behavior because common offenses such as vandalism, shoplifting, underage drinking, and using drugs go largely unreported by most states and provinces, due to juvenile protection legislation of various kinds.

Today, it is estimated that one in four teens is involved (as victim or perpetrator) in a gang-related crime. The U.S. Department of Justice reports that as many as 125,000 to 250,000 young people are members of organized gangs today.

But, again, there is very little that is unusual even in this domain of contemporary teenagehood. Belonging to a gang, which is really a specific type of clique, has always been a part of adolescence, as exemplified in 1950s movies such as *Blackboard Jungle* (1955). The reason why it is more noticeable today is because of greater exposure to juvenile delinquency by the media.

Juvenile gangs are classified as *violent, delinquent,* or *social* by police forces across the continent. The activities of *violent gangs* revolve around violent crime, as the epithet suggests. Deadly warfare among such gangs is a common event, as they vie for territory in which to carry out their criminal activities (e.g., drug trafficking and prostitution). However, although intergang violence is sanctioned, violence within the gang is discouraged. The *delinquent gang* is a small cohesive group that carries out small criminal acts, such as petty thievery and mugging. Although violence may be used, the primary goal of such gangs is material gain. The *social gang* is really a type of clique. Although they call themselves gang members, individuals in such groups are held together primarily by a common interest in being perceived as physically aggressive and tough.

The social scientific explanations of why juveniles join gangs are hardly etched in stone. Not only do they vary widely, but they also tend to be culture-specific. Comparisons of the crime rates in various countries are, in fact, severely limited by wide variations in national legal systems, categories of criminal behavior, methods of reporting crimes, and definitions employed to define juveniles. Many theories within our own culture focus either on the individual or on society to explain juvenile crime. Theories centering on the individual suggest that teens engage in criminal behavior because they were not sufficiently penalized for previous delinquent acts or because they have learned criminal behavior through interactions with others. Theories focusing on the role of society in juvenile delinquency suggest that teens commit crimes in response to their failure to rise above their socioeconomic status or as a repudiation of middle-class values.

In my view, such theories tell only a minimal part of the story. The most important factor is the fact that many juveniles perceive gang membership as "cool." This was borne out by a 1991 survey by the National Crime Prevention Council, which found that teens who join gangs are primarily those who live in situations and locales where gang membership is perceived as prestigious or even as an obligatory coming-of-age rite. The survey also provided a useful breakdown of gangs (see box) according to the social objectives of the members.

The enormous emotional power of gang symbolism, with its tribal connotations, has probably much more to do with teen violence today than any of the traditionally accepted socioeconomic and psychological causes.[6] Psychologists who look for the causes underlying the increase in

---

GANGS

- Traditional street gangs, such as the Hell's Angels, the Bloods, or the Crips, hold a large appeal to streetwise teens searching for a family-type structure outside the family.
- Neighborhood gangs have only a local reach, attracting mainly teens living in the area for a limited period of time.
- Ethnic gangs base their membership criteria mainly on ethnicity (Hispanic gangs, Chinese gangs, and the like).
- Drug dealer gangs emerge spontaneously from teen cliques wishing to generate income for themselves through drug-related criminal activities.
- Hate gangs are motivated by racial prejudice and intolerance (for example, the Skinheads).

Source: National Crime Prevention Council, www.ncpc.org.

violence among teens in the social sphere (such as family background and class) are, in my view, more often than not barking up the wrong tree. Thirteen teens declared themselves to be gang members to the research team. The recurrent reason why they joined gangs was encapsulated in the response given by one of them: "It's cool, man! Nobody messes around with us!" Glorified by movies and music videos, gang membership affords many teens the opportunity to look and act tough *just for the sake of it* or, more accurately, *for the look of it.* One thinks, for instance, of the media glorification of ghetto teen gangs in the 1950s—a phenomenon captured brilliantly by American composer Leonard Bernstein (1918–1990) in his 1957 musical *West Side Story.* Incidentally, in this area of teen behavior, too, degendering has taken full effect (regrettably so, in this particular case). Females today are as prone to join gangs as are their male counterparts. And the activities of female gangs are no less violent.[7]

CULTS

Most people today over the age of 40 cannot help but shudder at the recollection of an event that occurred in 1969. That was the year in which the Tate-LaBianca murders made headlines. Screen actress Sharon Tate Polanski was murdered at her Bel-Air home in Benedict Canyon early in the morning of August 10 along with coffee heiress Abigail Folger, Folger's common-law husband Wojiciech Frykowski, Hollywood hair stylist Jay Sebring, and delivery boy Steven Earl Parent. Supermarket chain president Leno LaBianca and his wife Rosemary were murdered later in the day at their home in Los Angeles. What makes the memory of the event even more disturbing is the fact that the murders were planned and executed by members of a hippie cult family, led by an ex-convict named Charles Manson, for no other reason than to carry out Manson's personal vendetta against society. Manson had mesmerized and brainwashed his followers with drugs, sex, and pseudoreligious rhetoric, then ordered them to commit the horrific crimes.

The Tate-LaBianca murders dramatically brought to the surface the power that cult leaders have over some impressionable adolescents. *Cult* is the term used for a group that is usually religious; is devoted to a living leader, almost always male; and is committed to observing his teachings and practices. Cults range in size from a few followers to worldwide organizations directed by a complex chain of command. Since the 1960s, publicity about cults has altered the meaning of the term. Today, it is applied to groups that follow any self-styled leader who promotes unorthodox doctrines and practices. Cult leaders claim to possess truth exclusively. They also command absolute obedience and allegiance from followers, forcing members to release all their possessions to the group and expecting the female members to make themselves sexually available to them.

Why do teens join cults? Perhaps the reason can be found in the words of one informant: "I know a friend who joined a cult, because he wanted to be part of a family." The desire to be a member of an emotionally meaningful family-like structure is probably the primary reason for cult membership. Teens join cults so that they can immerse themselves into group life and thus leave decision making and all the risks involved with growing up to a leader. It is easier to be told what to do than to have to act independently. We sometimes forget this, living in a culture that stresses independence and individuality. Humans are gregarious animals. They need group structure in order to survive emotionally. With few exceptions—hermits and loners—people accept such structure as normal. Individuals who cannot cope with the burdens of individual decision making tend to join radical group formations. In effect, a cult acts like a surrogate family, providing the same kind of emotional shelter that the individuals probably felt as children within their real families. This is why those who join cults become so totally committed to them and may even end up dead because of it, as the most notorious incidents related to cults have made so obvious to all in recent years (see box).

There is statistical evidence indicating that several million Americans may be members of cults.[8] This does not make them necessarily weird or dangerous. It really depends on the situation. High-pressure groups

---

NOTORIOUS INCIDENTS ASSOCIATED WITH CULTS

- 1978: More than 900 members of the People's Temple, led by the Reverend Jim Jones, committed suicide by drinking cyanide-spiked grape punch in Jonestown, Guyana.
- 1993: Eighty followers of David Koresh's Branch Davidians died by gunfire or flames in an infamous and controversial battle with federal agents in Waco, Texas.
- 1994: Fifty-three members of the doomsday Solar Temple cult committed murder-suicide in Switzerland and Quebec.
- 1995: Twelve people were killed and some 5,000 injured when members of Aum Shinrikyo, a Japanese cult, released nerve gas in the Tokyo subway system.
- 1997: Believing that a UFO behind the Hale-Bopp comet would carry them to heaven, thirty-nine similarly dressed members of Heaven's Gate committed suicide in the United States.

targeting young people are perhaps the most dangerous ones, since they present themselves as perfect and as having all the answers. They also offer instant love and friendship, and they will simply not take "no" for an answer to their requests. Typically, they dupe the young person into membership by making him or her feel guilty, afraid, or ashamed.

INSIGHTS

Children depend upon their parents for protection and comfort. During early adolescence, this sense of dependence begins to decline while peer pressure starts to increase. Such pressure is particularly strong during junior high school and the early years of high school. It is only during middle adolescence, near the end of high school, that adolescents begin to act the way they think is right rather than trying to impress their friends.

"I can't stay without my friends; everything else is boring."
The pubescent individual's discovery that he or she thinks and feels the same way as someone else the same age becomes an important basis of friendship and is critical in how he or she constructs identity. As someone defined as "not quite an adult" but "no longer a child," the adolescent simply does not fit into the broader social matrix. This is why peers become important. In societies where adolescence does not exist as a social experiment, the need to be part of peer groupings does not emerge. This was noted by Mead already in the 1930s (see chapter 1). It is a "fact on file" in the annals of cultural anthropology.

Fortunately, the cliquing phenomenon has a lifecycle of its own. It is particularly characteristic of early adolescence, when pubescent individuals tend to yield to peer pressure in such matters as styles of dress, tastes in music, and choices among leisure activities. But already by mid-adolescence, most teenagers will turn to their parents and teachers when it comes to long-range questions concerning educational or occupational plans, or decisions involving values, religious beliefs, or ethics—whether they admit to seeking such guidance or not.

"All my friends do it; I mean, like, make out."
This statement was made in response to the question: "Does sex occur among your friends?" Clearly, it indicates that sex is not a random act negotiated by any two teens; rather, it unfolds within the confines of the tribal enclave. Although many parents may cringe at the thought that their "child" is having sex, it is virtually impossible to keep it from happening, as was mentioned already several times in this book. In fact, the very emergence of the tribal enclave (whether it be a clique, a gang, or some

Chapter 6

other peer configuration) can be explained as a response to sexual urges—
that is, it can be explained as a social system designed to allow adolescents
to engage in sexuality in a regular and meaningful way rather than in
some random fashion. The quest to satisfy sexual urges is a fact of life for
individuals reaching puberty; it cannot be so easily turned aside or redi-
rected by adult sanctions. Fortunately, it appears to be a fairly controlled
activity, constrained and regulated by the "mores" of the peer group.

By the time tweenies reach high school, they probably have had some
significant sexual experience. Centers for Disease Control (CDC) statistics
show that during the 1970s and 1980s, more tweenies became sexually active than in the past and became so at an earlier age. Paradoxically, surveys in the late 1990s indicated that this trend was leveling off, suggesting perhaps that recent generations of teens are more "responsible" than
their predecessors. But, despite the statistical surveys, my sense is that not
much has changed. I get this from the interviews and the ongoing dialogue I maintain with teenagers. As one teen told me recently: "If parents
knew what was going on, they'd freak!"

"That guy dresses like a freak, man; crazy!"
Peers have a significant influence on the development of gender identity. But this is not unique to adolescence. Even 3- and 4-year-olds have
ideas about "what boys do" and "what girls do," and they put pressure
on one another to act according to those ideas. When children engage in
behavior labeled as typical of the other sex, their peers may criticize them.
For example, classmates may ridicule a boy who wears a frilly pink shirt.
In addition, many children tend to select playmates of the same sex,
which reinforces traditional gender roles.

During early adolescence, the approval and acceptance of peers are
more important than the approval of parents when it comes to gender
roles. In high school, peer groups provide sharply defined ideas about
gender with implicit rules about proper behavior for males and females.
Individuals who do not meet peer expectations may be subjected to
ridicule, teasing, or ostracism.

Having said this, I sense that there is a growing tolerance of sexual difference in many schools today. Teens with different views about sexuality,
gender, and even sexual orientation are now more accepted by the general
peer group than they were in the past.

"No way, I belong to those creeps; my friends are different!"
The clique is dominant in shaping lifestyle and personality (at least
temporarily). A teen who sees himself or herself as a gangsta rapper,
for instance, will eventually develop a commensurate personality
with gangsta lifestyle—that is, the teen will typically manifest aggressive

behavior, utter obscenities regularly, wear certain gangsta fashions, listen to hip-hop music, and so on. The clique constitutes a "shelter" system, as mentioned several times, in which the teen can safely fashion an identity consistent with that of his or her peers. Ironically, the protection afforded by the peer group can, in itself, be a source of endangerment, since it tends to convey the impression to teenagers that "bad things will happen to others, not to us."

Gangs and cults have names, rituals, and symbols that give them away. The use of jackets, motorcycles, profane language, tattoos, and hand gestures are characteristic of gang lifestyle. Membership is through some violent initiation rite, which involves "proving oneself" by surviving some violent physical attack.

The thirteen gang members interviewed by the research team all pointed out that they joined their gang to be "cool" and "tough-looking," as in the movies. The teens came from diverse social backgrounds, incidentally, suggesting that no particular class of youths can be labeled "at risk" more than any other. Teenagehood has taken care of leveling the playing field for all teens; essentially any youth, no matter what his or her background may be, might decide to join a gang because it is cool.

Teens who join a cult, on the other hand, are those who might already experience a serious emotional gap in their family or peer relations. They try to fill it by becoming cult members. As a consequence, their personalities will change drastically. They will become totally devoted to the leader of the cult and claim to be so in no uncertain terms. A teen who becomes hostile to the family and to previous friends, who misrepresents the cult and its purposes during conversations, and who drops out of school is potentially someone who may have come under the emotional sway of a cult.

"I'm afraid; ya know if I rat on them, they'll come after me again!"
The peer group exacts uncompromising adherence from its members. Members who "rat on" the group, as our informant put it, will typically be subjected to some form of retaliation. Peers take justice into their own hands and dispense it on their own terms. Many of the so-called random acts of violence reported by the media in school settings are hardly "random." They are motivated by the dynamics of the peer group.

"Nah, I don't hang out with those guys any more; I'm my own man!"
The most predictable facet of the cliquing phenomenon is that most peer group formations forged in early adolescence are short-lived.

At its inception, a clique tends to be mainly unisexual (all boys or all girls) and isolated from other cliques. A little later on, the clique starts typically to become interactive with other cliques. During subsequent stages,

---

CLIQUING

- During the early teen years (12–15 years of age), there is a sharp increase in the amount of time adolescents spend with their peers compared to the time they spend with their families.
- In early adolescence, teen cliques tend to consist of members of the same sex (all boys or all girls).
- There is much more contact between peers of the opposite sex during the middle (16–18) and late teen (18–early 20s) years.

---

therefore, the clique opens itself up more and more to members of the opposite sex. Finally, the event that signals the disintegration of the clique is the romantic bonding that older adolescents seek out.

"I'm into heavy things, man, like my friends."

Satanic rites, vampirism, and other bizarre lifestyle practices among teen groups have received widespread media attention in recent years. In themselves, they generally mean no more than temporary choices. They are forms of escapism, expressions of group solidarity, or outlets for rebellion. However, there is cause for concern if the teen persists in being secretive over certain rituals and symbols, spends more and more time away from home, shows drastic clothing and appearance changes, constantly reads materials and listens to music with occult themes, and exhibits falling grades.

It is ironic to note, actually, that problems such as these are the result of the social experiment of adolescence and, thus, are part of a self-fulfilling prophecy. This is not to say that gangsterism is a product solely of adolescence. The Mafia, for example, originated in feudal times, when lords hired brigands to guard their estates in exchange for protection from the royal authority. In the United States, gangs of outlaws emerged in frontier sections of the country and wherever government was weak. Notorious were the Sydney Ducks of San Francisco (active in the 1850s) and the Hudson Dusters of turn-of-the-century New York City. But the rise of the youth gang as a group of adolescent "toughies" is something that was unknown before the advent of adolescence. It would seem that we will have to live with this sociopathic outgrowth of adolescence, whether we like it or not. On the other hand, if the cause (adolescence itself) is eliminated, then things might change. More will be said about this in the final chapter.

NOTES

1. Camille Paglia, *Sex, Art, and American Culture* (New York: Random House, 1992), 25.
2. R. W. Bibby and D. C. Posterski, *Teen Trends* (Toronto: Stoddart, 2000).
3. The research team found that only 2 (3.6 percent) of those in the late teen category (55) claimed that clique membership was vital to them, compared to 75 (97.4 percent) of the 77 in the early teen category. For more insights on this issue, see the interesting book by S. Shellenberger and G. Johnson, *Cars, Curfews, Parties, and Parents* (Minneapolis, Minn.: Bethany House, 1995).
4. Christina Hoff Sommers, *The War against Boys* (New York: Simon and Schuster, 2000).
5. See also V. Strasburger, *Getting Your Kids to Say "No" in the '90s When You Said "Yes" in the Sixties* (New York: Fireside, 1993), on this point.
6. Good treatments of the relation between culture and gangs are the ones by Jack B. Moore, *Skinheads Shaved for Battle: A Cultural History of American Skinheads* (Bowling Green, Ohio: Bowling Green State University Popular Press, 1993); and Daniel J. Monti, *Wannabe Gangs in Suburbs and Schools* (Cambridge: Blackwell, 1994).
7. Works on gang and cult membership—both popular and scientific—have been proliferating. This is strong evidence that such behavior has become a worrisome problem. See, for example: M. Webb, *Coping with Street Gangs* (New York: Rosen Publishing Group, 1990); and K. M. Porterfield, *Straight Talk about Cults* (New York: Facts on File, 1997).
8. See Porterfield, *Straight Talk about Cults.*

7

Tobacco, Alcohol, and Drugs

Interviewer	Do you smoke cigarettes?
Teen Informant	Of course I do.
Interviewer	Why do you say "Of course"?
Teen Informant	'Cause everybody, like, does it, you know, my friends and all people my age. It's, like, a cool thing, man.
Interviewer	Are you aware of the dangers?
Teen Informant	Yeah, but I don't care.

BACKGROUND

The late John Lennon (1940–1980), a founder of the Beatles, made a statement on the Dick Cavett television show on September 24, 1971, that resonates with relevance to this day: "Why do we have these accessories [cigarettes and drugs] to normal living to live? I mean, is there something wrong with society that's making us so pressurized, that we cannot live without guarding ourselves against it?"

Why does "everybody do it," as our teen informant observed, in such blatant defiance of the risks that smoking and drinking entail? Why have campaigns by concerned groups to dissuade teens from smoking or drinking proven to be largely ineffective? These are the questions to be taken up in this chapter. Understanding the role of such "accessories," as Lennon described cigarettes and drugs, in adolescence is clearly of critical importance to completing the portrait of contemporary adolescence, given that a significant number of teens continue to smoke, drink alcohol, and even take drugs as part of the whole "cool thing."

TOBACCO

Smoking cigarettes is a de facto "cool thing" to do, as virtually every informant told the research team, whether or not the teen actually does it. Even the brand smoked carries great significance. The team discovered, for instance, that Marlboro was, by and large, the preferred brand of most of the teens. "Camels," one female informant exclaimed, "are for grandmas and grandpas," a sentiment confirmed by a male informant: "Camels ain't cool; Marlboro is, like, a real cigarette, man."

As surveys indicate, cigarette smoking starts early. The average starting age is 12–13, among mainly white boys and girls (equally). For some unknown reason, fewer African American youths take up smoking. Moreover, it would appear that cigarettes constitute the main smoking prop among teens, although there is some use of cigars and chewing tobacco. As one informant put it: "Only those who want to be different and tough chew tobacco." Of the 200 interviewees, only 3 claimed to smoke cigars regularly and 9 to chew tobacco. The researchers also found that smoking percentages went up according to age group: 21 of 77 early teens (27 percent), 34 of 72 mid-teens (47 percent), and 38 of 51 late teens (75 percent) claimed to smoke on a regular basis; 30 of the 200 teens interviewed (15 percent) claimed that they did not smoke at all, with most of them finding smoking to be a "disgusting thing," to quote one particular informant.

According to the U.S. Food and Drug Administration from the early to mid-1990s, the proportion of teenage smokers in the United States rose from one quarter to one third. Since then, efforts to discourage teens from starting to smoke have been aggressive and widespread throughout the nation. I will give here only a selective accounting of such efforts.

A standard measure is taxation. An excise tax on cigarettes has, of course, been in place for decades. The rate rose from 8 cents per pack of 20 cigarettes in 1951 to 24 cents per pack in 1993. Currently, the tax is approximately 35–40 percent of retail price. In other developed countries, the cigarette tax rate is much higher, ranging from 50 percent in Switzerland to 85 percent in Denmark. Another measure is the use of "scare tactics." The U.S. Surgeon General's report on smoking in 1964, which led to the mandating of a warning on cigarette packages by the Federal Trade Commission, is an example of a scare tactic. A third is legislation designed to curb (and even prohibit) the advertising of tobacco products. In 1971, all cigarette advertising was banned from radio and television. Recently, the U.S. Food and Drug Administration agency increased its jurisdiction over the marketing and advertising of tobacco products with the specific aim of reducing smoking among teenagers. A fourth tactic is prohibiting smoking in public locales. Most cities and states passed laws requiring nonsmoking sections in most public places and workplaces in the early

1970s. The U.S. Occupational Safety and Health Administration agency has proposed that smoking be banned in all places, and this will probably come to pass in the near future (given recent attitude shifts in society at large with regard to smoking).

Various lawsuits have been brought against tobacco companies to reclaim damages due to disease or death caused allegedly by smoking. In part to avoid potentially ruinous lawsuits filed by states and diseased smokers, in 1997 the tobacco industry proposed a tentative settlement pledging over $368 billion to be spent over twenty-five years to compensate states for the costs of treating smoking-related illnesses, to finance nationwide antismoking programs, and to underwrite health care for uninsured adolescent smokers.

But despite all such measures and actions, teens continue to smoke, seemingly unperturbed by all the warnings and undiscouraged by all the prohibitions. The reason for this is not hard to figure out. Smoking is a desirable thing to do because it is associated with coolness and because it is forbidden by adults. Ever since it fell out of the social mainstream, smoking has entered the alluring world of the *verboten*. Anytime something becomes taboo, it takes on powerful occult symbolism—the more forbidden and the more dangerous it is, the more sexy and alluring it is. Smoking communicates rebellion, defiance, and sexuality all wrapped into one. No wonder, then, that regulations aimed at curbing the marketing and sale of tobacco products to young people have failed miserably in deterring them from smoking. As Tara Parker-Pope has aptly put it:

> For 500 years, smokers and tobacco makers have risked torture and even death at the hands of tobacco's enemies, so it's unlikely that a bunch of lawyers and politicians and the looming threat of deadly disease will fell either the industry or the habit.[1]

As mentioned in chapter 2, cigarette smoking constitutes a kind of implicit coming of age and courtship rite that is anchored in socially meaningful peer contexts. And, indeed, the informants who smoke gave answers such as the following when asked why they smoke: "Because the rest of my friends smoke," "It makes me look big," "To feel sophisticated," "The girls like it," and "It's cool, man."[2] In almost every era, cigarettes have had some connection to something that is erotically, socially, or intellectually appealing. Musicians smoke; intellectuals smoke; artists smoke. Smoking is a symbol of both sexual cool and intellectual prowess. Movies once told us that smoking is a prelude to sex and a form of relaxation afterwards; smoking seems to be the entire point of being mature; smoking is fun. Smoking is, in two words, a *taboo language* that allows teens to look cool in peer tribal settings.

In this area of teen behavior, too, degendering has taken full effect. In the 1950s smoking was reserved mainly for male teens. In the 1960s and 1970s females started to smoke more and more, joining their male counterparts in expressing their sexual cool openly and, more significantly, their equality to males. By the 1980s smoking became as de rigueur for females as it was for males. Today, statistics show that female teens on average smoke even more than male teens. In this brave new girl power world, the cigarette has become an intrinsic prop in the arsenal of female cool.

Where do teens pick up the association between smoking and coolness? There is no doubt in my mind that it once came from cinematic images that have become part of our communal memorate, the term used by anthropologists to refer to an unconscious pattern of thought that has become so common that it is no longer recognized as originating in some idea, trend, or event. The initial link can probably be traced back to the jazz club scene of the first decades of the twentieth century. The word *jazz* originally had sexual connotations, and to this day the verb form, *to jazz*, suggests sexual intercourse. The jazz clubs, known as *speakeasies*, were locales where young people went to socialize and to smoke (a habit that was not looked upon too favorably in society at large during the era). Cigarette smoking was portrayed by movies of the era as part of the whole scene. The association between smoking and sexuality was thus forged in our collective memory. It is that unconscious imagery that continues to sell cigarettes.

It is true that we see less smoking in movies now—a fact reflecting the change in social opinions on smoking. There are even movies that parody the association. I mention, as an early case in point, the 1980 movie *Caddyshack*, which contains a scene parodying smoking as a come-on, when actor Chevy Chase smiles at a woman as smoke comes out of his mouth in a ludicrous, farcical way.

Nevertheless, the "sexual allure" of the cigarette, so to speak, is alive and well among teens, and this might explain why measures taken by schools and communities to discourage smoking invariably seem to fail. When something with erotic connotations is forbidden or even downplayed (as witnessed by the conspicuous absence of cigarette smoking in the movies), it entices teens to do it even more so. Although statistics show that only one third of teens now smoke regularly, virtually every teen involved in a social scene with other teenagers (such as parties) will have the odd cigarette just to fit in. And, indeed, that is the good news. *Most teenagers are occasional smokers.*

One campaign that seems to have been somewhat successful in lowering the desire in teens to smoke was the one mounted by the state of Florida in late 1999. Using the nearly $40 million dollars a year that came as part of the settlement of the state's successful lawsuit against tobacco

SMOKING IN THE MOVIES

- Gjon Mili captured the "nightclub" allure of smoking memorably on film in his 1945 movie, *Jammin' the Blues*. In the opening segment, there is a close-up of the great saxophonist Lester Young inserting a cigarette gingerly into his mouth, then dangling it between his index and middle fingers as he plays a slow, soft, hazy kind of cool jazz for his late-night audience.
- Michael Curtiz conveyed the same kind of cool in his 1942 movie, *Casablanca*. Cigarettes are conspicuous sexual props in Rick's café. Swaggering imperiously in his realm, Rick (Humphrey Bogart) is rarely seen without a cigarette in his mouth or in his hand.
- So captivating was this image of sexual cool to cinemagoers that it became a paradigm imitated by hordes of young males in the 1940s and 1950s. Incidentally, that very paradigm was satirized by Jean-Luc Godard in his 1959 film, *Breathless*. In one scene, Jean-Paul Belmondo stares at a poster of Bogart in a cinema window. He takes out a cigarette and starts smoking it, imitating Bogart in *Casablanca*. With the cigarette dangling from the side of his mouth, the sexually cool Belmondo approaches his female mate with a blunt, "Sleep with me tonight?" The parodic intent is obvious.
- In Nicholas Ray's 1955 movie, *Rebel without a Cause*, the "sexual cool" associated with smoking comes out forcefully in the "car chicken" scene, in which teen idol James Dean can be seen dangling a cigarette from a side of his mouth just before he gets ready to duel his opponent to the death with his car (see also chapter 2).
- Starting in the 1990s, Hollywood became politically correct. Fewer and fewer movies involve smoking as part of a coolness performance. By the twenty-first century, virtually no mainstream movie includes cigarette smoking of any kind.

firms, Florida gave the assignment of finding strategies to curb smoking to the teenagers themselves. Nearly 10,000 teens were given total leeway to devise antitobacco ads, script them, and then produce them. Known as Students Working against Tobacco (SWAT), the campaign was unexpectedly successful in getting teens to consider the health implications of smoking. But more recent statistics from Florida show that new teens seem to be completely ignorant of the efforts of their older peers.

Except for SWAT's brief success, antismoking campaigns have never worked, no matter how effective they may appear to adult eyes. Some current TV campaigns showcase diverse casts of teens talking about why they don't smoke or describing tragic deaths due to smoking. The approach is emotionally powerful—at least, to an adult viewer such as myself. But the

Centers for Disease Control (CDC) reported in 2002 that such ads did little to deter smoking among teens, highlighting the fact that the antismoking media campaigns of governments and concerned citizen groups have little effect—one in three teens still smoke, a percentage that has not changed much since adolescents started smoking en masse in the 1950s. Even the use of horrific images on cigarette packages showing rotting teeth and decaying cancer-ridden lungs seem to have little effect on teens. One interviewee told me, in response to such images, "Cigarettes are nasty, man" and "Smoking is gross," but he nevertheless smoked because "I don't care," in an obvious display of bravado and defiance.

As Margaret Leroy has suggested, smoking is now part of our sexual traditions.[3] The history of smoking shows that tobacco has been perceived at times as a desirable thing and at others as a forbidden fruit.[4] But in almost every era, as Richard Klein has also eloquently argued,[5] cigarettes have had some connection to sex or to something that is erotically, socially, or intellectually appealing. As Michael Starr puts it, "Smoking is, in many situations, a species of rhetoric signifying certain qualities of the smoker."[6]

This characterization was saliently evident in videotapes I made of teens smoking in clique settings in the 1990s.[7] The tapes showed that smoking gestures were coded sexually. For example, females tended to take the cigarette out of its package with a slow, deliberate movement, inserting it coquettishly into the middle of the mouth, then bringing the flame of a match toward the cigarette in a laggard, drawn-out fashion. The males, on the other hand, tended to employ abrupt, terse movements to take the cigarette out of its package, insert it into the side of the mouth, and then swiftly light it. If sitting, females tended to keep their legs crossed, resting their arm on the table, with the cigarette between the index and middle fingers pointing upwards, periodically flicking the ashes, and inserting and removing the cigarette from the mouth, with graceful, circular, swooping motions. If sitting, males tended to keep their legs apart, leaning back in the chair in a regal manner, keeping the head taut, looking straight ahead during the puffing motions, holding the cigarette mainly between the thumb and middle finger, and guiding it to the side of the mouth with sharp, pointed movements.

The tapes also showed that females tended to draw smoke in slowly, retaining it in the mouth for a relatively protracted period of time (rarely inhaling it into the lungs), exhaling the smoke in an upwards direction with the head tilted slightly to the side, and, finally, extinguishing the cigarette in an ashtray—"squishing" it in a tantalizing way. In contrast to such gestures, the tapes showed males inhaling abruptly, holding the smoke in the mouth for a relatively short period of time, blowing it in a downward direction (with the head slightly aslant), and then extinguishing the cigarette by pressing down on the butt with the thumb, almost as if they were effacing or destroying evidence. If standing, the males typically flung the cigarette as far as they could with the middle finger and thumb.

The gestures and postures changed very little from high school to high school, from city to city across North America. In a phrase, they constitute an unconscious body language that keeps males and females sexually differentiated.

It is interesting to note that tobacco was part of many rites of the ancient Mayan peoples, who believed it had medicinal and powerful mythical properties. The Arawak people of the Caribbean, observed by Christopher Columbus in 1492, smoked it through a tube they called a *tobago*, from which the word *tobacco* originated. Brought to Spain from Santo Domingo in 1556, tobacco was introduced to France in the same year by the French diplomat Jean Nicot, from whom the plant derived its generic name, *nicotine*. In 1585 the English navigator, Sir Francis Drake, took it to England, where the practice of pipe smoking was subsequently introduced among the Elizabethan courtiers by the English explorer, Sir Walter Raleigh. Tobacco use spread quickly throughout Europe, and by the seventeenth century it had reached China, Japan, the west coast of Africa, and other areas of the world. From the moment of its introduction into European society, smoking was perceived either as a subversive act or as one laden with sexual connotations.

By the early twentieth century, smokers in the United States were consuming more than 1,000 cigarettes per capita each year. The general attitude of American society was that smoking relieved tensions and produced no ill effects, enhancing the attractiveness of the smoker. During World War II, physicians even endorsed sending soldiers cigarettes, which were consequently included in ration kits. Epidemiologists soon noticed, however, that lung cancer—rare before the twentieth century— had increased dramatically, beginning about 1930. The American Cancer Society and other organizations initiated studies comparing deaths among smokers and nonsmokers, finding increased mortality rates from cancer among the former. In 1964 the U.S. Surgeon General's report affirmed that cigarette smoking was a health hazard of sufficient importance to warrant the inclusion of a warning on cigarette packages. All cigarette advertising was banned from radio and television, starting in 1971. Today, smoking in public places, buildings, vehicles, and many other kinds of places (restaurants, movie theaters, and the like) is generally strictly controlled or prohibited.

Yet people, especially teens, continue to smoke. The tribal symbolism of the cigarette has not as yet been erased from the memorate. Smoking is a largely unconscious coming-of-age rite rooted in a body language that keeps the two sexes highly interested in each other. Let's scrutinize the typical female's smoking gestures described above. The sequence of holding the cigarette invitingly between her index and middle fingers and then inserting it into the middle of her mouth, slowly and deliberately, constitutes a highly erotic sequence—at any age, for that matter. Her hair-tossing movements, slightly raising a shoulder to highlight her breasts, also constitute powerful erotic signals. Needless to say, these same gestures can be observed in females in cinematic roles and in advertising.

The male teen's gestures form a patterned counterpart to those of the female, emphasizing sexual differentiation. Her movements are slow, his are abrupt; she crosses her legs, he keeps his apart; she puffs her smoke upwards, he blows it downwards; she holds the cigarette in a tantalizing manner between the index and middle fingers, he holds it in a sturdy way between the thumb and middle finger; she puts out the cigarette with a lingering motion, he crushes it forcefully (or else flings it energetically away). Her gestures convey sensuality, voluptuousness, and sultriness; his communicate toughness, determination, and control.

These gestures are so familiar and understandable to us because, as mentioned several times, they constitute a memorate. The particular performance will vary in detail from locale to locale, and from individual to individual, but its basic features will remain the same. Smoking allows teens to assume a role in sexual acting. Incidentally, when such structured patterns are altered in any way, they indicate a change in gender roles and relations. To wit: punk males and females smoke in the same "aggressive fashion." I have also noticed, in a recent follow-up to the study I conducted a few years ago, that female smoking actions and gestures are approaching those of males more and more. The reverse has not, as far as I can determine, yet occurred.

Such differential displays are not unique to the human species. The biologist Charles Darwin (1809–1882) called certain displays "submissive" when they send out the message, "Notice me, I am attractive and harmless." The female's coy glances and movements have parallels in the behaviors of females of other species as signals to prospective mates for compliance and pursuit. They are, in effect, opening gambits in a continuing series of mating negotiations. But human courtship is not controlled exclusively by biological mechanisms. Cigarette smoking has nothing to do with evolution. A cigarette is a ritualistic prop. It is a key element through which sexual messages are encoded.

ALCOHOL

Like smoking, drinking alcohol is part of the enactment of coolness. It was so even when the writer of this book was a teen himself in the late 1950s. Imbibing alcohol with friends at parties has always been "part of the cool scene." Adolescents experiment with alcohol for no reason other than because it is the thing to do and, of course, because it flies in the face of adult opposition. It emphasizes alienation from adult authority and, like smoking, it bespeaks sexuality.[8]

Surveys show that alcohol use among teens has reached mind-boggling proportions. In our own survey, we found that nearly all of the informants claimed to have consumed significant quantities of alcohol in the company of peers at least once in their lives. However, only later teens claimed to be regular consumers of alcohol. The breakdown according to category is especially revealing, showing a dramatic increase in the number of drinkers from the early period onwards: 10 of 77 early teens (13 percent), 21 of 72 mid-teens (29 percent), and 45 of 51 late teens (88 percent) claimed to imbibe regularly. These findings are in line with those documented by agencies, such as the U.S. Drug and Food Administration, suggesting that drinking is seen as a sign of maturity by teens in direct correlation to aging. In a phrase, by the last year of high school, most teens drink. It is also revealing to find that, on average, as many females as males drink. Our survey showed that rather clearly: in all three age categories, as many girls as boys claimed to drink regularly. Again, this is not a surprising finding, given the degendering forces at work generally that are introducing unisex habits into virtually all domains of social behavior.

The last comment requires further elaboration here. Pop culture initiated a society-wide movement known as "girl power" in the mid-1990s, as mentioned several times previously. This was welcomed by many as a concrete way of eliminating gender stereotypes in the media, where males have traditionally been represented as the heroes, the warriors, the intellectuals, and so on and so forth, and females as the sweethearts, the beauty queens, the housemakers, and so on. The new heroines of prime-time TV and the big screen became more muscular, they were trained in the martial arts, they were intelligent and technologically clever, and they had no compunctions about punching or kickboxing their way through life. Be it a Charlie's Angel or a Dark Angel, it was obvious that the new brand of female was hardly "angelic" in the traditional feminine sense; she was more akin to an "angel of fear" in the traditional masculine sense. The fashion industry, too, jumped on the bandwagon, introducing "hard styles" such as black patent leather, lace-up pants, and conical bras as part of the new feminine look.

Although images of physically strong women have a long history in Western representation, from ancient mythic female warriors to early television heroines such as Wonder Woman, never before have there been so many as today in the media. Even cartoon programs now showcase tough females for the preschool audience, and shows such as *Buffy the Vampire Slayer* (now off the air) do the same for a primarily teen audience. But I detect a dose of hypocrisy in all this. First, why must women behave in such an aggressive way? And why is the new female "tough" still portrayed as *necessarily* desirable sexually? Is there still a double standard? What is going on, in my view, is a ploy by the entertainment industry to cash in on the degendering process—no more, no less. Female toughness now sells. Tattoos, cigarettes, leather clothing, and all kinds of fetishistic jewelry props have crossed over from the world of the dominatrix to that of every woman, and the result has been commercially profitable. It is play-acting, albeit of a harmless variety. And, as in all cultural clouds of this kind, I see a silver lining. Like the history of cosmetics, the history of "feral womanhood," which has mythic origins, is ultimately a good thing, since it allows females the opportunity to be whatever they want, even in a physical sense.

However, some changes come with risks. Alcohol abuse, for instance, is now a degendered phenomenon, as virtually all informants pointed out: "Yeah, girls drink more than guys, sometimes, becoming drunks like everyone else," "Sure I drink, like all my girlfriends; so what if I get drunk?" The research of the association known as Mothers against Drunk Driving (MADD) shows that alcohol use among teens of both genders is, in fact, becoming a problem of alarming proportions.

I would like to suggest that one of the causes of alcohol abuse among teens is the very fact that alcohol is viewed so ambiguously by American society generally. It is seen as something prohibited, yet desirable.

The Puritan legacy in this case has been absolutely devastating. In societies where children and teens are allowed a moderate use of alcohol at specific meals or festivities in the company of adults, statistics such as those reported by MADD simply do not emerge. Like smoking, teens drink mainly to look cool at parties and at other types of get-togethers.

FINDINGS OF MADD

- As many adolescent females as males are alcohol users and abusers.
- Alcohol is often a factor in automobile accidents, the leading cause of death among American teenagers.
- Adolescent alcohol abusers expose themselves to long-term health risks.
- Adolescents who consume alcohol regularly are 7.5 times more likely to use illicit drugs and fifty times more likely to use cocaine than teens who never drink alcohol.
- Poor grades correlate with an increased use of alcohol.
- Alcohol is implicated in over 40 percent of all school-related problems and 28 percent of all dropouts.

Smoking, drinking, and sex seem to go hand-in-hand in teenagehood. They form a link that reverberates with coolness.

DRUGS

Drug use as a social activity among teens has been highly popular since the hippie 1960s. A 1995 survey conducted by the National Institute on Drug Abuse (NIDA) pointed to an increase in the use of a variety of drugs at earlier ages. Marijuana remained the most commonly used illegal drug. The proportion of students that reported using it over the previous year rose to 16 percent of eighth graders, 29 percent of tenth graders, and 35 percent of twelfth graders. Nearly 1 in 20 (4.6 percent) high school seniors and roughly 1 in every 35 tenth graders (2.8 percent) claimed to be daily users.

Use of LSD and other hallucinogens, amphetamines, stimulants, and inhalants also continued to drift upwards in the 1990s. Although heroin use

---

FINDINGS OF NIDA

- More than 1.5 million teens aged 12 to 17 use illicit drugs on a regular basis.
- The average age at which a child initially uses marijuana is 12.
- Drug abuse occurs in all areas of society, not only in the inner cities.
- The University of Toronto research team was able to corroborate many of NIDA's findings with its limited sample of 200.

Source: NIDA, 1995, and author.

Slang Names for Common Drugs

- Amphetamines or methamphetamines: speed, ecstasy, A's, meth, bennies, black beauties, chalk, copilots, crank, crystal, footballs, ice
- Barbiturates: barbs, candy, goof balls, rainbows
- Cocaine: coke, Charlie, crap, dust, flake, snow
- Depressants: downers
- Hashish: hash, ganja, rope
- Heroin: brown, china white, H, horse, junk, scag, scat, smack, speedball (= heroin with cocaine)
- LSD: acid, beast, cubes, sunshine
- Marijuana: pot, joint, grass, Acapulco gold, MJ, primo (= marijuana with cocaine), roach, weed
- Mescaline: mesc, cactus
- PCP: angel dust, hog

remained rather low, a statistically significant increase in annual heroin use nevertheless was registered by the study. Levels of use were two to three times higher than they had been a few years earlier.

Why are drugs so cool? The association of drugs with teen rebellion was established, as mentioned, in the hippie 1960s, although the use of drugs as part of one's lifestyle goes much farther back than that.[9] It was a practice in early tribal rituals and, of course, it became a wide practice among jazz musicians. But it was in the counterculture 1960s that it became part of the symbolism of adolescent rebellion. The teen counterculture rejected traditional bourgeois life goals with an "in-your-face," public use of drugs. Many good things, of course, also came out of that era (as mentioned in the opening chapter)—civil rights activism, the women's movement, the gay rights movement, and the environmental movement. Each, to varying degrees, changed government policy and, perhaps more important, how almost every single North American lives today. Equal opportunity and equal rights became the law of the land for all citizens regardless of their race, ethnicity, or gender. The veil of secrecy that surrounded much of North American foreign policy was, at least partially, removed. The health of the continent's environment became a priority.

But the same movement also had its negative side to it, introducing the social use of drugs among teens and, thus, instituting a trend that continues to characterize adolescent tribalism. For some reason, the hippies' association of drugs with youthful rebellion has stuck. To this day, references to drugs in pop music lyrics abound.

Some statistics suggest that things may be changing, but not as much as it is claimed. Drug use among teens (along with smoking and drinking) fell significantly in 2002, according to a survey conducted by NIDA that was reported widely by the media. But the survey, known as "Monitoring the Future" and carried out by the University of Michigan's Institute for Social Research, found a drop only in the use of ecstasy, with heroin, cocaine, and crack cocaine use remaining virtually unchanged. The survey did find, however, a decline in smoking. The proportion of teens who said they smoked fell by several percentage points. Since 1996, the proportion has dropped significantly, according to the survey. Nevertheless, estimates from various sources still indicate that nearly one third of teens engage in some form of smoking (from casual to habitual). Similar declines were found for alcohol use.

In my interviews with teens, the allure of the cigarette, of alcohol, and of drugs continues to be there. These props are part of the whole "cool thing." The percentages may go up and down, but there will always be percentages of some kind as long as adolescence is around. I should also mention that, as I write, there seems to be an increase in teen use of the prescription painkiller OxyContin. This came out in one of the last interviews conducted by the research team. An informant who used the drug claimed to us that "it's a common thing, man, and it's getting bigger." I subsequently called up a rehab center in downtown Toronto to confirm the claim and was told that it had substance. The case worker also pointed out to me that OxyContin seems to be the drug of choice among affluent white teens, whereas "heavier" prescription drugs, such as methadone, continue to be used mainly by lower-class teens.

INSIGHTS

The study of smoking, drinking, and drug use among adolescents contains several implicit insights, of which the most important is that anything forbidden takes on a mystique and an appeal all its own. Teens are aware of the dangers of tobacco, alcohol, and drugs at a rational level, but emotionally they find it simply too difficult to resist using them in peer settings.

"You can easily tell if your friend is, like, takin' drugs; he really changes."
Drug abuse causes a visible change in behavior. The first sign is a drastic alteration in the energy level of the teen. If he or she becomes restless or listless in an uncommon way, it might be a danger sign. Increased levels of sustained aggressive, hostile, and bellicose behavior also constitute danger signs, as do abrupt changes in friendships and in lifestyle patterns.
As in most attempts at decoding danger signs, the problem is that they can be connected to many other facets of teen behavior. Feelings of euphoria, manifestations of decreased alertness, and so on may be due to reasons other than an intake of drugs. In this, and in all other cases, the operative word is *consistency*. If such signs are consistent, regular, and unmistakable, then further investigation is required.
As indicated throughout this chapter, the primary reason for taking drugs is to fit in socially with peers. It was the hippies who introduced drug use as a means of going on *trips*, as they were called, to discover the self. There are, of course, many other less risky ways to induce trips—through Zen meditation, through music, and so on. In the research conducted for this book, the teen informants were asked if they were aware of these alternative means of "getting high." Surprisingly, nearly half of the informants, cutting across all three age categories (early, mid-, and late adolescence), showed a rather high degree of sophisticated knowledge of the alternatives, with meditation being the one most mentioned (112 out of 200). However, they also admitted that they probably would not take them into consideration because they were not cool among their friends and because they "took too long" to produce the desired "trip effect."

SIGNS OF DRUG ABUSE

The teen will tend to:

- Become more restless, listless, or both
- Become more aggressive and hostile toward others
- Change friends and lifestyle abruptly and radically
- Suffer significant slippage in school grades

Symptoms Associated with Drugs

Barbiturates (Nembutal, Seconal)
Short-term: Relaxation, euphoria, decreased alertness, drowsiness, impaired coordination, increase in the frequency of sleep (2–16 hours), slurred speech, stupor, hangover
Long-term: Sleepiness, confusion, irritability, severe withdrawal

Inhalants (aerosols, glue, amyl nitrate, nitrous oxide)
Short-term: Relaxation, euphoria, impaired coordination (1–3 hours), stupor
Long-term: Hallucinations, damage to liver or kidneys, brain damage

Narcotics (codeine, heroin, Demerol, methadone, morphine, opium, Percodan)
Short-term: Relaxation, decreased alertness, euphoria, hallucinations (3–6 hours), convulsions, stupor
Long-term: Lethargy, constipation, weight loss, withdrawal

Marijuana, hashish, THC
Short-term: Relaxation, euphoria, increased appetite, impaired coordination (2–4 hours), trancelike states, panic, stupor
Long-term: Not entirely known; may include states of paranoia and panic

Hallucinogens (LSD, mescaline, psilocybin, PCP)
Short-term: Some loss of vision, increased energy, hallucinations, panic, anxiety, vomiting, tremors
Long-term: Increased delusions and panic

Amphetamines (benzedrine, dexedrine, ketamine, MDMA or "ecstasy," methadrine)
Short-term: Increased alertness, excitation, euphoria, decreased appetite (2–4 hours), rapid speech, restlessness, irritability, insomnia, convulsions
Long-term: Insomnia, excitability, hallucinations, delusions

Cocaine
Short-term: Self-confidence, exhilaration (4 hours), irritability, fever
Long-term: Blood vessel damage, anxiety, depression, organ damage

As perhaps off-colored as this suggestion might appear to readers, maybe the time has come to introduce into our schools courses or training sessions in the meditative arts. This might make them appear to be "cool activities" and, as a byproduct, take away the attractiveness of doing mind-altering drugs. It may or may not work. But, in my view, it is certainly worth a try. I would also make the study of classical music as important as anything else in school, for the same reason.

Knowledge is power. Knowing what kinds of drugs are out there, and what physical and psychological effects they produce, will put adults in a better position to take appropriate rational action in response to their teen's drug use. Observing and listening to what a teen says may also provide crucial information about drugs. Many of the code words for drugs are known to society at large. But there are many more such terms that adults may not know. Generally speaking, the more terms in use to describe a particular drug, the more likely its popularity among teens. Some of these are given here (see box).

"Yeah, I smoke, like every one of my friends."
Smoking, drinking alcohol, and taking some drugs are worrisome facets of the "portrait of adolescence" being drawn in this book. Smoking and the occasional taking of alcohol at parties in themselves generally mean nothing more than temporary socialization activities. They are activities that allow teens to act big and appear cool. However, this should in no way undervalue the dangers of the activities. Narcotics have a lasting effect on those who use them, even in an occasional fashion, and those who abuse alcohol in adolescence regularly are at risk of becoming alcoholics.

NOTES

1. Tara Parker-Pope, *Cigarettes: Anatomy of an Industry from Seed to Smoke* (New York: The New Press, 2001), 168.
2. See also D. E. Green, *Teenage Smoking: Immediate and Long Term Patterns* (Washington, D. C.: Department of Health, Education and Welfare, 1979) for teenage smoking patterns.
3. Margaret Leroy, *Some Girls Do: Why Women Do and Don't Make the First Move* (London: HarperCollins, 1997).
4. Jordan Goodman, *Tobacco in History: The Cultures of Dependence* (London: Routledge, 1993).
5. Richard Klein, *Cigarettes Are Sublime* (Durham, N.C.: Duke University Press, 1993).
6. Michael E. Starr, "The Marlboro Man: Cigarette Smoking and Masculinity in America," *Journal of Popular Culture* 12 (1984): 45–56.

7. The details of the study were published in Marcel Danesi, "Smoking Behavior in Adolescence as Signifying Osmosis," *Semiotica* 96 (1993): 53–69.

8. R. Vogeler and W. Bortz, *Teenagers and Alcohol: When Saying No Isn't Enough* (Seattle, Wash.: Charles Press, 1992), provide a useful commentary on the reasons why teens drink.

9. R. McFarland, *Drugs and Your Parents* (New York: Rosen Publishing Group, 1997) is a good overview of the reasons for drug use among teens. For an interesting discussion of the relation between drugs and writers (in their younger years), see Marcus Boon, *The Road of Excess: A History of Writers on Drugs* (Cambridge, Mass.: Harvard University Press, 2002).

8

School

Interviewer	Do you like going to school?
Teen Informant	Yeah, mainly to be with my friends. Otherwise, it's, like, boring.
Interviewer	Why is that?
Teen Informant	I dunno. I like math, but that's about it. I'm also afraid, sometimes.
Interviewer	What do you mean?
Teen Informant	You know, stuff happens at school. People sometimes get hurt real bad.

BACKGROUND

In his controversial 1999 book titled *The Rise and Fall of the American Teenager,* Thomas Hine fingers the unnecessarily long period of compulsory education in America as the cause of teen crime and drug use, since it keeps young people for too long in a dangerous "holding pattern."[1] In characterizing the school as the place where "stuff happens," our teen informant would seem to be implicitly in agreement with Hine's accusation.

Paradoxically, education for the masses became mandatory in Great Britain not only because the newly industrialized workplace of the nineteenth century required a more literate workforce, but also because many British social reformers believed (naïvely in hindsight) that it was the solution to all social ills. The reformers claimed that, by taking youths off the streets, the high school would preserve social stability, prevent crime, and eliminate poverty. The same belief system took hold of America at the turn of the twentieth century. As a consequence, by 1918 all U.S. states had passed mandatory school attendance laws. How ironic it is that today many American social critics, like Hine, blame the high school for causing the very problems that it was supposed to eliminate! Are such critics right? Answering this question is the objective of this chapter.

A CRISIS IN EDUCATION?

The reformers believed that a school system for one and all would create common bonds among people living in the increasingly diverse society that was taking shape in the industrialized cities of Europe and America. They argued that free elementary school education should be made available to everyone through public funds. Shortly thereafter, the first school attendance laws for children of elementary school age were passed. By the end of the nineteenth century, the reformers had largely achieved their objectives.

High school, however, was still largely the privilege of the rich. Only 10 percent of American youths aged 14 to 17 were enrolled in high schools. Most of them were from affluent families. Secondary education was mostly conducted by private tutors or privately supported academies.

After the introduction of strict child-protection labor laws in the early part of the twentieth century, and with increasing affluence in society at large, more and more youths began attending high school before entering the workforce or starting a family. As the twentieth century progressed, most states enacted legislation extending mandatory education to the age of 16. The rise in the high school graduation rate was one of the most striking developments in education during the century. From 1900 to 1996, the percentage of those who graduated from high school increased from less than 6 percent to over 85 percent.

Early on, high schools came to be seen not only as places where students could prepare for the practical demands of the workplace but also as self-contained communities for them in which to grow to adulthood. The high school thus became the locus for adolescents not only to gain an education but also to socialize with peers. As the socialization function of the high school increased gradually throughout the century, its schooling function concomitantly took a beating.

By the late 1980s, this situation had evolved into a problem of major concern as virtually all states started to give unprecedented attention to high school education standards. Much of the initiative stemmed from the publication of a report by a federal commission in 1983 that indicated unprecedented low academic achievement in American high schools. The

---

**HIGHLIGHTS IN THE HISTORY
OF EDUCATION IN THE UNITED STATES**

- After the American Revolution (1775–1783), the founders of the United States argued that education was essential for the prosperity and survival of the new nation.
- Thomas Jefferson (1743–1826) put forward an education plan that envisioned free schooling for all children in the state of Virginia for three years. Jefferson's proposal failed to gain widespread support. Nevertheless, it formed the model for education systems developed a little later.
- In 1794, New York became the first state to establish a board of regents to oversee public education. Eventually, every state established a department of education and enacted laws regulating the financing of schools, the hiring of school personnel, student attendance, and curriculum structure.
- The modern American school system originated in the 1830s when a committed group of social reformers attacked the tradition of localized education, claiming that all children should be schooled and that the content of education should be the same for everyone.
- Massachusetts passed the first compulsory school attendance laws in 1852, followed by New York in 1853. By 1918, all states had passed laws requiring children to attend elementary school.
- Catholics, however, believed that the moral values taught in public schools were biased toward Protestantism. They therefore created their own separate school system.
- Public financing for secondary education was rare until 1874, when a Michigan Supreme Court decision involving the city of Kalamazoo made it possible for communities to use local property taxes to support high schools.
- In 1925, the Supreme Court of the United States ruled that states could not compel children to attend public schools and that children could attend private schools instead.
- In the mid- to late 1990s, surveys conducted by educational agencies, such as the U.S. Department of Education, indicated that a small percentage of American students in elementary and secondary schools— around 10 percent—attended private institutions. Most of these were Catholic schools.

---

report, titled *A Nation at Risk,* presented alarming statistics suggesting that American students were outperformed on international academic tests by students from virtually every other modern society. It also found that standardized test scores were declining across the nation. Unsettled by the report, parents' groups, educators, and government officials across the country initiated a concerted reform effort aimed at overcoming the apparent shortcomings of American education. Because the perceived "crisis in education" was based largely on test score results, most states subsequently implemented curricula and pedagogical methods that emphasize more frequent testing and more state-mandated "standards."

What the writers of the report failed to realize, however, was the possibility that the decline in standards was due to the fact that, by and large, adolescents perceived the high school primarily as a locus for socialization with peers, not as a place of learning. The high school had become by the 1980s virtually no more than a milieu within which teenagers could center more and more of their social lives, not a place to learn mathematics, history, and other subjects. With its athletics, clubs, dances, parties, and other extracurricular activities, the high school had evolved into a social cosmos all unto itself, catering more to the social needs of teenagers than to their intellectual ones. To this day, teenagers tend to see it more as a place to interact with peers than as a place to learn about algebra, Spanish, or some other academic subject.

This is why since the 1970s many alarming facts about high school life have come to the forefront. The most frightful of all is the growth in the incidents of violence. From 1998 to 2000, incidents of reported violence in North American schools went up 65 percent (as reported by schools across the continent and documented by agencies such as the U.S. Department of Education). Similarly horrifying is the fact that those who are ostracized socially by their classmates are much more likely to drop out.[2] Our research team confirmed the general thrust of these findings. It found that virtually all the informants witnessed some incident of violence at their school. Nearly 50 of the 200 informants claimed to feel unsafe in their school, 160 of them had complained about being intimidated or attacked physically, 49 of them brought a weapon to school for protection (a knife, a tool, and even a handgun), and 76 had been in a fight at some point in their school life.

It is ironic and profoundly sad to note that an institution that was set up to solve social problems is now beset by so many of those very problems itself. Why? For one thing, the standard model of education is far too fragmented. Control over public education matters is assigned largely to local districts, raising the specter of local politics influencing curricula. Public schools also rely heavily on local property taxes to meet the vast majority of school expenses, making them, practically, "pawns" in local power struggles. For this reason, North American schools have tended to reflect parochial values and have been often limited by the financial capabilities of the communities in which they are located. This is why when students move from one community to another, they often encounter entirely different curricula, even though they are in the same grade. Even within a given school district, very different kinds of public schools can be found in different neighborhoods.

There is also a high degree of discontinuity between school levels in such domains as the delivery of learning, the relation between teacher and learner, and the like. In elementary school, the child has, typically, a single homeroom teacher who knows him or her personally; in junior high and high school, the student usually has a different teacher for each subject. In elementary school, the child is rewarded for trying hard; in secondary school, grades are based more on performance than on effort. In elementary school, children work under close supervision all day; in secondary school, young people must learn to work more independently; and so on and so forth. No wonder that so many students are temporarily disoriented during the transition between school levels.

But perhaps the greatest problem besieging the school system is that, despite its establishment to solve social ills, it has rarely resolved them. For example, it took a unanimous U.S. Supreme Court decision in 1954 to make racial segregation in public schools unconstitutional, reversing the position it had held since 1896. Since then, the federal courts have largely succeeded in eliminating segregation in schools. However, many educators continue to cite inequality in educational opportunities for both African American and Hispanic American students. In 1996, a report issued by the Presidential Advisory Commission on Educational Excellence for Hispanic Americans indicated that a disproportionate number of Hispanic American students attend schools that predominantly lack adequate educational resources.[3]

Discrimination against females too was, in the not-too-distant past, as pervasive as was discrimination based on race. Laws in the nineteenth century required states to provide equal educational opportunity for both boys and girls. Most public schools were coeducational, yet the Victorian society of the era subtly suggested to girls that a woman's place was mainly in the home rather than in schools, colleges, or professions—unless the intended career was teaching school. In the middle part of the nineteenth century, reformers established academies that provided female students with secondary and sometimes college-level instruction and offered subjects that were previously considered unnecessary for women, such as mathematics, science, and history. Only since the 1960s has truly equal opportunity education become a reality for young women.

Today, education critics argue that special programs and resources are essential for ensuring genuine equality of education to disadvantaged youth. Chapter I of the Elementary and Secondary Education Act of 1965 provided some federal funds for supplementary education programs targeted at poor and disadvantaged children, and some of those funds were spent in line with the prevailing theory of the era that educational disadvantages could best be eliminated at an early age, before their effects could become more difficult to reverse. For this reason, the federal Head

Start program created special education programs for preschoolers and remains one of the most admired achievements of the War on Poverty programs of the 1960s.

The federal government has also provided financial assistance for bilingual education programs. And in 1975, with the Education for All Handicapped Children Act, it has mandated individualized programs for students with disabilities, which require placing such students, whenever possible, in regular classrooms rather than separating them. In 1994, the Department of Education reported that 6.7 percent of all Americans below age 21 were enrolled in special education programs.

Yet, despite all kinds of measures, the fact remains that inequalities, problems of violence, disinterest, and lack of standards persist to this day across the board. North American society is split in identifying the causes of the perceived crisis in education. Some blame the fast pace of change in technology, others denounce our materialistic culture and the loss of traditional values, others still ascribe blame to the dilution of standards, and the list could go on and on. Presidential commissions and local school committees have been advocating a "back to basics" approach. A host of band-aid solutions are, seemingly, being envisioned on a daily basis in a desperate attempt to bring an end to the crisis. Clearly, something is amiss here. Perhaps the true source of the crisis is in the very structure and design of the school system itself. A growing number of educators have, in fact, started to look more closely at the unworkability of the concept of *one education system for one and all*.[4]

INTERVIEWS

To be sure, the high schools are filled with adolescents studying hard, striving to achieve well-defined goals. But it is also true to say that they face a challenge to be that way.

Violence at school, shootings, and increasing incidents of aggression in the schoolyard have gotten many people to reconsider the role of education in adolescence. Instead of seeking a "return-to-basics" solution or some other media-popularized solution, I believe that, as never before, schools should no longer think of themselves primarily as solvers of social problems and as "general knowledge and skill institutions." Unless there is a radical shift in society, the school cannot set itself up to be everything to everyone. This may mean, of course, that schools will have to redesign their curricula radically, to rethink their basic pedagogical practices, and to reinterpret the role that they should play in our society.

In fieldwork I conducted between 1998 and 2000, I found that the teens who are most adjusted to the academic life of the school and who go to school to develop their skills, and not just to be with peers, are those in "special" or "alternative" schools.[5] For, example, I visited several "schools for the arts" in four North American cities (Toronto, Detroit, Montreal, and New York). These offer students the opportunity to enroll in programs that suit their natural talents and career aspirations. In other words, they allow students to learn what they feel is best for them by themselves, not in accordance with what adults want them to learn. Virtually all the students interviewed told me that they enjoyed going to school because they were learning what they wanted to learn. Socialization with peers was seen as intertwined with learning, not separate from it. The students thus socialized without cliquing, and they perceived their friends to be partners in the overall academic goals of the school.

FIELDWORK QUESTIONNAIRE RESPONSES (1998–2000):
ALTERNATIVE SCHOOLS

Why do you come to school?

- "I love dancing, I want to be good at it."
- "To learn and be good at something."
- "I really like playing jazz; the school lets me learn it."
- "It's fun."

What do you like best about the school?

- "I get to do what I'm good at."
- "I like my teachers."
- "I don't have to argue with my dad; here, I get to learn something."
- "I'm not afraid like I used to be at my other school."

What do you not like about the school?

- "Nothin'; it's great."
- "Sometimes, I gotta do things I don't like, like math."
- "Pressure to get things done."
- "Phys ed.; like, what's the point?"

How do you find your learning experience?

- "Great."
- "Okay."
- "Better than last year at my other school, but I miss my friends."
- "Phat (excellent)."

FIELDWORK QUESTIONNAIRE RESPONSES (1998–2000):
REGULAR SCHOOLS

Why do you come to school?

- "I gotta'; I hate it."
- "To be with my friends."
- "I like to learn things, but sometimes it's scary; things happen."
- "Because of the vagrancy act."

What do you like best about the school?

- "Lunchtime."
- "My history teacher; he knows what I'm going through."
- "I'm away from my crib (home)."
- "I get to stay with my friends."

What do you not like about the school?

- "I'm scared sometimes."
- "Things get outta hand a lot."
- "Everything, man; a waste of my time."
- "Losers; I hate them."

How do you find your learning experience?

- "Bah."
- "Sucks."
- "Too much work."
- "Okay, sometimes."

Follow-up interviews with teachers and parents indicated to me that they too were highly satisfied with the objectives and methods of the school. Some parents worried about their teens' entry into college or into society because of the perceived "low career value" of the arts. But by and large, they also understood that their teens were learning much more than they would otherwise. I include here some of the answers I recorded to a few of the questions I posed to the students (see box). They will give the reader a general flavor of the type of responses I got.

The above pattern of findings stands in stark contrast to those I compiled from similar interviews I conducted with students in "regular" schools. These are places where classes consist of groups of twenty to thirty students with a teacher at the front of the room; instruction proceeds by lecture, demonstration, discussion, or silent work at a desk; and teachers often assign homework for the students to complete after class. Many of the students I interviewed told me that they perceived the school environment as a threat to their "physical survival," not as a place to hone their intellect. Cliquing in such schools was the norm. Those left out of cliques were fearful of being harmed by their peers. Many of them told me that they wanted to "get even" for all the insults they had received. A sampling of some of the answers I recorded to the questions I posed to the students is provided here (see box).

My follow-up interviews with teachers suggested that they were aware of everything that was going on. But they emphasized to me that they felt powerless to do something about it, because they sensed that the cultural forces at work in the school were beyond their control. In my view, the teachers in such schools are valiant gladiators fighting a losing battle. My interviews with parents were also highly revealing. All parents suggested to me that they expected more out of the school—certainly more than the school was able to provide.

SOME POTENTIAL SOLUTIONS

The high school clearly needs to be endowed with a new sense of purpose and perhaps given a broad new mandate to pursue many of the goals of the so-called alternative or special schools. Efficiency at solving quadratic equations is not perceived as cool or necessary by many teens. But the means to make such a skill appealing are probably right before our eyes. If alternative schools are indeed more successful in producing well-adjusted adolescent learners, then it is probably because they make academic achievement an attractive end in itself within the school environment by allowing the students to develop their native talents in a constructive and tutored way.

Needless to say, there is a host of problems associated with such schools that is beyond the present discussion. But if there is one lesson well worth learning, it is simply that they have been successful in removing the "fear factor" associated with cliquing and gangs within the school environment by allowing students to pursue what they are most inclined to do. Perhaps schools specializing in math and science, others in the humanities, and so on should be instituted. After all, the "specialization model" has been the operative one in many parts of Europe for over 150 years. Violence at school tends to be far less of a problem in Europe than it is in North America.

Are there any other solutions? Many have been proposed, and some of them have merit. Actually, most recall the child-centered ideas put forward in the first part of the twentieth century by the educator John Dewey

(1859–1952), which led to some early positive results. But Dewey's ideas have never really been incorporated in a systematic nationwide fashion at the high school level. The reasons for this are many and would require a separate treatment. Suffice it to say here that Dewey's work has traditionally been viewed as relevant to elementary schools, not high schools. The time has come to reconsider his ideas and those of other enlightened educators for the latter, as well.

Another solution may come from technology. The revolution in computer and communications technology holds out hope that students will connect with more information and more people than ever before. This might mean that learning will become more individualized and thus more appealing.

Since the 1980s, education policy makers and reformers have also given greater attention and provided more funding toward improving the quality of education in nonschool settings. For example, some educators now view the family as perhaps the most natural place for learning to unfold. Aware of this possibility, most schools have increased education programs designed specifically to ensure parent involvement. The media can also help in this regard. During the 1960s the pioneering work of the Children's Television Workshop, which created *Sesame Street* in 1969, was an early example of how television could advance, rather than retard, educational objectives.

But no matter what solution is adopted, the idea of teaching different subjects to all adolescents may have run its course and certainly its usefulness. In ancient cultures, the goal of teachers—usually priests, shamans, or elders—was to determine which kinds of functional skills and knowledge should be taught to the youths of society, in tandem with the society's practical needs and its beliefs. Learners incapable of handling certain types of knowledge and skill were assigned social roles that were deemed more consistent with their abilities. There was no concept of teaching all things to all children.

The structure of modern educational systems in the countries of the Western world can be traced to ancient Greece, where Socrates, Plato, Aristotle, and other famous philosophers saw education as a means of preparing young people to take leading roles in the activities of society. In later centuries, Greek educational concepts served as the basis for the liberal arts, the teaching of the various branches of philosophy, the cultivation of artistic practices, and the promotion of gymnastic training. However, until the end of the eighteenth century there was no conception of education as teaching everything to one and all. It was the French philosopher Jean-Jacques Rousseau (1712–1778) in that century who started the ball rolling by emphasizing that learning was not the privilege of a few but was a right of every child.

The nineteenth century saw the rise of national school systems and a proliferation of Rousseau's basic idea in the West. But rather than focus on the personal abilities and needs of students, Western education took its main thrust from what is often called Descartes's project.[6] In 1637, the philosopher René Descartes (1596–1650) elaborated the view that it was essential to teach children how to think logically by showing them how to classify knowledge into neat little boxes—from which we have derived the modern idea of subjects at separate times of the day, on a regular basis, for all learners. But if the current crisis in education has taught us anything worthwhile, it is that such grandiose schemes overlook the fact that students bring with them different personalities, needs, expectations, and talents to the classroom. Classifying knowledge into boxes for them simply does not seem to work. The interviews I conducted, along with a spate of recent motivational studies, show that adolescents find a learning syllabus tailored for adult interests of little or no interest. On the other hand, they perceive ideas and processes that relate to their own lives as much more meaningful.

There is nothing radical about suggesting the incorporation of the adolescent's specific type of needs into a curriculum. After all, curricula for young children are now synchronized with the reality of childhood. Elementary school education is, in fact, based on the philosophy that children learn best when the subject matter to which they are exposed makes sense to them, not only to their adult mentors. Similarly, what adolescents learn at school should unfold in terms of the themes and topics that are meaningful to their real-life experiences. This does not mean that the traditional curriculum should be discarded, only that it should be adapted in specific ways according to situation.

I recall teaching a tenth-grade class of so-called problematic inner-city children in the Toronto area several years ago how to appreciate the music of Beethoven, as part of a research project. At the beginning of my lesson, not one of the students had a positive image of classical music. Most said initially that they found such music boring and old-fashioned. So, I started by simply comparing Beethoven's *Moonlight Sonata* to a pop music love ballad that most of them knew at the time (sung by Jennifer Lopez). Together we listened and relistened to the two pieces of music in class. I commented on Beethoven's music; they commented to me on the main message of their beloved pop artist. We made points of comparison and discussed each other's musical preferences critically. I also told the class how Beethoven was an abused and disadvantaged child, like many of them apparently were, and then I discussed how he transferred his experiences to his music. By the end of the class, the very same students who had declared no interest in Beethoven's music were asking me to provide them with more samples of it. Needless to say, my lesson was atypical. But it showed that an "adult art" can become meaningful to young people once it is related to their experiences.

Having said all this, I am quite aware that, short of making schooling optional during the adolescent years, there are no simple solutions, no magical formulas, and no recipes for solving our educational problems. Perhaps the educational bureaucracy has become so Byzantine and self-serving that it is beyond repair and transformation. I certainly hope not. Moreover, I have found that institutions have a knack of adapting to cultural change *on their own*. The British anthropologist Mary Douglas once wrote that "institutions breathe" because they are made up of people and thus are really "organs" of the "communal body."[7] Like people and their cultures, institutions are prone to change.

But certain things are probably universal and will never change. During my research project, I noticed that teenagers universally responded to poetry and to other creative products of the imagination (music, drama, and the like) when these were put in relation to their emotional and social experiences. I also found that schools that focused more on the traditional humanistic subjects tended to stimulate in their learners a love of all learning. This is actually the approach that the ancient Greeks cherished. They did not see any need to separate the study of mathematics from that of philosophy or poetry. On the contrary, they believed that a true love of learning would emerge when a balance between studying the arts, philosophy, and the sciences was achieved. They also firmly believed that education was necessarily tied to larger social and personal realities.

The current crisis in education has made it obvious that the school can no longer act alone, apart from the family, the working world, and other social institutions, in solving problems. The primary goal of the school should not be only to impart knowledge and skill but also to impart wisdom, respect, and a sense of community. As the great writer T. S. Eliot (1888–1965) once remarked, school should be about preparation for life, work, and community, not just about solving equations and spelling correctly.

INSIGHTS

The foregoing discussion suggests one obvious insight: students should be allowed to study *what they are good at* and, thus, to go to a school that best suits them. This might require some sacrifices, but they are worthwhile. There are several other relevant insights discussed below.

"I can't stand going to school."

A teenager who constantly expresses a strong dislike of his or her school, or who becomes secretive about what he or she is doing at school,

---

SIGNS OF PROBLEMS AT SCHOOL

The teen tends to:

- Become secretive about school
- Show a lack of interest in going to school
- Suffer a significant drop in grades
- Withdraw from family and friends

---

might be a victim of name-calling, ostracism, and even physical attacks at school. If the teen becomes especially secretive about what is happening at school, shows a lack of interest in going to school on a regular basis, experiences a significant drop in grades, and tends to become more and more withdrawn, further investigation might be required. In recent years, some teens who have been "shunned" or constantly exposed to abuse have taken matters into their hands with tragic results (as the media have made so saliently clear).

When peer-related problems are identified as the source of the teen's distress, the best thing to do, in my view, is to convince the teen to go to another school or to enroll him or her in some special program. A change of milieu is crucial. A teen who remains in a desperate situation is greatly at risk. He or she may be more inclined to commit a criminal act, to take drastic action against others, to run away, and the like.

"Pressure, pressure, from all sides, from my parents, my friends, and my teachers; I've had it."

A 15-year-old who was being constantly criticized for not living up to his intellectual capacities made this comment. No one, at any age, can accomplish very much under pressure. Some variability in academic achievement will have to be tolerated by parents and educators. Only if it becomes chronic should it be considered to be a sign of danger. In any case, pressure tactics ("Why aren't you studying more?" "How come your grades are always dropping?" "You're always out; why don't you study more?" and the like) will rarely work. They might make the teen feel guilty, but they do not generally get him or her to change his or her ways.

"I like music, so why can't I study it?"

This statement was made by a teen who had considerable musical talent but who did very poorly in many school subjects because she considered them to be useless to her career plans. It brings out the need to review and revise our understanding of what education should be all about.

In most of Europe, children entering high school are given the chance of choosing a school that best suits their interests, talents, and life plans. Our informant would be better off in a conservatory to hone her musical talents further.

Having said this, I am also aware of the many obstacles that lie in the path of reforming an education system that has deep historical roots. Of course, the most radical course of all is the one that would envision high school as optional. As extravagant as this may sound to readers, it is nevertheless something that may have to be taken into consideration, given the number of dropouts that continue to characterize and plague modern-day schools. After all, obligatory schooling is only a relatively recent trend, as discussed in this and in the opening chapter. My prediction is that, even if high school becomes optional, most adolescents would go there just the same. However, by giving them the choice, we would in effect be giving them the right to choose and, thus, we would be putting the onus to treat the school as a learning place, rather than as a social one, on them directly. When given a choice to decide for themselves, teenagers tend to act much more responsibly and maturely.

I am aware, of course, that such a drastic change in mindset with regard to school is unlikely. Too many resources, human and institutional, have been invested into the current school system. Nevertheless, radical change is needed. The informant's statement points, in my view, to the path that education must take in order to truly transform schooling into a meaningful learning experience. The case of the late great pianist Glenn Gould (1932–1982) is a case in point. In a lecture he gave at the Royal Conservatory of Music of Toronto in 1962, which I attended as a student of the conservatory at the time, he quipped that he was always "lousy" at school because he couldn't wait to "get to my piano." As a consequence, he always performed below expectations at school and never went very far. He was, at one point, pegged as becoming a "nobody in life." Not only did he prove everyone wrong, but he was also a classic case of how schools cannot possibly serve the needs of everyone.

NOTES

1. Thomas Hine, *The Rise and Fall of the American Teenager* (New York: Bard Books, 1999).

2. On the issue of violence in schools, see M. Miller, *Coping with Weapons and Violence in Your School and on Your Streets* (New York: Rosen Publishing Group, 1993); and S. U. Spina, ed., *Smoke and Mirrors: The Hidden Context of Violence in Schools and Society* (Lanham, Md.: Rowman & Littlefield, 2000).

3. Readers interested in the issue of bilingual and alternative forms of education can consult the controversial book by Rose Pedalino Porter, *Forked Tongue: The*

Politics of Bilingual Education (New York: Basic Books, 1990). Although I do not necessarily agree with all her conclusions, she does draft a fairly complete assessment of the state of affairs in this domain of modern education.

4. In addition to Hines's book mentioned at the start of this chapter, readers can consult the recent book by J. Featherstone, L. Featherstone, and C. Featherstone, *Dear Josie: The Hopes and Failures of Democratic Education* (New York: Teachers College Press, 2003), which paints a vivid picture of how "democratic" education (education for one and all) is both a wonderful experiment and, often, a failure.

5. The research was funded by a grant from the Social Sciences and Humanities Research Council of Canada, to whom I am most grateful.

6. See, for example, P. J. Davis and R. Hersh, *Descartes' Dream: The World According to Mathematics* (Boston: Houghton Mifflin, 1986).

7. Mary Douglas, *Objects and Objections* (Toronto: Toronto Semiotic Circle Monographs, 1991), 27.

9

The Media

Interviewer	Do you watch TV a lot?
Teen Informant	Nah, not as much as I did when I was a kid.
Interviewer	Why is that?
Teen Informant	Nothing good's on, and, besides, I prefer being with my friends.
Interviewer	Do you not watch the music channel?
Teen Informant	Yeah, when there's, like, not much else to do. I like music videos; I can hear my favorite songs.
Interviewer	What about movies?
Teen Informant	We go, like, all the time, with friends I mean; it's cool.

BACKGROUND

In 1952, the American author Max Lerner wrote in the *New York Post*:

> Having a thirteen-year-old in the family is like having a general-admission ticket to the movies, radio and TV, because you get to understand that the glittering new arts of our civilization are directed to the teen-agers, and by their suffrage they stand or fall.[1]

In the first decade of the twenty-first century, the situation has not changed one iota. Virtually our entire pop culture industry today depends on capturing the "teen dollar" for its economic survival. For this reason, Hollywood, record companies, television networks, and Internet sites cater primarily to the adolescent and young adult markets.

There is (and always has been) a veritable synergy between the media and adolescent lifestyles—one influencing the other in tandem. Describing that synergy is the objective of this chapter.

JUVENILIZATION AND THE MEDIA

As our informant aptly put it, teens prefer being with their friends rather than alone in front of a TV. But it is also true that TV and other media cater primarily to adolescent social interests. And it is true to say that television may have been instrumental in shaping the changes in family structure that are now part and parcel of our social outlook on the family and on adolescence. The survey reported here indicates that parents' groups are, in fact, worried about how family life, moral values, and ethics are depicted on television, given its persuasive dominion over virtually every teen, whether he or she knows it or not (see box).

THE MOST AND LEAST "FAMILY-FRIENDLY" TV PROGRAMS, 2001

The Best

- *Touched by an Angel* (CBS)
- *Doc* (Pax)
- *7th Heaven* (WB)
- *Sabrina, the Teenage Witch* (WB)
- *Who Wants to Be a Millionaire?* (ABC)
- *Mysterious Ways* (NBC and Pax)
- *Daddio* (NBC)
- *Twice in a Lifetime* (Pax)
- *My Wife and Kids* (ABC)
- *Moesha* (UPN)

The Worst

- *Boston Public* (Fox)
- *WWF Smackdown* (UPN)
- *Buffy the Vampire Slayer* (WB)
- *Dawson's Creek* (WB)
- *That '70s Show* (Fox)
- *Friends* (NBC)
- *Ally McBeal* (Fox)
- *Angel* (WB)
- *Hype* (WB)
- *Big Brother* (CBS)

Source: Compiled by *Parents Television Council,* July 2001.

And there is real cause for concern. As social critic Todd Gitlin has aptly put it, the modern media spew out a relentless barrage of infantile humor, sensationalism, instant gratification, and nonstop stimulation; they fuel celebrity cults, paranoia, and above all else an ironic view of the world.[2] Already in the 1950s, movies, TV programs, magazines, and advertising styles were being designed to serve the interests and needs of the new and economically powerful teen market. By the mid-1950s, the media etched the image of the rebellious teenager into the social memorate of adolescence (the term *memorate*, introduced in chapter 7, refers to an unconscious thought pattern in the culture at large). Music, movies, and radio and television programs became increasingly more juvenilized in content. Teenage icons in the media became the norm. Before that era, it was difficult to find a movie that dealt with adolescence or that even involved adolescents as actors or characters. Since the 1950s, on the other hand, it is difficult to find a movie or other kind of media product that does not deal with some adolescent theme, involve adolescents as actors, or else revolve around them in some way.

Although there was an initial well-documented adverse reaction to the emphasis on youth in the media in the mid-1950s (especially to the perceived "moral danger" posed by rock and roll music), by the 1960s the entire society had started to accept the ever-growing influence of youth lifestyles as the norm. Indeed, as the era of counterculture dissidence approached, the business world coopted teenage lifestyles and ideologies as part of its overall marketing philosophy. The rock and roll culture of the 1950s had proven to be a profitable one indeed, no matter how iconoclastic it appeared to be to the self-appointed moral guardians of society. So, by the time of the hippie movement of the 1960s, the business world was inclined to pay very close attention to teen trends, realizing that it was in its own best interest not to fight the new images of youth insurgency but rather to embrace them outright and thus to "change with the times." One highly effective early strategy of this "If you can't beat them, join them" approach was the development of an advertising style that mocked consumerism and advertising itself!

The strategy worked beyond expectations. Being young and rebellious came to mean having a "cool look," and being antiestablishment and subversive came to mean wearing "hippie clothes." The image masters had cleverly "joined the revolution" by deploying the language and aesthetics of hippie rebellion to market their goods and services. The underlying subtext of this clever approach allowed common folk to believe (in a bizarre way) that the clothing they bought and the records they listened to ipso facto transformed them into revolutionaries without having to pay the social price of true nonconformity and dissent. This brilliant strategy continues to be used to this day. Never before in the history of humanity have so many spectacles (movies, TV programs, and the like) and products (CDs, cell phones, and so on) been created with an eye on trends within teenagehood.

The business world discovered fortuitously in the counterculture era how to incorporate the emotional power of adolescence into the "grammar" of everyday life. Truly brilliant advertising campaigns of the late counterculture era—such as the *Pepsi Generation* and the *Coke* universal brotherhood campaigns—can be recalled here. These directly incorporated the images, rhetoric, and symbolism of the hippie movement, thus creating the illusion that the goals of the hippies and of the soft drink manufacturers were one and the same. Rebellion through purchasing became the subliminal thread woven into many other ad campaigns. The *Dodge Rebellion* and *Oldsmobile Youngmobile* campaigns followed the soft drink ones, etching into the names of the cars themselves the powerful connotations of youth rebellion. Even a sewing machine company, alas, came forward to urge people to join its own type of surrogate revolution with the slogan "You don't let the establishment make your world; don't let it make your clothes." In effect, it was the marketing world that brought about the real revolution. This is why, since that decade, the worlds of advertising, marketing, entertainment, and teenagehood have become totally intertwined.[3] The counterculture threat passed because in the end the hippies joined the *Pepsi Revolution*. The only authentic rebel was, according to many, Abby Hoffman, whose *Steal This Book*—a handbook of how to survive by stealing that Hoffman wanted readers to shoplift from stores—was the only kind of subversive gesture that was truly hostile and menacing to the corporate world order. The other revolutionaries were, in hindsight, really adolescents doing no more than waging battles with their parents and with one another.

The signs of the amalgamation of the media, the business world, and teenagehood are unmistakable. Nowadays, the fashion trends of the young are recycled and marketed shortly after their invention as the fashion styles of all; teen music trends quickly become part of the music tastes of society at large; teen vocabulary surfaces in the everyday discourse of adults and is even given official status by reputable dictionaries; and the list could go on and on. Teenage cool has become social cool. Teen music has moved from the margins of American popular music to the center of a multi-billion-dollar global industry. Teen musicians influence fashions, language, attitudes, and political views. In effect, teen-based music plays a central role in the popular culture of the United States and, increasingly, the world.

Economic prosperity and the obliteration of the repressive authority traditions and structures of the past are, of course, good things. Today, because of movements spawned by young people, there are many more tolerant attitudes around. The hippie revolution was provoked by human

sentiments—by an abhorrence of social injustice, by a disgust over discrimination against specific groups (such as Blacks and women), and by
other inequities. As an aside, it is paradoxical, nay, perplexing, to note that
the very images of Western capitalism that the hippies deplored were
adopted by the youths of communist countries two decades later in order
to successfully topple their socioeconomic orders. Life is really much more
complicated than any cultural theory or historical analysis will allow!

But all this comes as a mixed blessing. Juvenilization has obliterated the
distinction between young and old, and this has led to several commu-
nally shared illusions. Today, most North Americans take it for granted
that a 13-year-old in the fifth grade is "behind schedule," that teens who
marry "too early" are looking for trouble, and that a 75-year-old is pleased
at being told, "You look young for your age." Almost nobody defines
himself or herself proudly as *old*. Old age is something to be avoided at
any cost. Such attitudes and beliefs would have been considered irrational
not too long ago.

It is also true that many of us, if not most, now take little notice of teen
trends. This is because pop culture is now virtually the only form of culture we understand. We live in a veritable "distraction factory," as the social critic Goodwin has designated it.[4] But therein lies the rub—as Shakespeare aptly put it. The factory is both good and bad. It produces such
ephemeral products as the *Scream* movies and high art such as *Amadeus*
and *One Flew over the Cuckoo's Nest.* In this factory, entertainers and artists
have become strange partners. The vocalizations of a Limp Bizkit or an
Eminem are promoted alongside the music of a Philip Glass or a Nino
Rota (the composer of the soundtrack to *The Godfather*). The media oli-
garchy has replaced the aristocracy and the church as a sponsor of the
arts—but it is a Janus-faced sponsor. In Roman mythology, Janus was the
god of gates and doorways, depicted with two faces looking in opposite
directions. Today, the media have become the gods of the "gates and doorways of aesthetics," looking in opposite directions—one pointing toward
distraction and the other engagement.

Pop culture has been basically a good thing, opening up the aesthetic
channels to one and all, not just the élite and the cognoscenti. It has made
personal choice a reality. However, it has also generated a widespread forever young syndrome. The effects this syndrome has had on individuals
are hard to identify and examine objectively, because they are so diffuse
and variable. One concrete effect is the widespread tendency of adults to
maintain their own adolescent lifestyles well beyond their adolescent
years. People hold on to the music of their teen years and continue wor-
shipping the media idols of their youth well into middle age (and even
old age). To wit: in 2002 the remix of Elvis's song, "A Little Less Conversation," a minor song from 1968 that was used on the soundtrack for the

even more minor film *Live a Little, Love a Little,* was spliced with techno sounds and with electronic warps and woofs and then made its way to the top of the charts. All that can be said is that Elvis has become a pop culture myth—a poor country boy who made good and became an international symbol. His memory continues to fuel a passionate denial of aging and extinction. His home, Graceland, has become a pilgrimage for forever young people to whom he remains an ageless hero.[5]

This pattern of behavior is ultimately destructive to a society because it does not encourage people to grow intellectually, aesthetically, and philosophically. In addition, it has gradually removed the concept of the "wise elder" from the social radar screen. Today, most people do not want to be considered old at any age. Even people in their eighties think of themselves as "still young enough" to take up things such as the martial arts that are hardly designed for their age group.

The blueprint for the distraction factory was designed in the mid-1920s. That was the era when radio had become, alongside film, a highly popular mass medium, shaping trends in music overnight. Radio could reach many more people, because it could span great distances instantly. Programming could thus be designed with mass appeal in mind. As a consequence, radio spawned pop culture—a culture for all, not just the élite.

The distraction factory was expanded considerably with the advent of television. The first television sets for mass utilization became available in England in 1936 and in the United States in 1938; in the United States, six television stations were established at first, each one broadcasting for only a few hours each day. After World War II, technical improvements and prosperity led to a growing demand for television sets. By 1948, thirty-four all-day stations were in operation in twenty-one major cities, and about 1 million television sets had been sold. By the end of the 1950s, national television networks were instituted in most industrialized countries. TV had emerged, in effect, to replace radio as the primary source of mass distraction across the world. As the twentieth century came to a close, TV entered the computer age with the advent of digital TV.

With the widespread growth of cable television and then of Direct Broadcast Satellite services in the 1990s, many new channels and types of programming became available. As a consequence, debates about TV's impact on children, world culture, politics, and community life have become common and widespread. On the one side, critics say that television feeds a constant stream of simplified ideas and sensationalistic images to unwitting viewers, that it negatively influences politics and voting patterns, that it destroys local cultures in favor of a bland Hollywood-based distraction culture, and that it encourages passivity in people. On the other side, defenders say that television provides a great deal of high-quality educational and cultural programming, and that it is the major source of local, national, and international news for many people who would otherwise remain uninformed. Whatever the truth, one thing is for certain—TV has turned out to be *the* medium that has consolidated what the great Canadian communications theorist Marshall McLuhan (1911–1980) called the "global village," because it has made the same pattern and kind of distraction (the same TV sitcoms, adventure programs, and variety shows) available across the globe.

And there is little doubt that in this village, one general outlook prevails—the tendency of its inhabitants to think of themselves as forever young and attractive, both physically and socially, just like the young sexy actors and personalities they see day in, day out on television, in ads, and in movies.[6] All this is not only good for business, but it is also indispensable for it. In its August 9, 2000, issue, the *Wall Street Journal* pointed out that there are more teens today than ever before, because in each of the years from 1989 to 1993, births exceeded 4 million for the first time since the early 1960s. It has been estimated that in each of the years between 2000 and 2002, teens spent over $150 billion annually, making them one of the most important market segments around. Not surprisingly, a cottage industry of consultants, ad executives, and marketing researchers have sprung up to help corporations find a way to access the increasingly lucrative, and conveniently unstable, teen market. This is why new gadgets of technology are directed at teens. Attracted by the images of cool that technological advertising promotes, it is little wonder that teens are often the household's "experts" when it comes to new digital products and, thus, the ones who will influence what parents will buy. Hordes of tweenies and teens now trek to school with cell phones, pagers, and Palm Pilots—all of which, incidentally, have become themselves advertising vehicles for all kinds of products.

Teens are also the major users of cyberspace. One teen put it as follows during the research for this book:

> I spend my time mainly playing games online, and checking out sites or communicating with friends online; maybe four hours a day. TV is boring, man, you just sit there; at least here I entertain myself any way I want to.

A computer has, in fact, become a radio, a television, a video game, a movie theater, a library, a magazine, and a newspaper all wrapped into one. The cell phone and the online form of communication are fast replacing all other forms. Soon, kids will know how to design a web page before they can spell. Even television is becoming increasingly sensitive to the new "digital teens." Networks and specialty channel programs are constantly emitting blurbs inviting viewers to visit them online.

All this will dictate the future course of adolescence and, perhaps, even transform it radically. As teens go online en masse, then cliquing and hanging out may become less fashionable as the "virtual clique" will likely replace the real one. Online chatting is already a source of trends. Written language, for instance, is being slowly altered. In a recent study of Internet language, which he labels *Netspeak*, the linguist David Crystal notes that spelling has become simplified so that a message can be sent in the shortest time possible.[7] Hence, sentences showing abbreviations and simplified spelling patterns, such as the ones listed here, now abound in English (see box).[8] Teens have also reintroduced a pictographic element to the written language through the creation and use of *emoticons*. These are keyboard characters lined up to resemble human gestures or expressions: for example, the emoticon :) or :-) signifies "smiling." New emoticons are being created on a daily basis.

The online generation is being increasingly called the *IM* ("instant messenger") *generation* because instant messaging is replacing the phone as a means of instant communication among peers. Young people are, clearly, in the vanguard of the processes that now undergird linguistic change as they exploit the possibilities of digital technology, radically changing the face of literacy.

IM, and more generally TM ("text messaging"), is a product of the information age, in which a "compression style" in coding messages seems

---

NETSPEAK

- :-P ("You're being sassy; I'm sticking out my tongue at you")
- 8-) ("I'm wearing glasses; I'm acting smart")
- afk ("Away from keyboard")
- brb ("I'll be right back")
- btw ("By the way")
- g2g ("Got to go")
- hhok ("Ha ha; I'm only kidding")
- how ya doin ("How are you doing?")
- i dont know why ("I don't know why")
- i fine ("I am fine")
- i got enuf ("I've got enough")
- imao ("In my arrogant opinion")
- imho ("In my humble opinion")
- it wuz lotsa fun ("It was lots of fun")
- pos ("Parents on site/parents over shoulder")
- tttt ("To tell the truth")
- u feeling better now? ("Are you feeling better now?")
- wanna know why? ("Do you want to know why?")
- you da right person ("You're the right person")

to be the norm. Starting with telegraphy, a process that may be called "acronymic" has become commonplace in written communications. Constraints of the space in which a message is to be written, and limitations of time in which to deliver it, have brought about a general tendency to abbreviate words. IM and TM are contemporary outgrowths of this more general tendency.

TELEVISION

As mentioned, TV has become highly juvenilized. TV comedy, for instance, has now become virtually adolescent in its humor. Some programs, in fact, can only be deciphered by teens. One of these was *Beavis and Butthead*, which was extremely popular in the mid-1990s. It was one of MTV's top-rated shows, hated by parents, loved by teens. Beavis had reddish brown hair, Butthead brown hair and braces. The two characters sat together at the back of a high school classroom, picking their noses and chattering away. Typical verbal exchanges between them included "cool," "sucks (school sucks, life sucks)," "nachos rule," "burn it," "dude," "chicks," "ass," "asswipe." They spent a lot of their time watching music videos and TV commercials. In a phrase, they were adolescent boors. But they were a hit, as was the 2002 DVD, *The History of Beavis and Butthead*. Capitalizing on its success, the TV moguls came up with a female counterpart in 1997. Her name was Daria Morgendorffer—an expressionless high schooler with black glasses, dispensing wry witticisms à la Beavis and Butthead. Incredibly, her "dorky look" was adopted by many females in society at large during that era as part of a new fashion trend.

The promulgation of adolescent humor is not restricted to teen-directed programs. It is noticeable everywhere. Take, for instance, *South Park*, a popular cartoon sitcom that began in the 1990s and is still going strong as I write. It can only be characterized as a "comedy of vulgarity," parodying digestion, defecation, flatulence, and copulation. It is a kind of *Beavis and Butthead* program gone amok. Although the satirical thrust of the sitcom is rather transparent, its vulgar style makes it little more than an outlet for adolescent humor. Its subtext is bluntly: *the more vulgar and disgusting, the funnier.* There have, of course, been other programs of this type. But they really never degenerated to the level of vulgar buffoonery that is obvious in *South Park*. Many ancient satirists, too, delighted in putting vulgarity on the stage. But in all cases, the displayers were adult, and the mode of humor was in line with a certain literary tradition.

In a way, *South Park* is preferable to many of the soppy sitcoms and adult crime, lawyer, and adventure shows that now saturate the airwaves. At least *South Park* is not so sanctimonious and vacuous. Nevertheless, it is juvenile. It gets airtime because it is sophomoric in a juvenile way. Its type of humor has invaded mass culture. Blatant or suggested flatulence, for example, has been used in such mainstream movies as the *Mighty Ducks, Lion King,* and *Little Giants,* all made for young audiences. Irreverent logos and expressions now appear regularly on T-shirts and caps—*Snot Candy, Gummy Boogers, Monster Warts,* and so on. Wholesomeness simply does not sell in a market that is driven by teen tastes.

But how realistic are such media portrayals of teens? In my interviews, I found a fairly widespread critique of the media on the part of adolescents themselves. Moreover, the media have forgotten that teens can find as much delight and inspiration in artistic expression as adults. As I will discuss in the next chapter, young people are very much aware of the distinction between expressions that are designed primarily for distraction and those for engagement.

The research team found, significantly, that TV programs such as the family sitcom are of virtually no interest to teenagers. One informant put it as follows: "Those shows are stupid; they really don't know real family life at all!" The two exceptions seem to be *The Simpsons* and *Buffy the Vampire Slayer.* It is hard to fathom why the former—a cartoon parody of family life and of social mores generally—has enjoyed so much success, given the ephemerality of television programs in general. Undoubtedly, the program's writers—many of them Harvard graduates—are in tune with what people consider funny today. The program also engages famous people in conversation with Homer Simpson, ranging from physicist Stephen Hawking to pop music stars such as Mick Jagger and Paul McCartney. And it is in step with changes in lifestyle and in cultural groupthink. Its humor is subversive and delightful at the same time; it is perfect for the television medium—swift, to the point, and abrasive. The teens interviewed generally liked the TV show, because it reflected their sense of humor perfectly. As one teen put it: "It's funny, man; it tells us not to take things too seriously." However, when asked if it has any influence on them, virtually all answered that *The Simpsons* bears absolutely no direct meaning to their lives.

Many of the informants also claimed to watch *Buffy the Vampire Slayer* on a semiregular basis. It was, in fact, one of the few TV shows that dealt directly with teenagehood on its own terms. Driving the narrative of its weekly episodes was the theme of mortality.[9] Through an amalgam of pop culture genres—comic-book superheroism and vampirism—the sitcom depicted the horror of teenagehood itself—a world of nasty cliques, of anti-intellectualism, of perverse coolness, and of inane adult bureaucratic structures that have grown up around adolescence. Buffy's father had deserted the family, and her mother was largely "clueless" as to what was going on in young people's lives. In early 2002, Buffy went on to college, where, seemingly, more maturity and sanity prevailed (at least in the early episodes).

Fans of the show proved to be extraordinarily dedicated to it. They supported a *Buffy the Vampire Slayer* industry that produced the obligatory T-shirts, posters, trading cards, jewelry, quarterly magazine, books, and websites. Its appeal lay, in my view, in the fact that it portrayed average kids, in average relationships, battling the problems of teenagehood personified by vampires, demons, and monsters. One of the show's central subtexts, as I read it, was that teens need their parents and their teachers much more than they need peers. Alienation can occur within the home, but it is more likely to occur outside.

But when it comes right down to it, Buffy was no better or no worse than any other family sitcom/drama. At the risk of sounding élitist, I firmly believe that the TV medium cannot possibly provide a forum for the engagement of its audiences in understanding the "human condition," with half-hour programs. *The Simpsons* and *Buffy the Vampire Slayer* are good shows because they are reflective of reality. Whether or not they have an effect on teens or are relevant to their lives are open questions, as our research team found. As mentioned above, teens seem to be more into movies and digital media, with TV starting to take a back seat to them.

As a final word on television, I cannot help but mention reality shows, such as *The Bachelor/Bachelorette* and *American Idol*. When asked about these programs, most of the teens interviewed found them to be extremely humorous. Significantly, about half of them (sixty-four females and thirty-two males) expressed a desire to be on one of them, feeling that they provided an opportunity to achieve celebrity status. However, unlike many TV critics, I see nothing especially new or radical about these shows. In the 1960s and 1970s, television featured such shows as *A Day in the Life* . . . (if memory serves me correctly) and *The Dating Game*, which also featured average people getting catapulted into celebrity status. These shows have always borne testimony to the veracity of Andy Warhol's (1930–1987) prediction that everyone in our pop culture society desires to have their "fifteen minutes of fame."

Such programs combine elements of narrative with those of documentary and drama to produce a TV sociology of everyday life that piques everybody's latent tribal interest in the affairs of others. Reality TV is voyeurism for the digital age. With the use of webcams, millions of people throughout the world are now even letting strangers into their daily lives. It would seem that a growing number of people simply find "living in public" more exciting than living privately. Clearly, the boundaries between the private and the public have been eroded through the influence of TV. Everyone, from celebrities to homemakers, is airing personal laundry in public for everyone to see. Maybe at some deep unconscious level, we are all trying to understand what human life is all about through such artificial people watching. Who knows? But it certainly seems to be a bizarre way of doing so.

OTHER MEDIA

The research team asked the informants if they read magazines designed for teenagers and, if so, what they thought about them. Virtually all the 200 subjects claimed to have read and bought such magazines and to have been influenced by them to some extent. One teen put it as follows: "I read magazines so that I can keep up with fashion trends and with what's happening in music." The reason for the popularity of magazines can be traced, in my view, to the power of the photographic image. Photos of models or stars in magazines provide visual models, which then set the style for clothing, coiffure, and overall "look." The success of magazines such as *YM* and *Seventeen* is a testament to the staying power of the magazine medium.

The subjects were also asked if they read magazines regularly. Significantly, it was the female informants who claimed to do so. And, indeed, most teen magazines seem to be designed primarily for girls. Replete with stories and ads about makeup, jewelry, clothes, and male music icons, many magazines are really little more than marketing tools, although they may at times engage their readership in intellectually stimulating ways. However, the latter function is not perceived as relevant for the magazine medium by most of the teens interviewed. One informant stated bluntly: "If I want to read about issues, I'll buy a book; the 'zine is about what's going on."

As mentioned above, of all the media available today, movies remain the most popular among teens—a fact that has always characterized teenagehood. In the 1950s and early 1960s, the drive-in movie theater was a place where teens went to socialize and, perhaps above all else, to engage in romance and even sex. As one parent put it to the research team: "Yeah, in my days the drive-in was where the action was; the car was, I guess, a mobile bedroom."

Movies and youth culture go hand in hand. Since the 1950s, cinema has been catering to the teen market. Starting with movies such as *The Wild One* (1954) and *Rebel without a Cause* (1955), Hollywood sensed the economic potential of that market. In today's juvenilized culture, blockbuster films based on comic-book characters or adventure heroes tend to blur the dividing line between young and mature audiences even more. Movies such as those in the *Harry Potter* and *Lord of the Rings* series that cross books, video games, and digital effects now appeal to children, teens, and adults alike. This is why it is not surprising to find crossovers from the video game sphere to the movie one—I mention *Tomb Raider* and *Final Fantasy* as two cases in point.

To conclude the discussion on media, it behooves me to elaborate further on the idea of distraction versus engagement, since it has been implicit throughout it. In actual fact, it is a subjective distinction, because it is almost impossible to distinguish between what is art and what is mere distraction. The operas of Giuseppe Verdi (1813–1901), as great as they are, had an initial distraction function—people went to them to be entertained, plain and simple. The fact that his music has risen above its initial function is a consequence of various factors, not the least of which is the musical genius of the composer. Everyone in our pop culture world can easily locate a jingle such as the Alka Seltzer one ("Plop, plop, fizz, fizz, oh what a relief it is") at the distraction end of the "aesthetic continuum" and a musical work such as Mozart's powerful *Requiem Mass* at the other. As apparent as this line of reasoning is, it nonetheless brings out concretely that people, by and large, can discern quality in the smorgasbord of options that our media culture makes available. The problem lies in media products that fall on other parts of the continuum, creating cultural confusion. These include programs such as *The Simpsons* and *Buffy the Vampire Slayer*, mentioned above.

As also just mentioned, personal taste is a major factor in determining where someone will locate a specific text on the continuum. Human beings are not automaton-like consumers of cultural meanings; they are creative users of these meanings. The problem with our mediated culture is that the critics and defenders of media are both right. The goal of the distraction industries is to promote a consumerist lifestyle. Day in and day out, the fragmented images of life coming out of the media are bound to influence our overall view that reality is illusory and surreal, that human actions are a montage of disconnected desires and feelings, and that the only achievable goal in life is pleasure through consumption. It is also true, as media critics argue, that the messages of consumerism are modern-day surrogates for traditional forms of religious discourse, whose goal has always been the promulgation of the "good news." But within this same world, it is possible to expose the banality of consumerism and the dangers of technology, as do many pop culture artists and social critics. Therein lies the paradox of modern pop culture. As one teen informant put it: "There's, like, a lot of junk in the movies today; but there's also a lot of good things that make you think about life."

INSIGHTS

The media today showcase teen trends on a daily basis. As a result, as I said at the beginning of this chapter, there is a veritable synergy between the media and adolescent lifestyles—one influences the other in tandem. That is perhaps the greatest insight that can be derived from the foregoing discussion.

"Me and my friends love going to the movies; it's phat, man."
   Surveys show that over 90 percent of 12 to 19-year-olds go to movies regularly. This is because Hollywood has kept in step with teenagehood since the 1950s. Teen movie idols, from James Dean in *Rebel without a Cause* and John Travolta in *Saturday Night Fever* to contemporary icons such as Kirsten Dunst and Angelina Jolie, have become as much a part of teenagehood's history as have rock and rap musicians. Movies today tend to showcase the themes that young people are interested in, and movie theater complexes have become places for teen socialization. Movies ranging from the *Scream*-type genre to the *American Pie* and *Dumb and Dumber* types are tailor-made for large teen audiences.
   A movie theater is also popular among teens because it is a locus for dating. Watching a movie, eating popcorn, drinking soda, and holding hands in a theater constitute dating activities that have been carried out since at least the 1950s, and probably even before.

"Nah, there's nothing much on TV, maybe rap videos, I prefer to play video games."
   There is little doubt that the computer screen is taking on more and more of the load of providing entertainment to children and teens. Video games in particular seem to have a particular stranglehold on the teen imagination—after that come music videos and CDs. Teens spend a large portion of their money on such entertainment paraphernalia. When adding in the cost of cigarettes, alcohol, and movies, the teen budget adds up to a significant amount of money spent on entertainment.
   Many parent groups believe that video games and television may have a negative effect on teens. The theory that the mass media can directly influence behavior is called *hypodermic needle theory* (HNT). It claims that media representations are capable of changing mental processes in the same way that a hypodermic needle can alter physical processes. The social diffusion of junk food is often cited in support of this theory. Promoted by effective advertising campaigns, junk food has become part of the common diet. But the consequences on health have been disastrous. The inordinate consumption of junk food is, in fact, one of the main factors contributing to the rise in obesity.

But the HNT view ignores the historical record. The ravages of diet are not just contemporary phenomena induced by exposure to the media. They have always been symptomatic of the excesses of affluent lifestyles. It is more accurate to say that the media influence people only in ways that they are already predisposed to be influenced. This in no way implies that the media have no impact on individuals. But then, this raises the question of what content is "kosher," so to speak, and, more important, who has the right (if any) of deciding what goes into the media. The danger in attacking certain representations as "harmful" and others as "acceptable" smacks of mind control and dangerous fanaticism, which, as such horrific movements as the Inquisition in Europe and McCarthyism in the United States have shown, were much more injurious to social well-being than were the actual "heresies" they denounced and censured.

"I love the Internet; it's cool, I can do things my parents can't."
Tweenies and teens today are in tune with technology, and they accept technological innovations much more readily than anyone else in our culture. Inevitably, the computer has replaced the traditional print media (books, comics, and the like) as the primary source of information for teens. Instant messaging in particular has become widespread. This is a good thing, in my view, for such activities take away from the time many teens would otherwise spend simply "hanging around" with friends, with little else to do but "waste time."

"I'm on my cell phone all day, man; it keeps me in touch."
Cell phone and electronic text messages have become intrinsic accoutrements of teenage communication. Of the thirty-eight informants interviewed in the last month of the project (December 2002), only one did not have a cell phone. The other thirty-seven teens all carried it with them to school and elsewhere, although only five claimed to pay the phone bills.

NOTES

1. Max Lerner, *New York Post*, June 4, 1952.
2. Todd Gitlin, *Media Unlimited: How the Torrent of Images and Sounds Overwhelms Our Lives* (New York: Metropolitan Books, 2001).
3. For an overall critique of the blurring of the lines between youth culture and advertising style, see Frank Thomas, *The Conquest of Cool* (Chicago: University of Chicago Press, 1997).
4. A. Goodwin, *Dancing in the Distraction Factory: Music Television and Popular Culture* (Minneapolis: University of Minnesota Press, 1992).
5. Both Greil Marcus, *Dead Elvis: A Chronicle of a Cultural Obsession* (New York: Anchor Books, 1991), and Gilbert B. Rodman, *Elvis after Elvis: The Posthumous*

Career of a Living Legend (London: Routledge, 1996), argue, in fact, that the reverence for Elvis is now part of an American mythology enmeshed with debates over what constitutes legitimate "culture." Interestingly, the 2002 animated movie *Lilo & Stitch*, put out by the Disney Corporation, used the music of Elvis Presley in its soundtrack and as part of the actual script. Given that the Elvis fan in this case was a little girl, it would seem that the "Elvis myth" is indeed a myth in the real sense—an unconscious narrative used to create stories for and about childhood.

6. See, on this point, J. Lopiano-Misdom and J. De Luca, *Street Trends: How Today's Alternative Youth Cultures Are Creating Tomorrow's Mainstream Markets* (New York: Harper Business, 1997).

7. David Crystal, *Language and the Internet* (Cambridge: Cambridge University Press, 2001).

8. See also Guy Merchant, "Teenagers in Cyberspace: An Investigation of Language Use and Language Change in Internet Chatrooms," *Journal of Research in Reading* 24 (2001): 293–306.

9. For a detailed synthesis of the themes and plots on *Buffy the Vampire Slayer*, see Kathleen Tracy, *The Girl's Got Bite: The Unofficial Guide to Buffy's World* (Los Angeles: Renaissance Books, 1998).

10

Ending the Experiment

Interviewer	What makes you angry?
Teen Informant	Adults. They, like, think they know it all, but they don't.
Interviewer	What do you mean?
Teen Informant	Like, they always think they know how we should, duh, run our lives. They have no idea how we really are.
Interviewer	Do you dislike being put into the same category as everyone else your age?
Teen Informant	I dislike categories, period! What good are they?

BACKGROUND

Ten years before his death, the American philosopher Eric Hoffer (1902–1983) stated rather bluntly that "a modern society can remain stable only by eliminating adolescence, by giving its young, from the age of ten, the skills, responsibilities, and rewards of grownups, and opportunities for action in all spheres of life."[1] Is Hoffer right? Is the elimination of the cultural experiment known as adolescence, necessitated by social circumstances over 150 years ago in Great Britain, the only way to solve the problems that continue to plague the coming-of-age period in contemporary cultures? I think so. The portrait of adolescence that I have attempted to sketch in this book is becoming more and more comparable to that of Dorian Gray. In Oscar Wilde's (1854–1900) moral fable, *The Picture of Dorian Gray* (1890), a man's portrait in the attic ages and grows ugly as a reflection of his moral corruption while his actual appearance remains

159

the same. The time has come to take the portrait of adolescence out of our cultural attic and take a long serious look at it.

As our informant astutely understood, adolescence can be eliminated only if the adolescents themselves, not just adults, take a major role in the elimination process. My encounters with teens over two decades have led me to believe that a slow, agonizing process of *cultural maturation* may be taking place on its own. The holding pattern into which pubescent individuals are projected is being questioned like never before by the adolescents themselves.[2] This is a sure sign that, as a cultural experiment, adolescence may well be on its way out in the next few generations. In the meanwhile, myths about adolescence and problems connected with it, continue to persist.[3] Thus, a starting point for eliminating the experiment is dispelling the myths and taking a hard look at the unnecessary perils these have engendered.

MYTHS

One widely held myth is that teens are "idealistic." This comes from our Sturm and Drang, or "Young Werther," view of adolescence captured brilliantly by J. D. Salinger in *Catcher in the Rye*. But the idealism of Werther is hardly what the research team found. The research tapes reveal that the most important preoccupation in adolescents' lives is coping as best as possible with the practical exigencies of everyday life.

A second widely held myth is that teenagers require "special handling" and that adults know what is best for them. But there is no right or wrong way to deal with teenagers. Each situation is different and cannot possibly be handled systematically or scientifically. As parents of troubled teens know all too well, things simply have to work themselves out. This does not mean that so-called professionals cannot help somewhat. But they are not diviners with all the right answers. I have found that they offer more solace to the distressed parent than anything else. Adolescents, on the other hand, are especially wary of adult professionals, whom they see as patronizing.

The teenagers have a point. The very people who dispense advice to teens—adults—are the ones who quickly take to their music styles, language, and fashions. As British writer, actor, and director John Wells (1936–) aptly put it in 1989, the awe we hold for all things adolescent "is possibly the hallmark of our generation."[4] Just as many grown-ups as teens enjoy rap music, comic books, video games, and superheroes such as Batman, Superman, and Spiderman (all once considered strictly kid stuff). In 2002, the Mattel Toy Company established a Planet Hot Wheels website where users could download toy-car games. The website even offered up-

---

SOME RELEVANT FACTS

- Teens spend billions and billions of dollars on everything from sneakers to posters of media stars in the United States.
- Parents do not understand trends initially because they relate specifically to teenage lifestyle shifts.
- Trends do not survive for long among adolescents once they are adopted by the mainstream culture.
- The only "constant" in teen trends is "constant change."

---

grades for "virtual vehicles" and a Motocross 1950s drag race—all free with a Hot Wheels purchase. In this way, the company was successful in equating its toy product with lifestyle cool for people of any age.

Teenagehood has been good for business. Statistics show that teens are among society's greatest spenders. Without them, modern economic systems would be altered radically. A recent national marketing study found that in the average teen pocket sits $107 of disposable income (per *week*). No wonder, then, that they are seen by business to be the trendsetters.

A third myth is that adolescents know more about sex today than at any other time in history. It is true that they are much more aware of sex, not only because of explicit sexuality in the media but also because of open discussions about sex at school. Still, when it comes to engaging in sexual activities, teens today, like teens in the past, continue to be influenced more by peers than anyone else.

In the 1950s, parents' groups made classroom guidance films on dating with titles such as *Age of Turmoil* (1953) and *Social-Sex Attitudes in Adolescence* (1953) that clearly revealed a concern over the risks of adolescent sex. The underlying assumption in such films was that teens would become sexually responsible if they were to be shown positive role models. By the 1960s and 1970s, the films became brutal, reflecting the growing horror that parents of that era felt vis-à-vis the sexuality flaunted openly by the new teen generation. Those newer films were "cautionary tales," showing teens slaughtered in automobile accidents, suffering from venereal diseases, or ravaged by drug use. By the 1980s, such films were finally discontinued as explicit courses in the biology of sex and on courtship were given in classrooms by teachers. But nothing seems to work to deter teen sex. Surveys taken in the first years of this century by agencies such as the Centers for Disease Control (CDC) and others show that half of the adolescents under the age of 15 and nearly three quarters under the age of 19 report having consensual sex, and most also report not having taken any precautions to protect themselves from disease or to avoid pregnancy.[5]

In actual fact, adult treatments of teen sexuality are somewhat patronizing, even if they come under the rubric of a "Sex 101" type of approach. They are useless, moreover, because they are motivated by the assumption that all teenagers are alike—sexually immature individuals incapable of making up their own minds.

A fourth myth, which is probably the greatest myth of all, is the view that the traumas and emotional crises of adolescence are "natural" consequences of adapting to puberty. As I have tried to argue throughout this book, this is simply not true. Adolescence is solid proof that human beings are highly susceptible to accepting the belief systems of the culture in which they are reared as commonsensical. As a teenager myself back in the late 1950s and as a parent of a teenager in the early 1980s, I, like most other people in my society, assumed that adolescence was a natural stage of development, as inevitable as flight is to birds. But since becoming directly involved with teens both as students and as subjects of research projects, I have come to understand firsthand what the anthropologist Margaret Mead (chapter 1) warned us all about back in the 1930s: namely, that culture has intervened in the continuous pattern of growth that children follow from one age to the other in other kinds of societies. The view of adolescence as a traumatic period is, simply put, a case of a self-fulfilling cultural prophecy, not a process guided by Mother Nature.[6]

As discussed in the opening chapter, the idea of making adolescence a specific period for psychologists to study was proposed in 1904 by Stanley G. Hall. As Hall was formulating his ideas on adolescence, Sigmund Freud was publishing case studies of troubled young persons who had become this way—according to Freud—because of negative childhood experiences. As it turns out, the Hall-Freud view of adolescence has been a lucrative one for the hordes of professionals whose job it is to give advice about how to raise adolescents. But rearing is not a science. There simply is no right or wrong way to deal with teenagers. Each situation is different and cannot possibly be handled according to scientific principles. Rarely have we in our culture stopped to consider that this whole line of attack may be seriously misguided.

Adolescence has been especially good for the disciplines of psychology and psychiatry. The number of practitioners involved in counseling adolescents, not to mention the number of psychology books written and sold on the problems of adolescence, have reached ludicrous proportions. These two disciplines have, in effect, declared ownership over adolescence. In 1970, a group of pediatricians formed the Society for Adolescent Medicine, which became a board-certified branch of pediatrics in 1995. In that year, the society declared that adolescence ended at the age of 26. In 2002, the society increased it by eight years to 34. Does this mean that every seven years, the age of adolescence will be extended by eight years?

I am positive that in their wildest imaginations, the dramatists of the theater of the absurd could not have thought up anything more absurd than
this. Probably influenced by the whole psychological approach to adolescence, it is relevant to note that in the same year, 2002, the National Academy of Sciences of the United States defined the period of adolescence as
stretching from puberty to 30 years of age. In the same year, the McArthur
Foundation went one step further, also pegging the end of adolescence at
the absolutely mind-boggling age of 34! Something is amiss here. How far
can we, as a society, allow such views to go unchallenged?

What the psychologists have ended up doing is nothing short of de-
priving young people of the right to assert themselves as adults. They
have joined forces with economists in promoting a self-serving view of
adolescence. This simply must stop. I cannot but agree with the great
American writer Henry Miller (1891–1980) who pointed out, disparag-
ingly, "In America youth means simply athleticism, disrespect, gangsterism, or sickly idealism expressing itself through thinly disguised and
badly digested social science theories acted out by idiots who are desper-
adoes at heart."[7] There is even a movement afoot within some states to require married couples to take courses in childrearing from professionals
before they become parents. Spurred on by the many child abuse cases
that seem to plague the modern family, the promoters of the movement
truly believe that there is a rational scientific approach to the upbringing
of children and adolescents. But only in our psychological age is such an
idea even thinkable. In actual fact, most teens prefer to get by in a difficult
family situation rather than be sent away to be under the care of strangers.
Only in serious abuse cases has any teen ever expressed to me the desire
to leave home, and even then it is with great trepidation and unease. Incidentally, it is significant to note that in 2002, one of the top teen hits was
the artist Pink's heart-wrenching song "Family Portrait," in which a little
child pleads with her parents, through tears, to stay together for the sake
of love and of the whole family. With its wistful and poignant melody, the
song became a hit because it touched a soft spot in the teenage heart. Its
subtext was obvious—despite problems in the family, only within it can
solutions be found.

Our obsession with finding scientific solutions to the problems of adolescence is also the reason why there is a constant barrage of pop psychology "studies" that are continually making it to the *New York Times*
bestseller list. One such study is the book by Rachel Simmons, *Odd Girl
Out: The Hidden Culture of Aggression in Girls*.[8] Although its description of
the cruelties that females perpetrate on each other in high school is something that I can certainly confirm, the general "this-is-the-way-it-is" tone
of the book is what makes it somewhat nerve-wracking. One is never sure
in reading such books who is being scolded—the teens, society, or both.

As well-meaning as they are, they end up simply capitalizing on parental dread by portraying school as littered with beaten-down adolescents.

RECONNECTION

At the start of the twentieth century, the sociologist Émile Durkheim (1858–1917) suggested that *anomie* (his term for "alienation") was the main cause of suicide. He traced its source to affluence, implying that the Western world's blatant materialism had brought about the social conditions that induced an all-pervading sense of disconnection within our spiritual selves. This disconnection, Durkheim claimed, tended to induce persistent feelings of anxiety and dissatisfaction in some individuals who, in turn, sought a way out by taking their own lives.[9] In my view, Durkheim's notion of anomie might explain not only the increase in suicide among teens but also the constant penchant for rebellion among modern-day youths in general. In a sense, the adolescent years are all about anomie. Generally speaking, this means a period of separation from the adult world with an attendant lifestyle (as we have seen in this book). But increasingly, it also entails serious consequences, such as eating disorders, suicide, aggression against peers, and the like.

The subtext I have tried to interlace throughout this book is, in fact, that teen life is regulated by a disconnection syndrome of which few teens are consciously aware. The time to reconnect the emotional, social, and sexual components of personality in adolescence by declaring the social experiment of adolescence a failure is long overdue. As the poet and critic Louise Bogan (1897–1970) has aptly put it, "Childhood prolonged, cannot remain a fairyland; it becomes a hell."[10]

But, one may legitimately ask, from where will the impetus for reconnection come? In my view, it has already started to come from young people themselves. From my interviews and daily interactions with them, I sense that a change is imminent. Although a large segment of the adolescent population continues to live in a virtual fog about everything around them, an increasing number of teens tell me bluntly that they are tired of being manipulated by the media-entertainment industry. One teen put it to me as follows: "Do the media guys really think they can fool us with the grossness of *South Park* and 'Disposable Teens' [a grotesque video by Marilyn Manson]?" Another aptly critiqued the self-serving egoism of programs such as *Sex and the City* with the following words: "That show is supposed to help us understand people today. It's stupid. Who really wants to be like those characters?"

Eliminating adolescence implies several radical changes in social groupthink. First and foremost, our culture will have to restore importance to the family in matters of upbringing and not look constantly to the theories and advice of experts in psychology and psychiatry.[11] When I use the term *family,* I am not referring to any particular form of that institution. Single-parent families are also families, as are those with homosexual parents. I once interviewed a teen who was raised by homosexual parents and who expressed his total love for them, indicating to me that his family was a true one "based on love and understanding," as he so aptly put it. Indeed, his explanation is the only real definition that can be given to the word *family.* Whatever form it may take, its defining characteristic is love.

Second, we will have to start ignoring the "sitcom view" of family life perpetrated by television and, often, movies. Humor and satire alone cannot solve family problems. And, along with it, we will have to reconsider our current attitudes toward marriage breakups. All the teens of divorced parents interviewed by the research team (seventy-six in all) found the breakup of their family to be the most agonizing experience they had ever undergone. Our culture has weakened the family institution much too much in the last five decades in order to promote individualism at any cost. The time has come to strengthen it once again. In no way do I intend to imply that divorce is always an inappropriate solution to marital problems. In cases of physical and emotional abuse, it is probably an unavoidable way out of the situation. But it is true that the experience of divorce will always be traumatic for children when they are going through it and, in many cases, will leave a lasting effect.

Third, reconnection implies treating adolescents as mature citizens of society, not as "half children, half adults." I started off this book by citing Antonio Gramsci's remark that the only two real phases in the human lifecycle are before and after puberty. Gramsci's simple model of the lifecycle is the only truly realistic one. Thinking of the period right after the arrival of sexual maturity as constituting a transitional phase characterized by the many problems discussed in this book is an idea pattern that should be seriously questioned. Individuals who have undergone sexual maturity are adults—end of matter. That's the way it always was and continues to be in many other parts of the world. The temporary disconnection of young people from adulthood was brought about by human intervention—by a practical need that emerged 150 years ago. That intervention has had profound effects on our institutions, legal processes, and general outlook. A *Gramscian reconnection* to adulthood will entail a radical revision of our institutions and legal practices. Bur we owe it, at the very least, to the children who are approaching maturity. It is ludicrous to continue denying them the right of entry into adulthood by disconnecting them from it socially and juridically and, consequently, by allowing them to wallow in a bizarre state of existence for a period of time—a period that we have been extending continually since the origins of the social experiment.

INSIGHTS

As annoying as they may appear to adults, most of the teen behaviors described in this book are really no more than temporary matters. They will disappear gradually as teens grow up—sooner or later. But some may lead to situations of real danger for both teenagers and parents. I will discuss these in this final "Insights" section.

"Everyone has sex, man; with or without precaution."
According to a 2002 CDC report, nearly one in ten people report having had sex before the age of 13, up 15 percent from 1997. And according to the Henry J. Kaiser Family Foundation, despite a decrease in the teen birthrate between 1991 and 1999, 20 percent of sexually active teen females still get pregnant each year. A 2002 Planned Parenthood survey found, even more revealingly, that two thirds of graduating high school seniors have had some form of sex, and one in four new sexually transmitted diseases occurs in adolescence. The use of "abstinence-only education programs" in some parts of the United States has obviously not worked. Nor can it, unless these new moral guardians find a way to stop sexual urges from occurring at puberty!

Of particular concern are sexually transmitted diseases, especially AIDS. AIDS was first identified in homosexual men in the early 1980s. Some continue, mistakenly, to consider it a homosexual disease. But the HIV virus is a blind one—it can be transmitted from male to female or from female to male. The virus can also be transmitted through needles and syringes. It may even be spread by tattooing or body piercing if the instruments were previously used on an infected person.

Feeling indestructible or that "bad things happen to others" is what puts teens at risk with regards to AIDS. It is a topic that must be discussed frankly, with no inhibitions or moralizing approaches. The teen's life literally depends on it. The CDC estimates that half of all new HIV infections in the United States occur in people under the age of 25. Although teens are well informed about the AIDS peril through school and the media, the "devil-may-care" attitude that is characteristic of teenagers often takes over their better judgment. It is thus practical, to my mind, to make such things as condoms available to teens with or without "adult consent" to preclude their sexual activities from becoming fatal.

"I live with my friends on the street, man; it's tough out there."
Risk taking of a physical nature, often meant as a show-off performance to peers (e.g., dangerous driving, engaging in physical confrontations, and taking drugs), is another area of great concern. Particularly worrisome are the dangers that teens running away from home face. Parents

have frequently told me that they felt like prisoners in their own house and slaves to the whims of their teens, but that they preferred such a situation to the danger of their sons or daughters leaving home to face the peril of the streets. And their fears are not unfounded: a million teens run away from home every year; the teen homicide rate has increased by 232 percent since 1950; 1 million teenage girls become pregnant yearly, most of them living away from home; and the list could go on and on.

There is no one single reason why teens run away from home. Family conflicts, peer lifestyles that are conducive to "living on the streets," and a need to cut the umbilical cord decisively are all factors. It depends on the individual and on the situation. A good relationship in the past, based on shared responsibilities and trust, will provide a basis for the runaway to reenter the home in due course.

"Yeah, I lost my best friend to suicide; he couldn't take it any longer."
Any danger sign of suicide demands immediate attention. Suicide is the second-leading cause of death, after accidents, among white adolescents aged 15 to 24, according to statistics published by the U.S. Department of Health in early 2000. The suicide rate has tripled since the 1950s. The causes for suicide have been studied by social and behavioral scientists. From their research, it is obvious to me that suicide is virtually unpredictable, although five factors in particular seem to place an adolescent at risk: (1) suffering from low self-esteem or an emotional problem; (2) being under constant stress, especially in school or because of a romantic relationship or conflict in peer situations; (3) experiencing family disruption or family conflict; (4) having a history of suicide in the family; and (5) having known a close friend who committed suicide.

POSSIBLE INDICATORS OF SUICIDE

The teen may show:

- An inability to tolerate frustrations
- A serious neglect of academic work
- A noticeable loss of interest in pleasurable activities
- A marked personality change
- Signs of drug and alcohol abuse
- Withdrawal from friends, family, and regular activities
- A persistent moodiness
- Constant feelings of hopelessness
- A drastic change in eating and sleeping patterns

Everybody experiences situations that bring about stress and depression, but most people do not contemplate suicide as a way out. So why is the suicide rate among teens so high? It is certainly not for me to give any expert opinion with respect to this truly devastating area of concern. Let me simply say that the question of suicide came up several times in interviews. The danger signs are well known. These include persistent feelings of emptiness, hopelessness, and guilt, along with a noticeable loss of interest in school and in carrying out ordinary activities. Other signs include disturbances in eating and sleeping patterns, restlessness, and irritability. Truly troubled teens will tend to discuss with others that they are contemplating drastic solutions to their problems. Thus, peers are crucial sources of insight and should be listened to very carefully.

What has brought about the increase in teen suicide? From my interviews with teens, I would like to suggest that our media-driven, forever young culture is itself to blame in some part. Many adolescents think seriously about the meaning of life. But our society, as a whole, seems to have little time or interest in discussing "life's greater questions" with adolescents, or with anyone for that matter. This induces a feeling of anomie (as Durkheim suggested) that is widespread among adolescents. Many simply attempt to cope with it as best they can; a few take the suicide route. The fixation on suicide as a kind of permanent answer to anomie is, in fact, a recurrent theme in some of the music lyrics that adolescents listen to. The lyrics of such bands as Nine Inch Nails and Nirvana, to mention but two, are all about despair and alienation. Expressions such as "I'd rather die," "my hatred grows extreme," "my head is filled with disease," "I really don't know who I am," and "this world of piss" are interspersed throughout the songs of Nine Inch Nails. Significantly, in 1994, Nirvana's lead singer Kurt Cobain committed suicide, showing his fans that his words were not vacuous, that he meant what he said.

Another definite cause for concern is ostracism from peer groups or constant ridiculing by peers. That is what brought about the homicide-suicide pact that we witnessed at Columbine High School in Colorado in 1999. The two students in that case murdered their peers and then took their own lives. "Getting even" for the constant ridicule they suffered appears to have been their primary motivation.[12]

"I'm afraid to get fat, and that's why I don't eat. I hate food."
As discussed briefly in the third chapter, anorexia nervosa is a disorder that is probably brought about by an abnormal fear of becoming obese. A feeling that they have no control over their lives and a desire to take control also motivate anorexics. It is beyond the scope of the present treatment to offer insights into the "causes" of anorexia. Suffice it to say that it is largely a product of an image-obsessed culture. Bulimia nervosa is char-

---

SIGNS OF ANOREXIA AND BULIMIA

The anorexic teen may:

- Show an obsession with food and recipes
- Develop unusual eating habits such as, for example, eating food in tiny pieces or eating only the crumbs that others leave behind
- Tend to feel constantly cold
- Undergo considerable weight loss
- Become involved in excessive exercise, spending hours at a gym, going on daylong walks, and the like

The bulimic teen may:

- Eat voraciously but show very little weight gain
- Become inordinately sensitive and secretive about food and eating
- Vomit secretly after meals
- Tend to have a chronic sore throat and hoarse voice

---

acterized instead by a frequent and uncontrollable desire to overeat. Bulimics eat until they are too full to eat any more. After bingeing, they purge the food by making themselves vomit or by taking large doses of laxatives to help empty the bowels.

As incredible to the Western mind as it may appear, anthropologists have found that there simply is no such thing as anorexia nervosa or bulimia nervosa among people reared in other cultures, such as Malaysians and Native Americans. These disorders clearly have a cultural etiology. In my view, the main cause of such unnecessary disorders can be found in the media images that are perpetuated daily of ultraslim fashion models and movie stars. No standard therapy for anorexia nervosa exists, nor can it exist, given its cultural source. Most cases of successful recovery show self-resolution without relapses. In my view, the most meaningful form of therapy is to get the anorexic or bulimic teenager away from such images. This may mean sending the teen to a place where such images have no impact, as implied by the statement made by one astute informant who had an anorexic friend: "I can tell you that my friend got much better by moving in with her aunt; that's because they have no TV and she had to help tend to the farm; at least that's what I think."

"My son is an alien."

The parent who uttered the phrase "My son is an alien" after one of the public lectures I gave several years ago (see the introduction) wanted to convey to me that she saw the identity her son had fashioned for himself as being at odds with the one that she thought it would turn out to be on the basis of a very close relation she had with her son in childhood. To her eyes, her son had become "an alien" because he looked, talked, walked, and behaved very differently from when he was a child. Interestingly, the same alien image of the adolescent was used by E. Burkett in his 2001 book titled, appropriately, *Another Planet*.[13] That woman's metaphor was, in fact, more discerning than she may have thought. The notion of alienation was developed originally by Karl Marx (1818–1883) and Georg Wilhelm Friedrich Hegel (1770–1831) to explain something very similar: namely, the solitary identity that individuals who feel estranged from their society tend to assume.[14]

The thematic thread that I have attempted to weave throughout this book is that the alienation of adolescents from the adult world is the product of a 150-year-old social experiment. In the last few decades, there has been a growing recognition even among psychologists of this fact. However, some continue to cling to the Hall-Freud view of adolescence, searching for new kinds of empirical evidence to support their case. To wit: some neuropsychologists are now claiming that the brain at adolescence undergoes drastic changes that, purportedly, constitute the source of the stress, depression, and mood changes that are manifest in teens.[15] A new biological theory of adolescence is thus starting to foment—one that is clearly going to put the blame on nature again.

But the evidence against this brave new attempt to explain away adolescence is overwhelming. Luigi Luca Cavalli-Sforza and Francesco Cavalli-Sforza, for instance, have shown that no such depressions occur among the youth of contemporary Pygmy society.[16] Life expectancy at birth in that society is an incredible 17 years. The "young" in Pygmy culture hardly have the time to go through an adolescent form of depression due to brain physiology.

In a phrase, culture has more of an effect on us than many current social scientists would allow. Carl Jung (1875–1961), the great Swiss psychoanalyst, was fond of recounting how culture had the power to affect physical processes. During a visit to an island tribal society that had never been exposed to illustrated magazines, he found that the people were unable to recognize the photographs in the magazines as visual representations of human beings. To his amazement, the islanders perceived them as smudges on a surface. Clearly, their erroneous interpretation of the photographs was not due to defects of intelligence or eyesight. On the contrary, the tribal members were clear-sighted and highly intelligent hunters. It was due to the fact that their primary assumptions were different from those of individuals living in Western culture—assumptions that blocked them from perceiving the pictures as visual signs. Human brains are, clearly, malleable organs. If the brains of Western adolescents are indeed different from those of adults, then it is because brain physiology has been refashioned by cultural tradition. I suspect that a comparison of the brains of Western teens and Pygmy youth, for example, would yield rather significant differences.

Anatomical peculiarities, not to mention diseases, make sense only if defined culturally. For example, in the lexicon of Western psychotherapy there is no mention of the condition called *zar* by the people of North Africa and the Middle East, whereby a person is believed to be possessed by a spirit that causes him or her to laugh uncontrollably. Nor is there any mention of *latah*, a syndrome that Malaysian, Japanese, Indonesian, and Thai peoples believe results from sudden fright; nor of *dhat*, a state of severe anxiety associated with the discharge of semen and feelings of exhaustion that is reported by East Indians, Sri Lankans, and some Chinese. There are indeed many syndromes that are not recognized by Western clinical practice. How would a modern-day psychotherapist treat what the Japanese call *taijin kyofusho*, a morbid dread that someone will do something that will embarrass other people? To claim that nature has culture on a leash is pure nonsense, no matter what social scientists claim.[17]

The portrait of adolescence that I have attempted to paint in this book, primarily with the help of the words of the adolescents themselves, can be compared, in the final analysis, to the fictional portrait of Dorian Gray. Like Dorian, we too have hidden the truth in the attic. It is simply unwise to continue on in this way. The time has come, as I have said before, to take the portrait out of the attic and take a very close and serious look at it.

NOTES

1. Eric Hoffer, *Reflections on the Human Condition* (New York: Harper and Row, 1973), 12.

2. This same kind of point has been made forcefully by Vappu Tyyskä, *Long and Winding Road: Adolescents and Youth in Canada Today* (Toronto: Canadian Scholars' Press, 2001).

3. See E. Burkett, *Another Planet* (New York: HarperCollins, 2001), for an overview of the kinds of behaviors that are considered to be typical of adolescents.

4. In Ronald Bergan, *Beyond the Fringe and Beyond* (London: Virgin, 1989), 4.

5. The patterns cited here were put together by two members of the research team from online reports provided by a number of agencies, such as the CDC.

6. In her book, *Kids: How Biology and Culture Shape the Way We Raise Our Children* (New York: Doubleday, 2001), Meredith F. Small looks at the culture versus nature debate from a historical perspective.

7. Henry Miller, *The Wisdom of the Heart* (New York: New Directions, 1941), 9.

8. Rachel Simmons, *Odd Girl Out: The Hidden Culture of Aggression in Girls* (New York: Harcourt, 2001). Among others written in the same vein, I mention here the

following two for the simple reason that they received more attention than others on the part of the mainstream print media. Their titles alone give an indication of how far our "pop psychological" view of adolescence has gone: Sharon Lamb, *The Secret Lives of Girls: Sex, Play, Aggression, and Their Guilt* (New York: The Free Press, 2002); and Rosalind Wiseman, *Queen Bees and Wannabes: Helping Your Daughter Survive Cliques, Gossip, Boyfriends, and Other Realities of Adolescence* (New York: Crown, 2002).

9. Émile Durkheim, *The Elementary Forms of Religious Life* (New York: Collier, 1912).

10. Louise Bogan, *Selected Criticism: Poetry and Prose* (New York: Noonday Press, 1955), 5.

11. This view is now held by a growing number of social critics, such as Frank Furedi, *Paranoid Parenting: Why Ignoring the Experts May Be Best for Your Child* (Chicago: Chicago Review Press, 2002).

12. Readers worried about this topic can consult the sites given in the appendix.

13. Burkett, *Another Planet.*

14. Karl Marx, *Economic and Philosophical Manuscripts,* trans. R. Livingstone and G. Benton (1844; reprint Harmondsworth, UK: Penguin, 1975).

15. Some of the research is discussed by Small, *Kids,* and taken up as part of his overall biological theory of human nature by Steven Pinker, *The Blank Slate: The Modern Denial of Human Nature* (New York: Viking, 2002).

16. Luigi Luca Cavalli-Sforza and Francesco Cavalli-Sforza, *The Great Human Diasporas: The History of Diversity and Evolution* (Reading, Mass.: Addison-Wesley, 1995).

17. See, for instance, Steven Pinker, *The Blank Slate.*

Internet Sites
and Associations

INTERNET SITES

There are many Internet sites available for anyone seeking information on adolescence. Some of the ones that may prove especially useful are the following.

Sites Dealing with Adolescence in General

http://education.indiana.edu/cas/adol/adol.html
Maintained by the Center for Adolescent Studies at Indiana University, and known as the Adolescence Directory Online, this site provides links, information, and resources on adolescent issues in one easy-to-use location.

www.aacap.org
This site is sponsored by the American Academy of Child and Adolescent Psychiatry (AACAP). The "Facts for Families" section has dozens of information sheets.

Sites Prepared by Adolescents

www.cloud9.net/~thorpy/TEEN.HTML
The site features survey results compiled by teens who poll young people to find out about current teen trends and language. Results are reported on even the most trivial trends, including popular brands of razors, deodorants, and nail polishes.

http://wings.buffalo.edu/student-life/ccenter/
This site is maintained by the State University of New York at Buffalo. It is aimed at college students, providing information and advice to them on such issues as body image and safe sex.

www.gurl.com/
With humor and insight, this site—known as *gURL*—deals with issues facing young women today, such as body image, sexuality, relationships, jobs, school, beauty standards, fashion trends, and so on.

www.teenadvice.org/
At this site, a group of adolescent volunteers offers advice to their peers on how to resolve emotional problems and cope with life's dilemmas, from issues of body image to awkward dating situations.

Sites Dealing with Eating Disorders

www.news:alt.parents-teens
At this site, the reader will find insights into the causes of eating disorders. There is a support group on call daily to answer questions, offer guidance, and share wisdom. Responses are usually immediate (or at least within a day or two), so problems can be addressed as they occur.

www.news:alt.support-eating-disord
This site provides information on anorexia and bulimia. Parents who fear their teen may be suffering from an eating disorder will get support and information at this site.

www.news:soc.support.fat-acceptance
This site deals with problems associated with obesity. Messages posted offer advice on how to deal with derogatory comments.

Sites Dealing with Sex-related Issues

www.oneworld.org/avert/young.htm
This site answers basic questions about AIDS and sexuality.

www.missouri.edu/~shape/
This site is maintained by the Sexual Health Advocate Peer Education Program of the Student Health Center at the University of Missouri, Columbia. Here one will find valuable information about sexually transmitted diseases.

www.mcms.dal.ca/dme/hsex/gay.html
This site offers frank discussions about sexuality in a straightforward, nonjudgmental, and factual manner. It also includes useful links to related Internet sites.

http://noah.cuny.edu/pregnancy/march_of_dimes/pre_preg.plan/teen fact.html
At this site, one will find facts and statistics about the pregnancy complications that are more likely to occur in teenage mothers, the health risks to babies born to teens, and the issues connected with raising a child in adolescence.

Sites Dealing with Slang

www.abcnews.go.com/onair/hiphop/glossary_hiphop_popoff.html
This site is maintained by ABC News. It can be consulted for a constantly updated list of slang terms.

www.slanguage.com
Amateur linguist Mike Ellis maintains this popular site, providing examples of new slang.

http://members.tripod.com/~LisaY/S2N.html
This site is aimed at teenage girls, but it also keeps an updated list of slang expressions used by teenagers across the country.

Sites Dealing with Gang-related and Cult-related Issues

www.geocities.com/Athens/4111/index.html
This site is maintained by a group devoted to helping parents whose teens may be involved with gangs and drugs. Information on gangs can also be obtained from the National Youth Gang Center Institute for Intergovernmental Research, P.O. Box 12729, Tallahassee, FL 32317 (904-385-0600).

Parents of teens in trouble with the law should know that there are several programs for juveniles run by the bureau of the U.S. Office of Juvenile Justice and Delinquency Prevention, which aim to deter juvenile crime and to improve state and local juvenile justice systems.

www.csj.org
This site assists cult victims and their families.

This site, maintained by the American Family Foundation, provides useful information on cults and what can be done about a teen who has joined one. The address of the foundation is P.O. Box 2265, Bonita Springs, FL 34133 (914-533-5420).

Sites Dealing with Pop Music and Media Issues

www.thinkcap.com/tc/fim.html
This site contains interviews with pop music personalities and discussions of issues related to media culture and content.

http://hoshi.cic.sfu.ca/adbusters/
This site is maintained by Adbusters, an agency that aims to expose the advertising business. It has clever parodies of current advertising campaigns as well as articles on how one can recognize media manipulation.

ASSOCIATIONS

There are several agencies and associations that provide information and practical advice on alcohol and drug abuse:

- Mothers against Drunk Driving, 669 Airport Freeway, Suite 310, Hurst, TX 76053 or P.O. Box 541688, Dallas, TX 75354-1688 (817-268-6233), www.madd.org.
- National Clearinghouse for Alcohol and Drug Information, P.O. Box 2345, Rockville, MD 20852 (301-468-2600), www.health.org. This association makes available a pamphlet titled *Tips for Teens about Alcohol*.
- American Council for Drug Education, 24 Monroe Street, Suite 110, Rockville, MD 20850 (301-294-0600).
- National Parents Resource Institute on Drug Education (PRIDE), 3610 Dekalb Technology Parkway, Suite 105, Atlanta, GA 30340 (404-577-4500), www.prideusa.org.
- Al-Anon and Alateen, AFG Headquarters, Inc., 1600 Corporate Landing Parkway, Virginia Beach, VA 23454-5617 (800-356-9996).
- Families in Action, Drug Information Center, 2296 Henderson Mill Road, Suite 300, Atlanta, GA 30345, www.emory.edu/NFIA/.
- National Clearinghouse for Alcohol and Drug Information, P.O. Box 2345, Rockville, MD 20852 (301-468-2600). The following free pamphlets are available from this agency upon request: *Marijuana Facts Parents Need to Know* (NIH Pub. No. 95-4036) and *Preventing Drug Use Among Children and Adolescents* (NIH Pub. 97-4212).

The following hotlines may also be useful:

- Alcohol and Drug Helpline: 800-252-6465
- Clearinghouse for Alcohol and Drug Information Line: 800-729-6686
- Cocaine Helpline: 8000-COCAINE or 800-662-HELP
- Just Say No: 800-258-2766

The following agencies offer advice on educational issues:

- Council for Basic Education, 1319 F Street, N.W., Suite 900, Washington, DC 20004, www.c-b-e.org
- Families in Action, 2296 Henderson Mill Road, Suite 300, Atlanta, GA 30345, www.emory.edu/NFIA/
- National PTA, 330 North Wabash Avenue, Chicago, IL 60611-3690, www.pta.org.
- Partners in Education, 901 N. Pitt Street, Suite 320, Alexandria, VA 22314 (703-836-4880)

Here are other useful addresses and phone lines:

- The Centers for Disease Control and Prevention is the best source for information on HIV/AIDS. Their AIDS Hotline operates on a twenty-four-hour basis: 800-342-AIDS.
- The organization known as Teens Teaching AIDS Prevention operates a phone line, 800-234-TEEN, in the after-school hours, Monday through Saturday, which is answered by teenagers trained to answer relevant questions about HIV/AIDS.
- Parents and caregivers worried about the sexual orientation of their own teens can write to Parents, Families, and Friends of Lesbians and Gays, 1101 14th Street N.W., Suite 1030, Washington, DC 20005 (202-638-4200), www.pflag.org.
- The National Youth Advocacy Coalition, 1711 Connecticut Avenue, N. W., Suite 206, Washington, DC 20009 (202-319-7596) can be contacted by gay and lesbian teens for emotional support.
- The American Association of Suicidology, Suite 310, 4210 Connecticut Avenue, N.W., Washington, DC 20008 (202-237-3380), www.cyberpsych.org, provides general information and a list of critical intervention addresses for preventing suicide.
- For troubled teens generally, Covenant House (800-999-999) is always a good source of help, as is the Youth Crisis Hotline (800-448-4663).

- The National Runaway Switchboard phone line, 1-800-621-4000, handles crisis situations and referrals for runaways. Runaways can leave messages for parents and vice versa. It operates twenty-four hours, seven days a week.
- The National Youth Crisis Hotline, 1-800-HIT-HOME, provides counseling for youths involved with drugs or worried about pregnancy, molestation, and suicide. It makes referrals to local drug treatment centers, shelters, and counseling services. It operates twenty-four hours, seven days a week.
- The National Association of Anorexia Nervosa and Associated Disorders, Box 7, Highland Park, IL 60035, 708-831-3438, provides written materials, referrals, and telephone counseling.

Glossary

acronym   Word formed from the first (or first few) letters of a series of words: for example, *AIDS*, from *acquired immune deficiency syndrome*

adolescence   Period of psychological development that characterizes pubescent individuals living in modern cultures

adolescent   Individual between the ages of 12 and 19 with recognizable emotional and social behaviors that are different from those of children and adults

AIDS   Acquired immune deficiency syndrome, a group of diseases that results from infection by the human immunodeficiency virus (HIV)

anorexia nervosa   Disease of the mind whereby individuals actually starve themselves to keep their weight down

antilanguage   Language used consciously to convey opposition, negativity, and reprobation

bisexual   Person who is attracted sexually to both men and women

body image   Subjective concept of one's physical appearance based on self-observation and the reactions of others

bulimia nervosa   Eating disorder whereby individuals overeat and then force themselves to vomit to avoid gaining weight

clique   Small, exclusive group of peers

coolness   Adoption of a specific type of look, walk, and talk that is considered to be stylish and voguish

counterculture   Nonpolitical movement of the 1960s that rejected traditional bourgeois values

cult   A group, often living apart from society, with a charismatic leader who indoctrinates members with unorthodox or extremist views, practices, or beliefs

degendering   Society-wide trend blurring the traditional lines between the genders

egocentricity   Behavior common among teenagers whereby everything is related to self-interest

emotional noise   Behavior that, like a noisy sound, is unexpected, discordant, and thus likely to cause a negative reaction

gang   Group of youths usually banded together for delinquent purposes

gender   Sexual role that is assumed by an individual according to cultural conventions

groupthink   General sense of understanding or agreement reached within a group

heterosexual   Person who is attracted sexually to the opposite sex

homosexual   Person who is attracted sexually to the same sex

identity crisis   Confusion whereby teenagers wonder about what their "real" personality is

juvenilization   General view of people that it is possible to hang on to one's youth for a longer period of time than ever before

memorate   Pattern of thought that has become so common that it is no longer recognized as originating in some idea

metaphor   Figure of speech containing an implied comparison, in which a word or phrase ordinarily used for one thing is applied to another

middlescent   Individual in his or her twenties or thirties who behaves and acts as if he or she were still a teenager

neomania   Abnormal craving for new objects of consumption, engendered by consumerism

onomatopoeia   Formation of a word by imitating the natural sound associated with the object or action to which it refers

peer pressure   Pressure felt by teenagers to conform to what their peers do, say, and believe

persona   Role that a person assumes in a particular social situation

pieces   Elaborate murals that may include characters from cartoons, proverbs, and so on

puberty   Arrival of sexual maturity in the lifecycle

pubilect   Slang used by adolescents; the term is intended to bring out the fact that such slang functions as a social dialect

pubescence   Process of becoming sexually mature

self-consciousness   Excessive preoccupation with one's appearance or behavior

self-definition   Definition of one's identity, character, abilities, and attitudes, especially in relation to other persons or to things

self-esteem   Positive self-image

self-presentation   Ways in which one behaves and looks in differing social situations

sex   Anatomical and behavioral features that differentiate males from females

sexuality   Sexual activities that characterize human behavior in a specific culture

tag question   Sentence that ends in an expression such as *right?*, *don't you agree? do you follow me? don't you think so?* and the like

tagging   Making of graffiti in marker, spray paint, or shoe polish representing the chosen street name of hip-hop teens

tattooing   Method of decorating the skin by inserting colored substances under its surface

teenagehood   Period of social development that characterizes pubescent individuals living in modern consumerist cultures

teenager   Individual between the ages of 12 and 19 who participates in a particular kind of lifestyle with peers

throw-up   Hip-hop practice of writing names in bubble, block, or other expansive styles

transsexual   Person whose sense of gender and sexuality is not consistent with his or her anatomical sex

tribalism   Tendency of individuals, especially adolescents, to group together as if in a tribe

tribe   Group of people sharing customs, language, and territory

tweenie   Child who behaves and acts like a teenager but has not yet reached the age of puberty

Index

T-shirts, 16
tweenie, 2, 38, 181

U2, 85
unisex, 41, 44
uptalk, 56
USA Today, 85

Valens, Richie, 10
Valley Girl slang, 58–59
verbal danger signs, 70
Verdi, Giuseppe, 88, 155
video games, 156
Vines, The, 46
violence, 6, 132, 139, 140
vocabulary creation techniques, 60
vocalism, 56–57

Wachal, Robert, 69, 73
Walker, Madam C. J., 49
Warhol, Andy, 11, 153
Washington Post, 55, 69

Watson, Johnny, 76
Wells, John, 160
West Side Story, 103
Wham!, 89
White, E., 38, 54
White Stripes, The, 46
Who, The, 11, 78, 80
Wild One, The, 154
Wilde, Oscar, 68, 73, 159
Williams, Hank, 76, 77
Wonder, Stevie, 86
Wonder Woman, 42
Woodstock, 78
World Health Organization, 34

Xena, 39

young vs. old, 14
Young, Lester, 115
youth organizations, 8

Zappa, Frank, 58–59, 77

About the Author

Marcel Danesi is professor of anthropology, semiotics, and communication theory at the University of Toronto. He is the author of numerous books, including Cool: *The Signs and Meanings of Adolescence.*